Reconstructing the
Welfare State

Reconstructing the Welfare State

A Decade of Change 1980–1990

NORMAN JOHNSON

HARVESTER
WHEATSHEAF

NEW YORK LONDON TORONTO SYDNEY TOKYO SINGAPORE

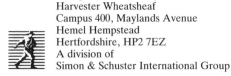

First published 1990 by
Harvester Wheatsheaf
Campus 400, Maylands Avenue
Hemel Hempstead
Hertfordshire, HP2 7EZ
A division of
Simon & Schuster International Group

Typeset in 10/12pt Times by
Keyboard Services, Luton, Beds

Printed and bound in Great Britain by
Biddles Ltd, Guildford and King's Lynn

British Library Cataloguing in Publication Data

Johnson, Norman, *1936–*
    Reconstructing the welfare state: a decade of
    change, 1980–1990.
    1. Great Britain. Welfare state, History
    I. Title
    361.650941

    ISBN 0–7450–0498–9
    ISBN 0–7450–0812–7 pbk

---

5 6 7 8 9   98 97 96 95 94

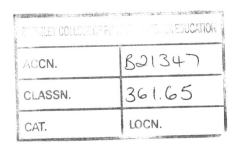

For Ruth, Karen and David

CONTENTS

TABLES

ix

ACKNOWLEDGEMENTS

I wish to thank colleagues at Keele and elsewhere for their help and encouragement. I am also grateful to past and present students at Keele for their stimulation. I would also like to acknowledge the useful comments made by two anonymous readers. My editor, Clare Grist, has been unfailingly patient and helpful. As always, my main debt is to my wife, Ruth, for her support and for many helpful suggestions during the course of writing the book.

CHAPTER 1

INTRODUCTION

In 1987 Mrs Thatcher won her third successive election. The Conservatives had a majority of 101 seats over all the other parties.

To put this victory into perspective, however, it is necessary to recognise two features of the result. First, the Conservative Party received only 42.3 per cent of the votes cast. Second, there was a very sharp North–South divide in the distribution of the votes. The electorate in the South and East voted overwhelmingly for the Conservatives: in Northern England, Wales and Scotland the Labour Party predominated with particularly strong support in the Northern cities and in Scotland. There were, of course, pockets of Conservative support in the North – mainly in the more rural and prosperous areas – and pockets of Labour support in the South – mainly in the more urban and deprived areas. There has always been stronger support for Labour in the North and stronger support for the Conservative Party in the South, but the 1987 election saw an intensification of this tendency.[1]

The political divide is a reflection of divides along other dimensions such as unemployment, income, and wealth. Unemployment is higher in the North; income and wealth are higher in the South. Writing in 1986, Deakin says:

Considered in the broadest perspective, the outstanding characteristic of British society after seven years of Conservative rule is its divisions. These divisions extend in a number of different directions, but overlap and reinforce one another. The most immediately evident of all are the regional divisions, reflected in contrasts in employment patterns and job

1

opportunities and in standards of living between different parts of the country.[2]

Since the election of 1987 the divides referred to by Deakin have widened.

THATCHERISM

Mrs Thatcher's election victory in 1987 meant that during her third term of office she became the longest serving Prime Minister this century. That she should also be Britain's first woman Prime Minister is another mark of distinction.

The term Thatcherism has entered the language to signify a particular brand of Conservatism. Gamble says that Thatcherism 'has come to stand for the distinctive ideology, political style and programme of policies with which the British Conservative Party has been identified since Margaret Thatcher became their Leader'.[3]

Various attempts have been made to explain and interpret Thatcherism. Gamble identifies three approaches: Thatcherism as a class or accumulation strategy; Thatcherism as statecraft; and Thatcherism as a hegemonic project. Although Gamble accepts that the first two of these offer useful insights, he finds them too narrow, and he prefers to analyse Thatcherism as a hegemonic project. Such an approach does not ignore the significance of class and statecraft but it integrates them into a broader framework which 'allows proper weight to be given to ideology, economics and politics'.[4] Thatcherism is interpreted as an attempt to clear the way for the replacement of the already crumbling social democratic consensus with a new consensus based on a free economy and a strong state.

Mrs Thatcher identified herself with the ideas and policies of the New Right which, as King demonstrates, is consistent with an analysis in terms of a free economy and a strong state. King sees the New Right as an alliance between free market liberals and conservative authoritarians.[5]

There are discussions within the Conservative Party about the meaning of Thatcherism and the relationship it has to traditional Conservative concerns. Some see Thatcherism as a decisive break with the recent past, rejecting the politics of compromise which characterised the 1960s. Some welcome this break, while others would wish to see the Party return to the centre ground. A competing interpretation of Thatcherism within the Conservative Party is that it signifies a welcome return to basic Conservative principles from which the post-war consensus was an aberration. This is the authentic voice of the New Right.

Throughout the 1980s Mrs Thatcher dominated British politics. Even those who disliked her style admired her energy, her determination and her ability to get things done. There were occasions when she appeared to be losing her grip, but, until the events of 1990, she always managed to re-assert her authority. Butler and Kavanagh note how Mrs Thatcher managed to control the political agenda:

The other parties tried to cope with the impact of Thatcherism on the public. Leaders of the parties recognised a greater public approval for the ideas of thrift, enterprise and self-reliance and hostility to restrictive practices. The government also appeared to have shaped decisively the agenda on such issues as the role of trade unions, the sale of council houses to sitting tenants, and the transfer of state services and enterprises to the private sector.[6]

RECONSTRUCTING WELFARE

In the early 1980s there was much talk of a crisis in the welfare state in Britain and elsewhere. It was claimed that the social democratic consensus sustaining the expansion of the welfare state had broken down.

In truth, the evidence was less clear cut than the critics of state welfare would have us believe. There is ample evidence to show that public support for the ideas underpinning the welfare state is as strong as it has ever been. Some disillusion there may have been in the late 1970s and this may have led to reduced enthusiasm for the welfare state, but the 1980s (especially since 1983) have witnessed a revival of support for welfare expenditure.[7] Some explanation is therefore required of how the notion of a crisis in the welfare state developed and became the accepted dogma of the late 1970s and the early 1980s.

The end of the Second World War was followed by a steady increase in social expenditure, and in the 1960s there was general confidence that the continuation and development of the welfare state was assured. However, this confidence began to evaporate with the onset of economic problems stemming from the oil crisis of 1973. The rate of economic growth slowed down and the economy actually contracted between 1973 and 1975 as investment and profits fell and unemployment increased.

The New Right theorists used the economic problems to argue for the changes that they had long wished to see. The reduction of public expenditure, they urged, was now not only desirable but absolutely essential if Britain's economic ills were to be remedied. They were particularly anxious to see a reduction in social expenditure, which could be achieved by transferring responsibility for the provision of education, health and other social services to private markets. When Mrs Thatcher came to power she was already convinced of the correctness of the New Right's ideas and set about attempting to translate them into practical policies.

After the war a mixed economy of welfare emerged in which the state predominated with smaller roles allotted to the voluntary and commercial sectors and in which domiciliary care was left largely to families. A broad consensus concurred with the balance struck between the statutory, voluntary, commercial and informal sectors. Mrs Thatcher and her colleagues sought to overturn these arrangements by reducing the role of the state and tipping the balance towards private markets, together with a greater contribution from the voluntary and informal sectors.

Private markets have certainly become a more prominent feature of the welfare state since 1979. Every sphere of social policy has been affected by this change in emphasis, but markets have made the biggest inroads in health services, housing, residential homes for elderly people, pensions and preschool nursery and child-minding provision. There will be greater emphasis on private markets in the personal social services when the government's plans for community care come into effect in 1992.[8] The changes in the NHS were also well underway by 1991 and will almost certainly serve to encourage further expansion of private provision.[9]

The government has also imported some of the features of the private market into the public sector through the introduction of internal markets and competition. This has been most clearly seen in the NHS and education, but it will also be a significant element in the community care services after 1992.

As is explained in Chapter 8, the government's attempts to cut public expenditure were not wholly successful. Between 1978/79 and 1989/90 public expenditure in real terms rose by 11 per cent. There were two main reasons for this. First, as unemployment rose, reaching a peak in 1986 and then falling slowly, expenditure on social security inevitably increased. Second, as a matter of deliberate policy the government increased expenditure on law and order and on defence. Thus what the government has done is to change the pattern of expenditure. Housing expenditure has been savagely cut: between 1978/79 and 1989/90 the housing budget was cut in real terms by 79 per cent. By contrast, expenditure on law and order increased by 63 per cent and expenditure on defence increased by 17 per cent over the same period. The increase in expenditure on education was well below these two, at 10 per cent. Although expenditure on defence declined slightly in real terms from 1984/5 onwards, it still exceeded expenditure on education in 1989/90. From the government's published figures it appears that health and personal social services have been treated more generously – an increase of 37 per cent in 'real terms' between 1978/79 and 1989/90. However, this figure is misleading; the retail price index is an inadequate measure of inflation in the NHS and extra expenditure is required to take account of demographic and technological changes. This is explained more fully in Chapter 4.

The government has guided legislation through Parliament bringing about major changes in every area of social policy. There have been Acts on social security, health, education, housing, and the personal social services. The changes are much more than cosmetic: they are fundamental; and by 1992 every service will have been substantially reconstructed.

PLAN OF THE BOOK

The book was originally designed to cover the period from May 1979, when the first Thatcher government took up office, to April 1990. After the book appeared in print, however, Mrs Thatcher was replaced as Prime Minister by John Major. To take this into account a short *Afterword* has been added, but the text of the book has not been altered.

Although the government first took up office in May 1979, most of the major changes they were planning required legislation and so the reconstruction did not really get under way until 1980.

Chapter 2 considers the aims of Conservative social policy under three headings: privatisation, curbing local government and promoting inequality. Chapters 3 to 7 look at five areas of ocial policy in some detail: social security, the National Health Service, education, housing and the personal social services. Chapter 8 is an attempt to assess the impact of more than eleven years of Conservative rule with Mrs Thatcher as Prime Minister. The Afterword is an attempt to assess the consequences of Mrs Thatcher's departure and her replacement by John Major.

NOTES

1. The best analysis of the 1987 election is D. Butler and D. Kavanagh, *The British General Election of 1987*, London: Macmillan, 1988.
2. N. Deakin, *The Politics on Welfare*, London: Methuen, 1987, p. 178.
3. A. Gamble, *The Free Economy and the Strong State: The Politics of Thatcherism*, London: Macmillan, 1988, p. 20.
4. *Ibid.*, p. 25.
5. D. S. King, *The New Right: Politics, Markets and Citizenship*, London: Macmillan, 1987.
6. D. Butler and D. Kavanagh, *op. cit.*, p. 9.
7. See Chapter 8 for further details.
8. Department of Health, *Caring for People*, Cm 849, London: HMSO, 1989.
9. Department of Health, *Working for Patients*, Cm 555, London: HMSO, 1989.

CHAPTER 2

THE AIMS OF CONSERVATIVE SOCIAL POLICY

It is possible to identify a number of unifying themes in Conservative social policy during the 1980s. This does not, however, imply either complete consistency or ideological purity, since in some instances ideology has given way to pragmatism and the underlying ideology of present day Conservatism is not without its contradictions.

It should be noted that this chapter is principally about social policy *aims*; the question of whether or not these aims have been achieved will be left to the final chapter. The aims will be considered under three main headings: privatisation, curbing local government, and the promotion of inequality.

PRIVATISATION

Privatisation, at its most basic, means a reduction in the role of the state and the transfer of some of its functions to private institutions. The private institutions may be commercial undertakings, formal and informal voluntary associations, or informal networks of families, friends and neighbours. It is important to stress that privatisation does not simply mean the sale of public assets and greater reliance on private enterprise and competitive markets.

Consideration needs to be given to those aspects of statutory activity that may be candidates for privatisation. Le Grand and Robinson identify three broad areas of state intervention: provision, subsidy and regulation.[1] A diminution of the state's role in any of these may be viewed as privatisation, and a closer look at each of these three areas may help to identify the privatisation strategies employed by the government.

Provision

Since 1979 the government has sold into private hands many of the nationalised industries; amassing £23.5 billion from sales between 1979 and the end of 1987. The most profitable privatisation during this period was the sale of British Gas which produced a £7.7 billion addition to government funds. The privatisation of water in 1989 also realised about £7.7 billion and the privatisation of the electricity industry in 1990 is expected to realise about £20 billion.

The significance of these sales is that the proceeds have been used to offset government expenditure and reduce income tax, thus contributing to greater inequality. The other major sale of assets under the Conservatives has been the mandatory sale of council houses either individually or of whole estates. Chapter 6 shows that between 1980 and 1987 slightly more than 1.1 million houses were sold.

Another way in which provision is privatised is through contracting out, where public authorities offer contracts to commercial undertakings or non-profit organisations who agree to provide a service wholly or in part at an agreed price.[2] Chapter 4 demonstrates that this is happening in the NHS with the contracting out of non-clinical services and the payments made to private hospitals to carry out operations on NHS patients; and the White Paper, *Working for Patients*, implies much more contracting out in the NHS in future.[3] Purchase-of-service arrangements of this kind are also likely to be a growing feature of the personal social services when the National Health Service and Community Care Act is implemented.[4]

Opting out, another form of privatising provision, has become one of the main ploys of the Thatcher governments. It has long been possible to opt out of the incomes-related element of the state pension scheme, but the Social Security Act of 1986 gave greater incentives to do so by reducing the benefits available under the state earnings-related pension scheme and by subsidising a switch to private pensions. Opting out has also become available under the Housing Act of 1988 which allows groups of local authority tenants to transfer to new landlords.

The term 'opting out' is also used in education and the NHS. The Education Reform Act of 1988 gave schools the right to opt out of local authority control. The funding of the schools, however, remained with the state, the responsibility transferring from local to central government. The NHS and Community Care Act allows hospitals to opt out of District Health Authority control while remaining NHS hospitals. The Labour Party claims that these changes are simply paving the way for future privatisation.

One of the most direct ways of privatising provision is simply through the restriction of state services, thereby forcing people to rely on other sources of help. We have already seen how this has occurred with the reduced benefits available in the state earnings-related pension scheme. Another example from social security is the abolition of exceptional needs payments and their replacement with loans from the social fund. Social fund officers are meant to explore other possible sources of help, such as charities, before granting a loan. If loans are refused, for whatever reason, people are forced to borrow from commercial companies, and the conditions attaching to social fund loans are such that some people may prefer credit companies.

Examples can be found in other services. In the personal social services, for instance, reduced support from the statutory community care services may have two consequences. First, it may ensure that responsibility for caring remains firmly, indeed increasingly, with families – especially women. Second, lack of adequate care in the community may persuade elderly people, for example, to seek residential care, and a shortage of places in local authority homes means that increasingly elderly people are being accommodated in the private sector.

In the health services, hospital waiting lists may be sufficient incentive for some patients to choose private treatment, and in housing, a shortage of local authority houses to let may force people into the private rented sector or into owner-occupation.

Subsidies

Subsidies are concerned with government financing of social and health services. Reductions of subsidies result from government efforts to contain or transfer the costs of provision, and subsidies may also be used to encourage activities favoured by government.

The state may reduce its provision of services, but retain its role as the chief source of finance. Thus reduced state provision does not necessarily mean a change in either the scale or the source of funding. As happens with contracted out services, the destination of the funds changes, since they are now directed towards profit-making or non-profit organisations.

In other circumstances, however, reductions in state provision may also mean a reduction in state finance. Indeed, reduced public expenditure may be the main object of cutting provision. Wicks, for example, claims that the government's commitment to community care is based on greater reliance upon families.[5] He sees this as 'a conscious attempt to shift costs from the governmental to the private, family sector'.[6] A quotation from the Audit Commission is used to illustrate this point:

authorities wishing to reduce their level of community care to the highly dependent would need to mobilise additional support from friends, relatives and the voluntary sector. If increased levels of support were following, and if an increased burden on friends and relatives were consistent with the authority's policies, the reduction in the authority's costs could be considerable. For example, a 10 per cent reduction in provision to the 'high public sector' dependency group could save £150,000 p.a. for a typical authority, or £17 million nationally.[7]

Community care policies may, then, mean a transfer of costs from the government to families. An example of transferring responsibility for finance from the government to the private sector is provided by changes in relation to housing associations. Following the enactment of the 1988 Housing Bill, it was announced that government financial support for housing associations was to be cut from 100 per cent to 75 per cent, forcing housing associations to raise 25 per cent of their funds from private sources.

The introduction or increase of charges has the effect of making recipients bear a greater proportion of the costs. The most obvious examples occur in the NHS. When the Conservatives came to power in 1979 the prescription charge was 20p an item; by 1990 it had risen to £3.05. Two new NHS charges have also been introduced: for ophthalmic and dental consultations. There have also been increases in charges for home helps and meals-on-wheels, and the White Paper on community care implies that charges are likely to be used more extensively in the personal social services.

Private provision may also be encouraged by fiscal measures.

Thus, tax relief on mortgage interest payments is a subsidy to owner occupiers and private pensions are also subsidised by tax concessions. The sums involved are substantial. In 1987–8 mortgage interest relief amounted to £4.75 billion and pension fund exemption totalled £4.1 billion.[8] Wilkinson calculates that between 1979–80 and 1983–4 the cost of relief to private pension schemes increased by 106 per cent.[9] The 1986 Social Security Act gave further encouragement to private pensions by granting to anyone who chose to leave the state earnings-related pension scheme or an occupational scheme and take out a personal pension a 2 per cent boost to their contributions. This subsidy will last until 1993. Hills demonstrates that between 1978/79 and 1986/87 mortgage interest tax relief more than doubled in real terms.[10] It is the better-off who benefit most from these tax reliefs.

The government has also taken steps to make private health insurance more attractive to people with modest incomes. After April 1982 employees earning less than £8,500 a year no longer had to pay tax on the value of employers' contributions to private health insurance schemes, and companies were also allowed to set the premiums they paid for their employees against corporation tax.

Public sector housing demonstrates how subsidies may be used in a discriminatory fashion. Council house tenants who wished to buy their homes were granted large discounts, while those who remained as tenants were faced with increased rents as subsidies were withdrawn.

Regulation

Privatisation may take the form of the removal, simplification or codification of government regulations. Regulations may relate to both public and private providers of social services, but it should be noted that a switch from public to private provision may entail substantially more regulation in an effort to protect vulnerable groups.

No unequivocal pattern emerges from an examination of the Conservatives' record. The government has portrayed itself as non-interventionist, but Young argues that 'at the heart of privatisation there appears to be a paradox. Its promotion depends on government playing an active and interventionist role on a continuing basis'.[11] The overall effect of Mrs Thatcher's years in office has been an increase in regulation. The deregulation that has occurred in some areas has been more than outweighed by increases in regulation elsewhere.

Three examples of deregulation can be cited. The most significant, in social policy terms, is the deregulation of rents. Under the 1988 Housing Act, all new private sector lets will have to be on the basis of either assured or assured shorthold tenancies, allowing rents to be set at market level and reducing security of tenure.

The second example is the deregulation of the labour market on several fronts. Workers' rights against unfair dismissal have been truncated. In 1986 wages council protection for all those aged under 21 was ended, and wages councils were restricted to setting a single minimum rate and a single overtime rate. The Sex Discrimination Act of 1986 allowed women to be employed on night-work and shift-work and gave them the right to work until the same age as their male counterparts. In 1989 the Employment Act swept away the restrictions imposed on the kinds of work available to women (e.g. work underground) and removed the restrictions on the hours of work of those aged between 16 and 18.

Bus transport provides the final example of deregulation. This measure, brought in by the Transport Act of 1985, was meant to increase competition among bus companies. However, in 1988 the Office of Fair Trading accused sixty-six companies of colluding to restrict competition.

There are many instances of increased regulation. One example is provided by the Education Reform Act of 1988 which left several areas to be clarified and extended by regulation. The Labour Party claims that this Act alone conferred 415 new powers on the Secretary of State. The whole of the educational system is now subject to much more central control than at any time in the past. The national curriculum lays down what is to be taught in schools and how it is to be examined, and the internal management of schools is subject to central regulation concerning the appointment and composition of governing bodies, finance, the involvement of parents and the publication of annual reports. There are regulations governing opting out, contracting out and charges in schools. The legislation introducing top up loans for students in higher education was in skeleton form only, leaving the Secretary of State free to fill in the details by regulation.

Increased regulation in the National Health Service has been concerned with cost and quality control through financial and medical audit. More concerned with cost than with quality was the introduction in April 1985 of a limited drugs list which had the effect of banning nearly 2,000 drugs from NHS prescription. *Working for Patients* proposes building on these arrangements through the introduction of indicative drug budgets.[12] The development of internal markets in the NHS will create a need for still more regulation to ensure the availability of a full range of adequate health care for all categories of patient.

The implementation of *Caring for People* will also involve a substantial increase in regulation. The NHS and Community Care Act requires local authority community care plans to be approved by the Secretary of State who can require modifications, and the White Paper indicates that the Secretary of State will be particularly concerned to ensure that the plans make the maximum possible use of the independent sector.[13] Guidelines are to be issued on the workings of the new assessment procedures and on registration and inspection, and the Social Services Inspectorate is to be strengthened. The White Paper is unequivocal about where the power lies: 'The Government will bring proposals before Parliament to enable the Secretary of State for Health to issue directions and give guidance over the full range of personal social services activities by local authorities'.[14]

A considerably enhanced role is anticipated for the independent sector, but it has proved notoriously difficult in the past to devise adequate systems of regulation and control. The general ineffectiveness of the Registered Homes Act of 1984 gives no cause for optimism. The White Paper proposes the establishment by local authorities of independent inspection units which will monitor standards in both public sector and independent homes, but it remains to be seen whether the new arrangements will be any more effective than those they replace.

As one might have anticipated, the regulation of the poor has become more pervasive under the Conservatives. For example, the changes made to the social security system have increased the use of means tests. Of course, means tests are themselves a device for regulating the poor, but they also lead to further regulations governing their operation. Furthermore, the social fund has increased the use of discretion and given rise to the Social Fund Manual.

During the 1980s the number of staff employed in social security offices has declined, with the exception of fraud investigators, whose number has increased, and the Department of Employment has established Regional Benefit Investigation Teams. We have also had the Restart Programme for 'counselling' the long-term unemployed. In 1986, when the programme started, it was restricted to those who had been out of work for at least twelve months, but in 1987 Restart was extended to anyone who had been unemployed for six months or more. In addition, the rules governing the payment of benefits to the unemployed have been tightened up by stages during the 1980s. Between 1982 and 1986 claimants were asked if they were prepared to take any work they could do, and if they were satisfied that adequate arrangements had been made for the care of dependants. In 1986 the test was made even tougher: claimants were obliged to take any full-time job, to work beyond the normal travelling distance and to make immediate arrangements for child care. The Social Security Act of 1989 goes even further by demanding that claimants should demonstrate that they are actively seeking work.

In summary, the privatisation measures taken by the government in terms of *provision* have included: the sale of public assets, the extension of market provision (including contracting out) and a greater reliance on informal and voluntary care. In terms of *subsidies*, the government has attempted to transfer costs to families (in some of its community care policies) and to individual consumers (through increased charges). Tax relief to the better-off has been matched by reduced subsidies for the poorer members of the community.

In many spheres regulation and the concentration of power in the hands of central government have increased under the Conservatives, while the deregulation that has occurred has damaged poorer people. This applies particularly to the deregulation of rents and the more restricted coverage of the wages councils. On the other hand, the poor, especially social security claimants, have been subjected to more regulation of an oppressive nature.

Thus, we have experienced increased private provision, increased private finance and increased regulation.

CURBING LOCAL GOVERNMENT

Expenditure

One of the major aims of Conservative governments since 1979 has been to exercise greater control over local government expenditure.

The government wasted no time, the first action to restrain local government spending coming in 1980 under the Local Government, Planning and Land Act. This allowed the Secretary of State to set expenditure targets for each local authority. Any authority exceeding its target was penalised by loss of central government grant, so that the more an authority 'overspent', the greater the proportion of block grant it lost: in the extreme case the whole of the grant was withdrawn. Greenwood and Wilson note that the local authority associations 'have generally deplored the imposition of targets . . . as an unwarrantable increase in central control'. They continue:

Centrally imposed expenditure targets not only infringe the rights of elected councillors to determine local spending needs and priorities, but also undermine their accountability to local ratepayers. What from the central perspective might be seen as an essential instrument for public expenditure control, from the local level might be seen instead as a threat to the fabric of local government itself.[15]

In 1982 further restrictions were placed on local authorities by the Local Government Finance Act which prevented authorities from levying supplementary rates and allowed the Secretary of State to withdraw grant in the middle of the financial year. The Act also established the Audit Commission to scrutinise local authority expenditure.

In spite of these attempts to limit local government expenditure, some authorities continued to spend above targets on the grounds of maintaining levels of service and avoiding job losses. Several authorities lost a good proportion, or all, of their block grant and made good the shortfall by raising rates.

The government's response was to introduce rate capping under the 1984 Rates Act. The Secretary of State was empowered by the Act to set upper limits to the rates levied by those he judged to be high spending authorities. In the first year of operation eighteen authorities were capped. A similar number have been affected in subsequent years and, as might have been anticipated, they are overwhelmingly Labour-controlled.

A variant of capping was introduced in the 1985 Local Government Act. The precepts of the Inner London Education Authority, those of the police, fire, civil defence and passenger transport authorities in the Metropolitan Areas and those of the authorities responsible for the fire and civil defence services in London, were to be automatically selected for limitation.

Financial control was, and remains, a source of much bitterness among local authorities, and by the mid-1980s central–local relations had reached a very low level with several local authorities engaged in acrimonious disputes with central government.

The most widely publicised of these disputes concerned Liverpool City Council. A key element in this dispute was the control of the council by Militant Tendency, an extreme left-wing organisation, subsequently banned by the Labour Party in 1986. The central figure was Derek Hatton, the deputy leader of the city council.

The dispute began in 1983 when the city council said that it had no plans to stay within spending targets, but nevertheless proposed to levy a rate for 1984–5 which would be insufficient to cover planned outgoings. This was intended as a direct challenge to the government.

There was an intensification of the dispute in 1985 when the city council simply refused to set a rate, but decided to continue with current spending plans. There were several court cases, teachers were served with redundancy notices, the bailiffs were called in and Liverpool City Council was on the verge of bankruptcy. The District Auditor served surcharge notices on forty-seven councillors, disqualifying them from sitting on any local authority council for five years. In November 1985 the council backed down and agreed to set a rate.

This was not quite the end of the story. A lengthy legal battle followed: the councillors appealed in the High Court against the imposition of both the surcharge and the ban. The High Court having refused the appeal, the case went to the Court of Appeal with the same result. Finally, in 1987, the House of Lords upheld the Court of Appeal's decision.

Two further extensions of central control of expenditure were introduced in 1986 and 1988. To avoid a repetition of the delays that occurred in Liverpool, the Local Government Act of 1986 required local authorities to set a rate by April each year. The 1988 Local Government Finance Act put a stop to sale and leaseback arrangements. Several local authorities had devised a novel way of increasing revenue by the sale of town halls and other local authority property (even parking meters) to banks who then leased the property back to the local authority. The Act banned this practice. It should be noted that once the full effects of the loss of functions in education and housing have been felt, local government expenditure may fall sharply.

The government was obviously not satisfied with the restrictions it had imposed on local government expenditure from 1980 onwards. One of the main objectives in scrapping the rating system was the hope that its replacement would entail even greater restraint. On several occasions the Conservative government promised to reform local government finance, issuing a Green Paper on the subject in 1981[16] and another in 1986. The Green Paper of 1986 formed the basis of the changes given legislative effect by the 1988 Local Government Finance Act.[17] In its manifesto for the General Election of 1987 the Conservative Party committed itself to the abolition of the rating system and its replacement by the community charge (more commonly referred to as the poll tax) and the national or uniform business rate.

Of all the Conservative innovations, the community charge has generated the fiercest opposition. In March and early April 1990 there was widespread unrest throughout Britain with angry demonstrations against the community charge up and down the country. Council meetings were disrupted and there were clashes with the police. Many people sustained injuries and there was some damage to property. A large demonstration in London led to more than 350 arrests and 58 police officers and 86 members of the public required hospital treatment. Although some extreme political groups and some criminal elements seem to have been involved, they were a small proportion only of those taking part in the demonstration.

Undoubtedly, opposition to the poll tax is not limited to a few activists but is spread throughout the community. Many Conservative MPs, many Conservative local councillors and many rank and file members of the party are deeply disturbed by the community charge. Eighteen members of the ruling Conservative group in West Oxfordshire resigned the Whip and continued to serve as independents. An ICM poll, conducted in April 1990, revealed that

70 per cent of respondents disapproved of the community charge.[18] A brief discussion of the charge may reveal some of the reasons for its unpopularity.

The community charge is a flat rate tax, which varies from one local authority to another. Thus, with a few exceptions, everyone over the age of 18 living within an area covered by a particular district council will pay the same amount. There are some exempted groups including: prisoners; nuns; monks; foreign diplomats; those resident and receiving treatment or care in a hospital, a home or a hostel; those who are severely mentally handicapped; 18-year-olds for whom child benefit is still payable; some of those who are staying in a charitable hostel or night shelter and those without a fixed address.

Full time students have to pay only 20 per cent of the charge. Maximum rebates of 80 per cent are available to people on income support and those whose incomes fall below income support levels. If a person's income is above his or her income support threshold then the rebate is reduced by 15 pence for every £1 by which income exceeds the threshold. In the original Bill 20 pence of rebate was forfeited for every £1 of 'excess income', but a backbench revolt forced the Secretary of State to make concessions. According to the Secretary of State this change brought approximately one million more people into the rebate scheme and increased rebate for a further four million. However, the disaffected MPs were not satisfied with this change and proposed a banded community charge related to the ability to pay.

As the scheme was modified it became ever more complicated. The government recognised that some people, especially those living in inner urban areas, would face huge increases (as compared with rates) when the scheme was introduced in England and Wales in April 1990 (the scheme was introduced in Scotland in 1989). If the tax was not to become even more unpopular, and indeed unworkable, some means had to be found of 'cushioning' those who would be hit hardest by the switch from rates to community charge. The government devised a system known as the safety net which involved community charge payers in some areas paying more to cushion the effect on those facing steep increases in other areas. In some instances this would have meant paying an extra £75 a head in the areas providing the subsidy, which were mainly in Conservative-held constituencies. Much resentment was expressed by those who claimed that the safety net meant that thrifty authorities would be subsidising high spending, and often Labour-held, authorities. It was agreed that while it was fair to cushion the effects of the change, it was unfair to expect low spending areas to bear the cost of £685 million.

In October 1989 the government accepted the force of this argument, no doubt being helped towards its conclusion by a *Local Government Chronicle*/National Opinion Polls survey which showed that in the fifty most marginal Conservative constituencies opposition to the charge had risen, and that on the present showing Labour would win forty-two of the fifty seats.[19] The government allocated an extra £1.5 billion to the transitional arrangements: about £300 million of this would be used to grant extra relief in the North and Northwest and there were similar arrangements for Scotland and Wales. No-one, according to the government, would be paying more than £3 a week more in community charge than they paid in rates provided they lived in areas where the council stayed within government spending limits. The bulk of the extra money would be used to ease the burden placed on 236 low spending councils by the safety net arrangements. The extra money meant that these areas would have to meet the costs in 1990/1 only, and that for a further three years the cost would be borne by the Treasury.[20]

The government estimated that the average community charge would be £278. In March 1990 it became clear that this figure was going to be exceeded and a national average charge of £354 resulted from the individual decisions of local authorities. In Labour-controlled councils the average charge was about £370 and in Conservative councils it was about £345.

These figures hardly support the government's contention that overspending is mainly attributable to Labour councils. What is also clear is that most people will be paying more in community charge than they paid in rates: a survey commissioned by the Labour Party claimed that 73 per cent of all adults were in this position.

The community charge has replaced only domestic rates. There is in addition a uniform business tax at levels set by central government, but collected on behalf of the government by local authorities. The total amount collected is redistributed to local councils in proportion to their adult populations. On very weak evidence, the government has consistently maintained that the high rates charged by high spending councils deterred businesses from setting up in the areas concerned and forced businesses already operating there to transfer to other areas. This was a particular problem, they claimed, in trying to regenerate the economies of the inner cities.

The government used two sets of arguments in support of the community charge: fairness and accountability. They argue that the charge is fair because it requires almost everyone to contribute equally to the provision of services. The use of the word 'charge' is interesting as Esam and Oppenheim observe:

The government responds to criticisms that the poll tax is unfair by arguing that it is not a tax at all, but rather a 'charge for services' – hence the official name, 'community charge'. They point out that in market transactions people pay for the use they make of services; and that charges are made without respect to income. The principle of charging for particular local services can therefore be extended to incorporate a general charge for the 'bundle of services' which individuals receive from local authorities.[21]

Yet the community charge *is* a tax and it is patently unfair if ability to pay is taken to be the hallmark of fairness in taxation. The community charge is sharply regressive, even more so than rates which at least varied with the size and amenities of the house occupied.

Accountability is identified by the government as the most significant attribute of the community charge. They argued that while there are 35 million voters there were only 18 million ratepayers, and that this disparity made for weak accountability. By contrast, virtually the whole of the electorate pays at least a proportion of the community charge, and the government also claims that the community charge makes a clearer connection between spending decisions and the revenue required to finance them. Electors will be able to express their views about the most appropriate level of spending through the ballot box, councils having to keep their spending in check if they wish to be re-elected. It is clear that the government is as much concerned with controlling expenditure as it is with democratic accountability.

Local accountability is not helped by the government's control of the national business rate and its ability to influence the levels of community charge by the manipulation of central government grants. Another restrictive feature of the community charge is that each year the Department of the Environment will announce what it thinks the charge should be and local authorities are obliged to include this figure in their demands and show by how much they are exceeding government spending limits. As Carey Oppenheim says: 'The intent is to make local authorities carry the blame for increased rates/poll tax rather than central government.'[22] Because local accountability has not produced the required reductions in local government expenditure the government has introduced a charge-capping procedure. In 1990/1 twenty-one councils were capped, none of them Conservative.

The community charge is inefficient in that it is expensive to set up and administer, and it is easier to evade than rates. The estimated cost of establishing the system in England and Wales was £387 million and the costs of collection are at least twice those of rates. Rates, being based on property, were difficult to evade, whereas the community charge is based on registration and is only as effective as the registration procedures. The government claimed that the electoral register and the community charge register would be compiled and maintained separately, but it is clear that some local authorities used the electoral register as a starting point in compiling their community charge registers. It is likely that when people register to vote, their names will be made known to the community charge registration officer. Even if this does not happen, people may very well assume that it does, and to this extent the community charge represents a disincentive to vote.

There are three particularly disturbing features of the registration procedures. First, the registration officers are empowered to obtain lists of names and addresses from other local authority departments, and, apart from the issue of confidentiality involved, people may be deterred from making use of services. Second, community charge registration officers have the power to impose financial penalties for non-registration without a court hearing, although there is a right of appeal. Local authorities, acting through their registration officers, are also given extensive powers to deal with default. Officers can apply to the magistrates' court for an all purpose liability order. Once this has been granted the local authority has several options open to it: it may go back to the court to apply for an attachment order which allows arrears to be deducted directly from earnings or from benefits, or it may decide to act through distraint – that is the seizure and sale of property. Third, community charge registration encourages 'snooping'. There were complaints when the registers were being drawn up that registration officers were asking questions of a very personal nature and probably breaching the Data Protection Act. Snooping is particularly intrusive in the case of couples because the Act makes couples, either married or living together, 'jointly and severally' liable for paying the community charge and this means that either partner can be made liable for the payment of the other. If one of the two falls into arrears, therefore, the other partner can be forced to pay. With couples who are unmarried but living together, however, a decision has to be made about the nature of the relationship if liability is disputed and this may mean inquiries about sexual relationships and financial arrangements.

The community charge and the uniform business rate are backed up by a new system of central government grants. The replacement of the rate support grant by the revenue support grant is more than simply a change of name. The allocation of the rate support grant took account of both differing needs and differing resources as between one local authority and another, whereas the revenue support grant takes account of variations in need but not of variations in resources (which arose because of differences in total rateable values). This change will most seriously affect deprived urban areas, the chief beneficiaries of resource equalisation in the old system. The new system is to be phased in over four years so that changes in the distribution of grant will not take place too suddenly.

The new financial regime in local government arises chiefly out of a desire to restrict local government expenditure. Clearly, however, the government had not anticipated the vehemence and extent of the opposition to the community charge. Although they claim that the disturbances were orchestrated by extreme left-wing groups, they cannot help but be aware that dissatisfaction is much more widespread and that this has contributed to their poor showing in the opinion polls and to their overwhelming defeat in the Mid-Staffordshire by-election.

The government was left with no option but to consider further modification of the community charge and a review was set in train. At the time of writing the results of this review are not known, but among the options being considered is the imposition of a cap on all councils, which would be a complete denial of the principle of local accountability. Other suggestions include a more generous rebate system and a reallocation of Treasury funds council by council.

Whether such changes will make the community charge more generally acceptable remains to be seen.

Governing the cities

It was a Conservative Act of Parliament that led to the restructuring of local government in 1974. The Act of 1972 was not concerned with London government which had been reformed in 1965 with the establishment of the Greater London Council and the London boroughs.

The reorganisation of 1974 distinguished between metropolitan and non-metropolitan areas. The metropolitan areas were the major conurbations: Greater Manchester, Merseyside, South Yorkshire, Tyne and Wear, West Midlands and West Yorkshire. The theory was that the special problems of the conurbations called for special treatment with a Metropolitan County Council covering the whole of each urban area.

The Metropolitan County Councils and the Greater London Council were all Labour-controlled and the government saw them as frustrating its plans to control local government spending. The councils, and more especially the Greater London Council, frequently found themselves in dispute with central government, and relationships deteriorated rapidly between 1979 and 1983. In its manifesto for the 1983 election the Conservative Party committed itself to the abolition of the Greater London Council and the Metropolitan County Councils. There was little justification for abolition in either financial or administrative terms, but the government was determined to destroy the power base of what it described as the 'loony left'. Legislation was passed in 1985 and the councils were abolished in the following year.

The abolition of the Greater London Council left the Inner London Education Authority (ILEA) intact, but it seemed only a matter of time before it, too, disappeared. The Education Reform Act was used as the vehicle for abolition. Initially, the Bill made provision for individual boroughs to opt out of ILEA, but if eight or more opted the remainder would be required to follow. At the committee stage the Bill was amended to the effect that abolition would follow if only five boroughs opted out, but at the report stage a further amendment provided for the outright abolition of the ILEA in 1990.

It is in its inner city policies that the government's hostility to local authorities becomes most apparent. The government has done everything it can to bypass local authorities. This has been most obvious in the lack of local government representation on the Urban Development Corporations which have virtually replaced local authorities as planning authorities. Housing Action Trusts also supplant local authorities.

Loss of functions

The most obvious loss of functions has occurred in the inner cities (as described above) in housing and education. In local authority housing we have had compulsory sales, Housing Action Trusts and provisions allowing council tenants to opt out of local authority control and choose a new landlord.

In education local authorities have lost their polytechnics and colleges of higher education. Schools have been allowed to opt out of local authority control and in those schools which remain within their control, the local authorities have had to cede greater financial autonomy to governing bodies and head teachers.

Contracting out may also entail some loss of function in terms of direct provision. As Kate Ascher explains, the use of outside providers is not new in local government, but the practice remained relatively undeveloped and uncontroversial until 1979/80 when pressure groups such as the Adam Smith Institute, and elements within the Conservative Party, began to press for compulsory competitive tendering.[23]

Competitive tendering became a hotly-debated political issue in the early 1980s when a small number of Conservative-led local authorities began to experiment with it.[24] The first central government action came in 1980 with the Local Government Planning and Land Act, with the stated aim of improving the efficiency of direct labour organisations. These would now be closed if in three successive years they failed to achieve a 5 per cent return on capital. Thresholds for particular categories of building work were set and if these were exceeded a certain percentage of the work had to be put out to private tender.

The government came under increasing pressure to introduce mandatory competitive tendering, but it delayed making any commitment to do so until 1985 when it issued a consultative document announcing its intention to introduce compulsory competitive tendering from 1987.[25]

In the event, the legislation introducing mandatory competitive tendering was delayed until 1988 when the Local Government Act was passed. The Act compelled all local authorities to put seven services out to tender: school meals, other catering, refuse collection, street cleaning, building cleaning, grounds maintenance and vehicle maintenance. The Bill, in its original form, outlawed all forms of contract compliance – the practice of writing non-commercial conditions into contracts – but the Commission for Racial Equality argued that the Race Relations Act placed a duty on local authorities to eliminate unlawful discrimination and to foster good relations between people of different racial groups. This meant that local authorities, in awarding contracts, should be able to insist that companies endorsed non-discriminatory employment practices.

The government accepted this argument and introduced an amendment to the Bill at the Report stage. However, the amendment was a grudging one in that the Secretary of State said that he would allow local authorities to ask only four to five questions relating to race and that these would be prescribed by him. Furthermore, the questions could be asked only before the award of a contract and councils would not be allowed to terminate contracts on race relations grounds.[26] A later amendment in the House of Lords permitted local authorities to ask those seeking contracts about their employment practices in relation to disabled people, and to take their answers into account in awarding contracts.

The competitive tendering provisions, which came into effect in April 1989, require councils to put at least one service category out to tender every six months and the whole process must be completed by April 1991 in the non-metropolitan areas, and by October 1991 in the metropolitan districts and the London boroughs.

During the passage of the Bill some of the more radical Conservative MPs tabled amendments which would have required local authorities to invite tenders on another forty-one categories of service. The government opposed these amendments on the grounds that the extension of contracting out would over-stretch local authorities' management capacity, but the Act gives the Secretary of State power to require competitive tendering in other local government services by Order in Council. One such Order, requiring local authorities to invite tenders for the management of sports and leisure facilities, has already been promulgated. The process will have to be completed by the end of 1992.

Whether the government will be satisfied with this level of potential privatisation remains to be seen. The recommendations of the White Paper on community care services stopped short of mandatory competitive tendering, but made it clear that local authorities would be expected to make the maximum possible use of private contractors. It appears that the absence in some areas of potential private suppliers was one of the reasons for non-compulsion.

PROMOTING INEQUALITY

Inequality has unquestionably grown under the Conservatives. This has not just happened through drift or as the unintended consequences of policies. Inequality has been used as a deliberate strategy. As Walker says:

There is . . . a systematic policy to pursue and exploit inequality. The government views inequality as being helpful to incentives at both ends of the income distribution and does not regard gross disparities in income and wealth as a problem. On the contrary it sees it as a measure of success.[27]

The objective of Conservative policy has been not only to promote inequality by direct means but also to create a system of values which accepts greater inequality as inevitable and desirable. The factors contributing to the creation of such a climate of opinion include the following:

1. The emphasis on the enterprise culture.
2. The promotion of popular capitalism.
3. The encouragement of a market philosophy and competition in all aspects of national life.
4. The almost complete disregard of the problems arising from poverty, and indeed claims that there is no such thing as 'real poverty'.
5. Blaming the poor and disadvantaged for their own condition which, it is implied, results from fecklessness, moral laxity, laziness or low intelligence: those dependent upon state benefits are depicted as scroungers.
6. As a special case of the above, developing programmes which

imply that people are unemployed because they are not trying hard enough to find work, or they are inadequately trained or lack job-finding skills.

7. Attempts to regulate and control the poor.
8. Tax policies which favour the rich and damage the poor.
9. The propagation of a crude form of materialism and conspicuous consumption which more than ever implies that personal worth is to be judged in terms of income and wealth.
10. Assertions which emphasise the individualistic as *opposed* to the social aspects of life: Mrs Thatcher's much-publicised assertion that there is no such thing as society is a good example.

An assessment of the government's success in attempting to change the way we view social life will be delayed until the final chapter. We now turn to specific strategies for promoting inequality. Again an evaluation of the success of the strategies will be made after the major areas of social policy have been looked at in some detail.

Fiscal policies

Titmuss identified fiscal welfare as one of the three systems contributing to the 'social division of welfare'.[28] This is an explicit recognition of the fact that raising revenue to finance public expenditure is not the only function of taxation, it also has important social and redistributive functions. Taxes related to the ability to pay have an equalising effect, and the system can obviously be manipulated to bring about more or less redistribution.

The Conservative government has used changes in the tax system to produce greater inequality. It has done this in a number of ways. For example, it has switched some of the tax burden from income tax to value added tax. In its present form value added tax is mildly progressive; but it is less progressive than income tax and the switch has therefore brought about gains for the better-off at the expense of the worse-off.

The major change has been a lowering in the rates of tax. The basic rate has come down from 35 per cent to 25 per cent, but more significant in producing greater inquality has been a massive reduction in the rate of tax applied to the top end of the income range, from 83 per cent to 40 per cent.

Other changes have included a reduction in the tax levied on investment income, and reductions in both capital gains tax and inheritance tax. Yet another major change took place in 1989/90 in Scotland, and in 1990/91 in England and Wales, when local government rates were replaced by the community charge or poll tax. Rates were by no means progressive but they were considerably less regressive than the poll tax. John Hills says of the tax changes:

This process has happened piece by piece, but each stage has moved gradually in the same direction – the tilt away from a tax structure in which people on higher incomes pay a greater proportion of their income in tax than those on lower incomes. The Poll Tax – under which everyone (except for the limited number receiving rebates) pays the same cash amount, representing the greatest proportion of income for the poor – is simply a logical extension of the process.[29]

Wages policies
Income tax cuts obviously increase the take-home pay of all taxpayers. However, as seen in the previous section, high earners have experienced a substantial fall in deductions from their pay while the low paid have done much less well. Indeed any gains made by the low paid have been eroded by higher national insurance contributions.

But differential tax cuts were not the only means used to bring about greater disparities in incomes. While leaving the wages of the highly paid to find their own levels, the government has taken several measures to hold down the wages of the lower paid. These include:

1. The scope of the wages councils has been considerably narrowed. The number of wages inspectors has been reduced, and the Wages Act of 1986 ended wages council protection for all those under the age of 21 and curtailed the protection offered to other workers. From time to time the government has threatened abolition of the wages councils and this remains a distinct possibility for the future.
2. The rates of allowances available in the Youth Training Scheme and the Employment Training Programme help to keep wages down, and this means that people may be better off even in the lowest paid jobs.
3. In 1982 the government abandoned the Fair Wages Resolution

in order to encourage contracting out. What it meant was that private contractors taking on public sector work were no longer subject to fair wage clauses.

4. The New Workers Scheme was discontinued in 1989, but, until its abolition, it contributed to the downward pressure on the wages of young workers by offering a subsidy to employers who took on young people. The subsidy was conditional upon the employer keeping wages below particular levels. The Jobstart Scheme, which began in 1986, performed a similar function in relation to older workers.

5. Rights against unfair dismissal have been successively eroded. In 1980 and 1985 the period of service required before workers became protected against unfair dismissal was lengthened, and in 1989 the Employment Act relaxed the law on the dismissal of employees by small businesses.

Social security policies

The changes in the social security system are covered in Chapter 3. The number of losers from the changes far outweigh the number of gainers. It is worth stressing the increased use of means tests and the increasingly onerous conditions placed on the recipients of unemployment benefit. For example, the Social Security Act of 1989 added the actively seeking work test to availability testing, and it must be remembered that failure to meet these conditions may lead to loss of further benefit.

Furthermore, after three months' unemployment claimants will not be able to refuse work outside their usual occupation or place of residence and low wages will not be considered good cause for refusing a job. While the refusal of a place on a government training scheme will not on its own constitute a sufficient reason for withdrawal of benefit, it will be taken into account when benefit decisions are being made. The Unemployment Unit says: 'It appears that we are moving rapidly towards something like the American system of "Workfare", where the unemployed are required to work, "train" or actively job search in order to demonstrate that they are eligible for their benefit payments'.[30]

Unemployment

Unemployment creates poverty and inequality. Several forms of inequality are involved. First, there is the general disparity between the living standards of the employed and the unemployed. Second, there are large regional and local differences in the rates of unemployment. Third, there are significant social class differentials in unemployment. Fourth, unemployment is more common among the members of ethnic minorities than among the rest of the population. Fifth, disabled people are more likely to experience unemployment than are non-disabled people. Sixth, there are gender differences in unemployment. Glendinning, quoting Equal Opportunities Commission figures, says that between 1979 and 1986 male unemployment rose by 143 per cent while female unemployment rose by 189 per cent.[31]

As unemployment rises these differences are accentuated, and under the Conservatives unemployment rose from 1.3 million in 1979 to 3.2 million in 1986 and then fell to 1.7 million in 1989.[32] However, these figures should be treated with great caution: between 1982 and 1990 twenty-nine changes were made to the way the unemployed are counted, all of them designed to make the figures appear more respectable. It should be emphasised, too, that the figures exclude all those on special government schemes.

Unemployment was the known result of the government's monetarist policies. The government evidently saw inflation as the main enemy and believed that the price in terms of unemployment was worth paying. Walker writes:

Rather than simply being the by-product of a world recession, the British government has consciously chosen unemployment as a tool of social and economic policy. It has been able to do so because the burden of unemployment is not borne equally. Thus, it is predominantly the same poor people in the benefit and low wage sectors who have experienced the lowest rises in income over the last eight years that have also been hit hardest by unemployment.[33]

Taming the unions
Increased unemployment had a useful spin-off for the government in that it weakened the power of the trade unions. The government was determined to face up to the unions and to limit their activities by means of legislation. In ten years, five major Acts dealing with trade unions have been passed: the Employment Act (1980), the Employment Act (1982), the Trade Union Act (1984), the Employment Act (1988) and the Employment Act (1990).

The Acts of 1980 and 1982: banned secondary picketing (the picketing of suppliers or customers of the company in dispute); prohibited sympathy or solidarity boycotts; and made closed shops more difficult to achieve by requiring an 80 per cent majority in favour of a closed shop in ballots to be held every five years.

The Trade Union Act of 1984 was concerned with what the government referred to as union democracy. The Act laid down procedures for the election of senior union officers and insisted upon ballots before every call for industrial action and upon ballots every ten years to decide whether the union is to continue to have a political fund.

The Employment Act of 1988 strengthened the provisions relating to secret postal ballots; enforced the *periodic* election of key union officials; and made provision for the establishment of a Commissioner for the protection of union members' rights. The most controversial aspect of the Act, however, was the guarantee of legal protection for any union member who continues to work during a dispute. This provision means that unions will have no right to discipline members for refusing to abide by a majority decision arrived at in a secret ballot.

In March 1989 the Department of Employment published a Green Paper which proposed further trade union legislation to outlaw the pre-entry closed shop and secondary action by workers who are not party to a dispute.[34] These proposals were put into effect in the Employment Act of 1990 which also gave employers the right to sack union leaders who they believe are behind unofficial walkouts.

During the 1980s the government was in conflict with the unions on several occasions, the two most publicised instances being the dispute over union membership at the Government Communications Headquarters (GCHQ) in 1984 and the miners' strike of 1984/5. The government won outright victories in both cases. Gamble says of the miners' strike:

The cost of the strike to the country and the Government was very high – approximately £2.5 billion. But the Government was prepared to write off this cost for the long-term benefits it expected from a clear-cut miners' defeat. These were not only the effects on the running of the coal industry, but the wider symbolic effects of defeating the group of workers who had successfully resisted the Heath Government. To gain this prize the Government made detailed preparations for a miners' strike, resisted all pressures to compromise, and won a complete victory.[35]

Contracting out has also been used as a means of reducing the power of the public sector unions in local government, the NHS and in central government. In a discussion of the ideological environment of contracting out Ascher writes:

> The numerous objectives that have been attributed to the policy generally fall into one of two categories: loosening the control of public sector unions or increasing competition and efficiency in the economy. The former is a covert set of objectives whilst the latter is overt. Competitive tendering is ideally suited to achieve *both* of these objectives simultaneously, and it is this simple fact which explains its widespread appeal to members of the Conservative Party . . . Competitive tendering and contracting out fit into the Conservative Government's comprehensive and sustained attack upon trade union power.[36]

Privatisation and inequality

Privatisation promotes inequality in a number of ways. The sale of public utilities, for example, may widen share ownership slightly by bringing new people into the equity market, but the main beneficiaries are in the middle and upper income groups. The alleged under-pricing of shares has led to quick profits for the few. The sale of council houses has been to better-off tenants, leaving fewer houses to rent for those who cannot afford to buy. Local authority housing is rapidly becoming a service for the poor and disadvantaged. The assisted places scheme in education and the growth of private facilities in the NHS chiefly benefit the middle classes. Perhaps a more important consideration, however, is that private provision corrodes social solidarity.

A general policy of cutting or restricting public expenditure and relying more heavily on the commercial, voluntary and informal sectors may in itself create greater inequalities. The commercial sector responds to the ability to pay; voluntary provision is unevenly distributed; and the informal sector relies on the unpaid work of, mainly female, carers.

How the aims identified in this chapter have been translated into actual policies in social security, the National health Service, education, housing, and the personal social services will be the subject of the next five chapters. The government's success in achieving its aims will be addressed in the final chapter.

NOTES

1. J. Le Grand and R. Robinson (eds.), *Privatisation and the Welfare State*, London: Allen and Unwin, 1984, pp. 1–14.
2. For a good discussion of contracting out see K. Ascher, *The Politics of Privatisation*, London: Macmillan, 1987.
3. Department of Health, *Working for Patients*, CM 555, London: HMSO, 1989.
4. For details of the proposals see Department of Health, *Caring for People*, Cm 849, London: HMSO, 1989.
5. N. Deakin and M. Wicks, *Families and the State*, London: Family Policy Studies Centre, 1988, pp. 19–36.
6. *Ibid.*, p. 30.
7. Audit Commission, *Managing Social Services for the Elderly More Effectively*, London: HMSO, 1985, para. 137.
8. Source: J. Hills, *Changing Tax: How the Tax System Works and How to Change it*, London: Child Poverty Action Group, 1988, p. 20.
9. M. Wilkinson, 'Tax expenditures and public policy in the UK', *Journal of Social Policy*, vol. 15, pt. 1, 1986, pp. 23–49.
10. J. Hills, 'What happened to spending on the welfare state?', in A. Walker and C. Walker (eds.), *The Growing Divide*, London: Child Poverty Action Group, 1987, pp. 88–100.
11. S. Young, 'The nature of privatisation in Britain, 1979–85', *West European Politics*, vol. 9, no. 2, 1986, p. 248.
12. Cm 555, pp. 57–9.
13. Cm 849, p. 6.
14. *Ibid.*, p. 41.
15. J. Greenwood and D. Wilson, *Public Administration in Britain*, London: Allen and Unwin, 1984, p. 157.
16. Department of the Environment, *Alternatives to Domestic Rates*, Cmnd 8449, London: HMSO, 1981.
17. Department of the Environment, *Paying for Local Government*, Cmnd 9714, London: HMSO, 1986.
18. *The Guardian*, 12 April 1990.
19. *The Guardian*, 6 October 1989.
20. *Ibid.*, 12 October 1989.
21. P. Esam and C. Oppenheim, *A Charge on the Community*, London: Child Poverty Action Group and the Local Government Information Unit, 1989, p. 36.
22. C. Oppenheim, *A Tax on All the People*, London: Child Poverty Action Group, 1987, p. 17.
23. K. Ascher, *The Politics of Privatisation: Contracting Out Public Services*, London: Macmillan, 1987.

24. *Ibid.*, pp. 33–5.
25. Department of the Environment, *Competition in the Provision of Local Authority Services*, London: HMSO, 1985.
26. *The Guardian*, 15 December 1987.
27. A. Walker, 'Conclusion I: A divided Britain', in A. Walker and C. Walker (eds.), *op. cit.*, pp. 129–38.
28. R. M. Titmuss, *Essays on the Welfare State*, London: Allen and Unwin, 1963, ch. 2.
29. J. Hills, *Changing Tax: How the Tax System Works and How to Change it*, London: Child Poverty Action Group, 1988, p. 11.
30. The Unemployment Unit, *Square Pegs in Round Holes*, London: The Unemployment Unit, 1988, p. 1.
31. These are the seasonally adjusted figures for October. They exclude school leavers.
32. C. Glendinning, 'Impoverishing women', in A. Walker and C. Walker (eds.), *op. cit.*, p. 51.
33. A. Walker, *op. cit.*, p. 132.
34. Department of Employment, *Removing Barriers to Work*, Cm 655, London: HMSO, 1989.
35. A. Gamble, *The Free Economy and the Strong State*, London: Macmillan, 1988, p. 193.
36. K. Ascher, *op. cit.*, p. 47.

CHAPTER 3

SOCIAL SECURITY: FORWARD OR BACKWARDS FROM BEVERIDGE?

Although its recommendations were never fully implemented, the Beveridge Report formed the basis of the British social security system for forty years.[1] There were some dissenting voices, but generally speaking the report was enthusiastically received as a blueprint for post-war social reconstruction. *The Times* said:

The Government has been presented with an opportunity for marking this decisive epoch with a great social measure which would go far towards restoring the faith of ordinary men and women throughout the world in the power of democracy to answer the imperious needs of a new age . . . The grand design of Sir William Beveridge's proposals has caught the imagination of the people and set new standards of what is possible in social reconstruction.[2]

The centrepiece was a contributory system of social insurance to provide cash support when earnings from work were interrupted through sickness or unemployment, or upon retirement or the death of a male breadwinner. The idea of wage-related contributions and benefits was rejected in favour of a flat-rate principle. Benefits should be sufficient, on their own, to maintain individuals and families at subsistence level, and the payment of maternity benefits would be a recognition of the extra expenditure before and after the birth of a child and a death grant would help with funeral costs.

It was assumed that a man's wages would be sufficient to support himself, his wife and their children and that unemployment would be minimal. However, since wages were not related to family size, a system of family allowances was thought to be necessary.

Underpinning the system of insurance, Beveridge recommended a non-contributory social assistance scheme financed from taxation. It is interesting to note that the assistance scheme was deliberately designed to be stigmatising:

Assistance will be available to meet all needs which are not covered by insurance. It must meet those needs adequately up to subsistence level, but it must be felt to be something less desirable than insurance benefit: otherwise the insured persons get nothing for their contributions. Assistance therefore will be given always subject to proof of needs and examination of means.[3]

The objective of the statutory scheme was the creation of a national minimum, leaving room for people to make private arrangements, one of the guiding principles of the report being that of partnership between the state and the individual. If benefits were too generous they might stifle initiative and discourage independence and the acceptance of individual responsibility. They might also damage the insurance companies and friendly societies.

Although the main features of the Beveridge plan were incorporated into post-war legislation, some of the recommendations were only partially implemented and some were completely ignored. Most important among those ignored were proposals for a marriage grant and for benefits to be paid to separated and divorced women, provided that they were not personally at fault.

A much more significant deviation from the report was the level at which insurance benefits were set (much lower than Beveridge had recommended) and limitations of the periods over which sickness and unemployment benefits could be drawn. This meant that insurance benefits were even less generous than means-tested benefits available under the national assistance scheme. This had far reaching and long-term consequences. It meant that the idea of insurance for all was compromised from the very beginning, with far greater numbers than Beveridge had envisaged dependent on means-tested benefits for topping up inadequate insurance benefits (especially pensions). The insurance principle was also breached by the payment of full pensions to elderly people retiring within the first few years of the scheme before they had built up entitlement on the basis of contributions.

Until 1987–8 there were no major overhauls of the social security system, but the cumulative effect of incremental change was considerable. By 1984, when a major review of the social security scheme was carried out, many of the principles of Beveridge had been abandoned or curtailed.

However, the piecemeal changes made to the social security scheme between 1948 and 1979 made it unduly cumbersome and complicated: no clear lines of policy had been followed and no review of the whole system had been undertaken. The return of the Thatcher administration in 1979 held out the possibility of a major re-structuring of the system.

SOCIAL SECURITY IN THE THATCHER YEARS

Modification and retrenchment

In September 1976 the Labour government asked a team of DHSS officials 'to take a thorough look at the supplementary benefits scheme'. The review team published its findings in July 1978 – nine months before the Conservatives came to power.

There had been considerable concern over a number of years about the operation of the supplementary benefits scheme. The review team claimed that the scheme was 'trying to handle too large a number of beneficiaries in too detailed and complex a way, with too extensive a reliance on discretionary payments',[4] and concluded that the social assistance scheme was 'having to play a role for which it was neither originally designed nor subsequently adapted'.[5] The theme of all of the team's proposals was the need for simplification, with clearer rules of entitlement laid down in legislation, a reduced reliance on special payments and a fairer deal for married women.

It was left to the Conservative government to implement the proposals in two Social Security Acts in 1980. The legislation resulted in a reduction of discretion, particularly in the area of special payments. Access to exceptional circumstances additions and exceptional needs payments was considerably diminished: both were restricted to specific listed items available only in carefully circumscribed circumstances. For example, lump sum payments would be made only if their lack would *seriously* damage or put at *serious* risk the health or safety of the claimant or of someone in his family.

Other changes introduced under the Social Security Acts of 1980 included the following:

1. The Supplementary Benefits Commission, which had possessed executive functions, was abolished and replaced by the non-executive Social Security Advisory Committee.
2. The link between average earnings and pensions was broken, so in future pensions would be uprated only in line with prices, resulting in smaller increases.
3. In calculating the benefits paid to meet the needs of strikers' families (no benefits being paid to meet strikers' own needs) it was to be assumed that strike pay was being received, regardless of whether or not unions were paying their members.
4. The position of women was slightly improved in that in future either the man or the woman in a couple could claim supplementary benefit or family income supplement.
5. As from January 1982, the earnings-related supplements to unemployment, sickness and widows' benefits were abolished.
6. Short term national insurance benefits were increased by 5 per cent less than the estimated rate of inflation. The government planned to make these benefits taxable and the reduction was to take into account the government's inability to introduce immediate changes in the tax system. Unemployment benefit became taxable in July 1982, but the 5 per cent cut was not restored, and then to unemployment benefit only, until November 1983.

Housing benefit was a matter of concern to the government: the system was complicated and expensive. When the Conservatives came to power there was a dual system of assistance towards housing costs: supplementary benefit claimants might have their rates and rent covered wholly by the DHSS while other people on low incomes could apply to the local authority for rent and rate rebates. One of the problems associated with this system was that some national insurance beneficiaries in receipt of rent and rate rebates were better off moving entirely on to supplementary benefit where the whole of their housing costs would be met.

The system was changed by the Social Security and Housing Benefit Act of 1982 which attempted to create a single unified scheme by transferring the DHSS's responsibility for paying claimants' rent and rates to the local authority. There were now two main types of housing benefit: first, certificated housing benefit for those on supplementary benefit who were required to obtain a certificate to that effect from the social security office and to present this to the local authority; and second, standard housing benefit – a new name for rent and rate rebates – obtainable directly from the local authority. A housing benefit supplement was made available to compensate those on low incomes who would have been better off moving on to supplementary benefit. Owner-occupiers on supplementary benefit had their rates covered by the local authority, but their other housing entitlement (mortgage interest and an allowance for repairs and insurance) were met by the DHSS.

It is doubtful whether this system was much simpler than the one it replaced, and recent changes (1988) have not altered its operating principles, although the benefits available have been much reduced.

One other set of changes must be mentioned before turning to the major restructuring under the Social Security Act of 1986. In April 1983 responsibility for the first eight weeks of sickness benefit was transferred from the state to employers: sickness benefit now became statutory sick pay during the first eight weeks' absence from work. In April 1987 the period of employers' responsibility was extended to 28 weeks and statutory maternity pay replaced the maternity allowance administered by the DHSS and the maternity pay scheme administered by the Department of Employment. These measures are significant because they represent a considerable increase in privatisation.

Restructuring

The government made it very plain that the changes under the 1980 legislation were no more than interim measures pending a more comprehensive examination of the social security system, although they waited until their second term of office before taking any further action.

In 1984, Mr Fowler, the Secretary of State for Social Services, named four teams to review supplementary benefits, benefits for children and young persons, housing benefit and pensions. Four separate reports had been anticipated, but in the event the recommendations of all four review teams were included in a single Green Paper with supplementary volumes, published in June 1985.[6]

The government was now in a hurry and the period for consultation was kept to an absolute minimum. In December 1985 a White

Paper setting out the government's intentions was published preparatory to legislation during 1986. The White Paper said that its proposals were the result of 'the most fundamental examination of our social security system since the Second World War',[7] and claimed that the serious shortcomings of the system made the case for reform overwhelming.

The major criticisms of the scheme were:

1. It was too complex; there were thirty benefits, each with separate rules of entitlement, and both claimants and those administering the scheme found the system difficult to understand.
2. It was too indiscriminate, failing to concentrate help on those in greatest need; families with dependent children were singled out as a priority group.
3. Some people were better off, or only slightly worse off, on benefit than when in work; and there were many who were trapped in poverty because any increase in wages resulted in higher tax liability and the loss of means-tested benefits.
4. People were discouraged from making their own provision and there were unnecessary obstacles to the growth of occupational provision.
5. The scheme was costly and committed the country to even greater expenditure in the future.

Most of the changes foreshadowed in the Green and White Papers were implemented in 1987 and 1988 under the Social Security Act of 1986. Before an assessment of these changes can be made, and the reasons for them analysed, a brief description of what they entailed must be given. They may be considered under five headings: income support, family credit, housing benefit, the social fund and pensions.

Income support
Supplementary benefit has been replaced by income support. There are two main elements to income support: a system of personal allowances, with additions for dependent children, and premiums (i.e. extra payments) for specific categories of claimant.

There are premiums for families, and there are extra payments for elderly people: a basic rate for those aged 60–79 and a higher rate for those aged 80 and over. There are also two disability premiums, the amount received depending upon the severity of the disablement.

The distinctions in the supplementary benefit system between long term and standard rates of benefit and between householder and non-householder have been eliminated, as have the exceptional circumstances additions. Responsibility for the lump sum exceptional needs payments has been separated from the basic income support system and entrusted to the social fund (see below).

Family credit

Family credit replaced family income supplement and, like its predecessor, it is means-tested. It is intended to help low income families with at least one dependent child and where at least one of the parents is working more than twenty-four hours a week. For each family there is a maximum benefit which varies with the number and the ages of dependent children. Each year the government will fix a 'threshold', and if the family's *net* income is below the 'threshold' then they will receive the maximum family credit. If net income exceeds the 'threshold' then family credit will be reduced by 70 per cent of the excess. That is, for every pound by which the family's income exceeds the 'threshold' they will lose 70p of benefit.

In its original form, family credit was to be added to the wage packets of the principal earner in a family which in most cases would have resulted in men being the recipients. This feature of family credit aroused considerable opposition both inside and outside Parliament, and, at a very late stage of its passage, the Bill was amended to ensure that family credit was paid to the main carers – usually mothers.

Housing benefit

The main structure of the housing benefit system remains intact but the rates of benefit have been much reduced. Savings of approximately £640 million have been achieved by tightening eligibility criteria, by tapering benefits more sharply as income rises above the base levels, by insisting that everyone must pay at least 20 per cent of their domestic rates (formerly full rebates had been available) and by dispensing with the allowance for water rates. For those on income support there was an amount built into the personal allowances which was meant to compensate for the 20 per cent rates payment, but this was based on average rates, so that claimants whose rates were above average were worse off. Rates have now been replaced by the community charge, but the same principle applies.

Social fund

The social fund is responsible for the administration of a range of grants and loans. The grants comprise maternity payments, funeral payments, cold weather payments and community care grants. The universal maternity grants and death grants were replaced in 1987 by maternity payments to those in receipt of income support or family credit and funeral payments, recoverable from the deceased's estate, to recipients of income support, family credit or housing benefit. A separate system of severe weather payments is made available to certain categories of income support claimants.

Community care grants are available to people leaving institutional care or in order to avoid the need for institutional care. Grants will also be made towards travel costs (e.g. to visit people in institutions) and to help ease exceptional pressures on families arising from illness, disability or breakdown of family relationships. In the allocation of grants, priority is to be given to the frail elderly, the physically and mentally impaired and the mentally ill, and priority will also be given to grants required for the purchase of essential furniture and domestic equipment, especially when it is needed by someone moving out of residential care into unfurnished accommodation.

The most far reaching change introduced by the social fund is the substitution of loans for exceptional needs payments. Apart from the few specific payments and the community care grants mentioned above, all other financial help will be given as interest-free loans which must be repaid out of income support benefits.

Two kinds of loans are available: budgeting loans and crisis loans. To be eligible for a budgeting loan a claimant has to have been receiving income support for at least six months. Budgeting loans are intended to be for the purchase of expensive items which have to be replaced infrequently, such as beds and cookers. Crisis loans, on the other hand, are to meet emergencies which could not have been foreseen: floods, fires, gale damage or loss of money or property through theft or burglary. Crisis loans cover a period of fourteen days after the disaster.

Pensions

The government seemed to have two concerns about pension arrangements: the present and future costs of the State Earnings-related Pension Scheme (SERPS) and the encouragement of occupational and private schemes.

SERPS, established with all-party agreement in 1978, was designed to provide those without an occupational pension with an earnings-related pension based on average earnings in the twenty years when earnings were highest. The earnings-related element was added on to the basic state pension, providing a pension equivalent to 25 per cent of earnings between lower and upper limits updated to take account of inflation. Since most non-manual jobs are pensionable and many self-employed professionals take out private schemes, the majority of the people on SERPS are manual workers.

The White Paper indicated that there were about 11 million people in occupational schemes with about 10 million dependent upon SERPS. The number of pensioners was expected to grow from 9.3 million in 1984 to 13.2 million by 2035, and this would lead to an enormous increase in the cost of SERPS. One of the problems with SERPS, according to the White Paper, is that it pre-empts resources and reduces flexibility for future governments. Another problem was said to be 'the very substantial financial debt we are handing down to future generations' and added the warning, 'We may make promises for the future – but it may be more difficult for our children to meet them.'[8]

The government had originally intended to abolish SERPS, but when this intention was revealed in the Green Paper there was a public outcry and the government was forced to alter its plans. The White Paper proposed the modification of SERPS in a downwards direction rather than its abolition. The position of anyone retiring before 1999 will be unaffected and there will be a transitional period from 1999 to 2009.

The scheme is being changed for the worse in three respects. In future, pension entitlement will be based on lifetime's earnings rather than on the best twenty years. Second, the amount paid will be 20 per cent of average earnings rather than 25 per cent; the reduction from 25 per cent to 20 per cent will take place by stages between 1999 and 2009. Third, widows will in future inherit only half of their husband's pension rights rather than the whole of them as at present.

The poorer returns available under SERPS obviously and intentionally make private pensions more attractive. In 1988 further encouragement to leave SERPS and take out a personal private pension or join an occupational scheme was given. Under the 1986 Social Security Act those leaving SERPS will be able to use the contributions which would have gone to the state scheme to pay for a personal or occupational pension; and, until 1993, the DHSS will add a further 2 per cent to the employee's own contributions. The same incentive is available to members of occupational schemes wishing to make private arrangements.

Assessment
When the Green Paper appeared in 1985, political and academic commentators were largely hostile. Donnison, for example, said that its proposals represented 'a decisive step backwards' and argued that government's main strategy was 'the product, not of honest economic and social analysis, but of an old-fashioned backlash'.[9] The Child Poverty Action Group, analysing the responses of sixty representative organisations, found that only the Institute of Directors and the Monday Club were in favour of the proposals.[10] If anything, the criticism has intensified and become more specific since the publication of the White Paper and the passing and implementation of the Act.

Initial analysis, based on the White Paper, suggested that there would be 3.8 million losers and 2.16 million gainers. Since that time there has been a continuous dispute about the percentages of gainers and losers. The government maintains that only 12 per cent are worse off because of the changes. The government's own Social Security Advisory Committee, however, says that 43 per cent are worse off; the Policy Studies Institute puts the figure at 48 per cent with 32 per cent having gained; and the Benefits Research Unit claims that just under 60 per cent are worse off, just under 25 per cent are in much the same position as before and fewer than one in five are better off.[11]

According to the White Paper the main gainers were said to be families with dependent children and, to a lesser extent, chronically sick and disabled people. This was said to be part of an overall policy of concentrating help on those whose needs are greatest. On the face of it, this seems a perfectly reasonable objective, provided of course that those in greatest need can be accurately identified and that they are willing to claim, but even if this can be accomplished, what in effect is happening is that favoured needy groups benefit at the expense of other poor people.

While families with dependent children and chronically sick and disabled people were to be the main gainers, the main losers were to be the young unemployed, elderly people, and unemployed child-less couples. Under separate legislation, many of those under the age of 18 are to be denied benefits altogether if they turn down a place on the Youth Training Scheme, irrespective of how unsuitable the place might be.

Evidence from the Benefits Research Unit and the National Association of Citizens' Advice Bureaux suggests that the policy of targeting benefits upon the two priority groups completely misfired. The Benefits Research Unit claims that 81 per cent of couples with children and 74 per cent of lone parents will lose.[12] The position has hardly been improved by the freezing of child benefits in 1988, 1989 and 1990 and the abolition of free milk and school meals for those on family credit and their replacement by a modest flat-rate allowance.

The Benefit Research Unit's estimates were made just before the Act came into operation. In November 1989 the House of Commons Social Services Committee, which is Conservative-dominated, issued a report assessing the operation of the Act. It indicated that single people had lost up to £8.84 a week and that single parents, childless couples and elderly people had lost substantial amounts. Couples with children had gained only marginally.

But these figures only compare income support levels with supplementary benefit rates, and take no account of the loss of one-off payments which were particularly significant to families with children. The Committee's Chairman has stated that the adverse effects on families were under-estimated in the report for another reason. Recipients of income support now have to pay 20 per cent of their rates and the whole of their water rates. The levels of income support are supposed to take this into account, but in many cases the amounts paid are insufficient to fully compensate people for the extra expenditure.[13] The National Association of Citizens' Advice Bureaux estimates that five out of six disabled people have lost on average £8.40 a week because the disability premiums do not compensate for the loss of special allowances for such things as special diet, laundry costs, extra heating; and because of the abolition of the long term rates of benefit.[14]

The social security changes have meant a very considerable increase in the use of means tests. Fran Bennett sums up this change of emphasis:

Under the Social Security Act, means-tested benefits become the fulcrum of the social security system. There is a shift in the centre of gravity of the benefits system away from benefits as of right towards benefits requiring a 'test of income' . . .[15]

Writing before the proposals were implemented, Alcock makes a similar point when he claims that 'the plans for the reform of social security in 1988 are based on the assumption that means-tested support will remain the major feature of benefit provision for the majority of claimants . . .'.[16] Two examples of an even greater reliance on means tests will suffice.

The first example concerns the operation of family credit. Initially it appeared that family credit meant replacing one means-tested benefit, family income supplement, with another. However, with the freezing of the universal child benefit for three years running, it became clear that means-tested family credit was to become the dominant means of child support and that child benefit might eventually be phased out. The Secretary of State, seeking to justify the decision not to increase child benefit, pointed out that it consumed nearly 10 per cent of the social security budget, and that help should be concentrated on those who most needed it. There is a problem of take-up in that only about 40 per cent of those eligible for family credit actually avail themselves of it. In 1989 a total of £6 million was spent on advertising the scheme, but initial indications are that this take-up campaign has failed: between April and June 1989 only about 10,000 new applicants came forward as compared with the target of 200,000 families.

The second example is the doubling of the contributions required before people can claim unemployment or sickness benefit from one year to two. According to a report by David Hencke this will mean that 350,000 people will lose their insurance benefits and be compelled to rely on income support, with married women who lose their jobs and young people without any work record among the main losers.[17]

The increasing use of means tests makes a nonsense of two of the stated aims of the government: simplification and a reduction in the number of people caught in the poverty trap. It is difficult to make a system dependent upon means tests simple to understand and operate, and, although there has been some standardisation of the tests, the application form for income support runs into nineteen pages. A report in July 1988 from the Select Committee on Social Services indicated that the number dependent upon means-tested state benefits had risen from 4.4 million in 1979 to 8.2 million in 1988.[18]

The poverty trap refers to the problem of people on low incomes who find themselves little or no better off when income rises because they lose means-tested benefits and they might move above the tax threshold. Figures produced by the Institute for Fiscal Studies when the White Paper first appeared indicated that as a result of the government's proposals the number of people losing between 60 per cent and 100 per cent of any increase in income would rise from 2½ per cent of taxpayers to slightly more than 5½ per cent.[19] A report from the House of Commons Social Services Committee, published in 1989, claims that the number of households in the poverty trap rose by 43 per cent between 1988 and 1989.[20] A study conducted by the Low Pay Unit looked at how the 1988 budget affected poor people. It claimed that the poverty trap was deepening, and that from every £1 gained from the tax cut a poor family would lose 70p in family credit, 6p in rate rebate and 19½p in rent rebate, leaving only 4½p out of the original £1.[21]

When a completely new system is introduced one can expect some initial administrative problems, but the problems experienced by the new social security system have been greater than might have been anticipated. A particular problem which can cause clients great distress is the very long delays in making payments. The National Association of Citizens' Advice Bureaux expressed particular concern about family credit payments, claiming that by the middle of July 1988, three months after the introduction of the scheme, 215,000 claims had been made and of these, 70,000 had not been dealt with; some families had been waiting three months. The Association claims that these delays are forcing families into debt, and the situation is made more serious by the fact that less than half of those expected to claim have actually done so.[22]

Robin Cook, the Labour Party's front bench spokesperson on social security, has raised the possibility of even greater delays, as long as thirty-one weeks, in the payment of housing benefit transitional protection; and the income support system has greater delays built into it: income support is now paid two weeks in arrears whereas supplementary benefit was always paid one week in arrears and one week in advance.

The two most controversial elements of the new system are housing benefit and the social fund; and the substance of the criticisms of both needs to be examined. The Social Security Advisory Committee has estimated that between April 1983 and April 1987 cuts in housing benefit amounted to £378 million. The changes made in April 1988 'will produce a further saving of £640 million compared with a continuation of the previous scheme'. The Committee states that 'the majority of households on housing benefit will receive less help with their rent and rates and over one million claimants will lose entitlement altogether'.[23] As Penny Waterhouse, the Housing Benefits Co-ordinator of Haringey Council, has written: 'Nearly everyone will lose as a result of changes to housing benefit, with the most needy among the most badly affected . . . Young people, elderly people and those with disabilities will be hit hardest . . .'.[24]

One of the bitterest complaints arose out of the withdrawal of housing benefit supplement – a payment formerly made to those whose incomes, even with housing benefit, left them worse off than they would have been on supplementary benefit. More than 400,000 people suffered a loss of income on account of the withdrawal of the supplement. The claim made by welfare rights activists was that, in spite of its name, housing benefit supplement was in effect supplementary benefit, not housing benefit. This distinction is of more than semantic importance because levels of existing supplementary benefit payments were protected for a transitional period after the introduction of income support.

Even the government's own backbenchers were far from happy with the housing benefit changes and threatened revolt. MPs from both sides of the House claimed that constituents in large numbers were registering their disapproval, a major cause for concern being the rule which reduced benefit if claimants had savings of more than £3,000 and cut it off altogether when savings exceeded £6,000. MPs said that the upper limit was far too low and that the people who suffered most from the application of the capital limit were retirement pensioners with very modest savings. There was pressure to raise the limit to £10,000.

Three weeks after the introduction of housing benefit the

government was forced to make a number of concessions in order to placate its own supporters. Robin Cook, shadow Social Services Secretary, claimed that there were 5.5 million losers and that the most compelling reason for concessions was that 55 per cent of them lived in Conservative constituencies. Three concessions were made:

1. The capital limit was raised from £6,000 to £8,000, benefiting 100,000 people and costing £30 million.
2. Those whose benefits were stopped because they had a house to sell would now be given six months to dispose of their property.
3. A transitional scheme was introduced to compensate recipients for any losses greater than £2.50 a week – 300,000 people would benefit from this at a cost of £70 million.

In spite of these concessions some of the problems of housing benefit remain. The capital limit of £8,000 is still too low – £10,000 would be more appropriate. Furthermore, the transitional scheme has run into problems. Three months after its introduction only sixty-eight claimants had received extra help; and instead of helping anyone who was more than £2.50 a week worse off, the scheme had helped only those who had lost £7 a week or more. Another shortcoming is the absence of an adequate means of reviewing housing benefit decisions, the only appeal being to a review board composed of local councillors.

The requirement that everyone should pay at least 20 per cent of their domestic rates and the whole of their water rates was also causing serious problems, as was the cut in levels of benefit generally. A report produced in August 1988 by the Institute of Housing suggested that rent arrears had increased dramatically since April: among the figures quoted were a 25 per cent increase in Leeds, a 32 per cent increase in Doncaster and a 48 per cent increase in Wales. The Institute claimed that failure to pay 20 per cent of the domestic rates had resulted in a number of enforcement actions in county courts and defaulters faced the possibility of losing their homes and other possessions.[25]

The most vehement criticism of the new social security system has been directed at the social fund. The replacement of single payments by loans has attracted widespread condemnation. Predictably, the policy is supported by such organisations as the Adam Smith Institute, the Institute of Economic Affairs and the Monday Club, but the overwhelming weight of opinion is hostile. The Social

Security Advisory Committee and the House of Commons Social Services Committee (with a majority of Conservative MPs) are opposed to the system of loans, as are all the groups representing the poor, the elderly and the chronically sick and disabled. Hostility towards loans is particularly significant because two-thirds of the £203 million allocated to the social fund is to be disbursed in the form of loans, and only one-third in the form of grants.

Between the end of December 1982 and the end of December 1989 the amount of outstanding consumer credit almost trebled, increasing from just under £16 billion to £46.9 billion. A report published by the Policy Studies Institute in 1990 claimed that 2.4 million families were in arrears with debt repayments: 560,000 households were in arrears with three debts and 170,000 were in arrears with five. Those most at risk of falling into arrears were the unemployed, single parent families and those on low incomes.[26] It is difficult to assess the extent to which this situation has been influenced by the social fund, but the replacement of grants by loans must have had some impact. Back street money lenders and loan sharks may be the only ones to benefit from the abolition of exceptional needs payments, because those who are refused a loan from the social fund may have no alternative.

The position of low income borrowers is improved where they have access to a credit union. Berthoud and Hinton describe a credit union as:

a co-operative society offering its members loans out of the pool of savings built up by the members themselves. A union is formed by a group of people with a common interest or 'bond' – working for the same employer, living in the same area or belonging to the same church, club or ethnic group. By agreeing to save regularly they build up a fund from which they can borrow at favourable interest rates.[27]

At present, however, there are only 141 credit unions in Great Britain.

Social fund loans are entirely discretionary, and this represents a complete reversal of the trend away from discretion observable in the early 1980s. To make matters worse, there is no independent system of appeals tribunals, but a rather long-winded system of internal review – first by the officer who made the original decision, and then, if that fails, by an assistant manager in a local DSS office, and finally by a social fund inspector.

Another problem is that the social fund is cash-limited and subject to rigid budgeting. Because each local office has an amount set aside for loans each month, claimants may be refused loans, no matter how strong a case they have, simply because the month's supply has run out: the budget, rather than need, may determine the outcome of an application. There is no system of queueing which would allow the client's claim to be considered in the following month. Once an application has been dealt with, no further claims can be made for six months. Variations between offices are inevitable, so that where a claim is made may be more important than criteria of need.

Clearly, people are going to be forced into poverty, since all the money borrowed has to be repaid out of future benefits. Weekly benefits are low enough already, and if 5, 10 or 15 per cent has to go towards repaying a loan, people simply will not be able to manage. The standard rate of repayment is 15 per cent over eighteen months which means that a claimant is expected to manage on 85 per cent of his or her income support entitlement. Berthoud compares this with the Netherlands where claimants retain 94 per cent of the higher base rates of income support and loans may be repaid over three years.[28]

Social fund officers are meant to offer money advice and debt counselling which are skilled tasks and may be thought to require extensive training. Officers, however, receive only three weeks' training to cover all aspects of their work.

Ever since the publication of the Green paper it has been clear that the government was hoping for the closest co-operation from social workers in the operation of the social fund, thinking, perhaps, that this would compensate for the brief training given to DSS officers. This view was confirmed by the Social Fund Manual which talked of 'a continuing need for constructive and close liaison between the local office and the SSD (Social Services Department) about the Social Fund.' Social workers would be involved in discussions 'about the relative priorities of different circumstances for community care grants and for loans.' However, the British Association of Social Workers was totally opposed to the social fund – especially the system of loans – and for a time it looked as though social workers would have nothing whatsoever to do with it; a similar attitude was taken by the Federation of Independent Advice Centres.

On the other hand, Ruth Lister, at that time Director of the Child Poverty Action Group, opposed a policy of total non co-operation, because it would work against clients' interests and leave social fund officers with a free hand. She recommended a policy of aggressive or determined advocacy, and this has now been adopted as the official line by local authority associations. What it means in practice is that social workers will give every help to clients applying to the social fund for a grant or a loan. They will, however, restrict themselves to the facts of the case: they will resist the pressure to provide judgements and they will not co-operate with social fund officers' attempts to set priorities. Social fund officers will not be invited to participate in case conferences, and there will be no joint visiting of clients by social workers and social fund officers. Tim Lunn, in a document advising social workers about the implications of determined advocacy for practice, recommends a concerted campaign to expose the weaknesses and unfairness of the social fund. He concludes:

Campaigning against the effects of the Social Fund will not get your client the help she needs. However, it will mean that the replacement of single payments by a thoroughly inadequate system of loans and occasional grants will not pass unnoticed. The only hope for changing the Social Fund is that its unfairness and meanness is clear for all to see.[29]

In view of social work attitudes towards the social fund, it is interesting to note that the Griffiths Report on Community Care recommended that the community care grants should be administered by local authority social services departments.

If this proposal were acted upon, grants and loans would be separated which would make a shift in the balance towards grants more difficult to achieve. The Social Security Advisory Committee, which has grave misgivings about the social fund, has recommended just such a shift, and it may be worth quoting the concluding comments and recommendations of this body in full:

We cannot support the social fund as it appears in the draft manual. It is dominated by a need to keep within the budget. It strikes what we regard as the wrong balance between loans and grants and between discretion and entitlement. We remain unconvinced that it will meet many of the genuine needs of some of the poorest members of society or command the confidence of agencies whose co-operation the manual itself sees as necessary. It sets awesome tasks for social fund officers. If the social fund is to have any chance of success in the longer term we therefore regard it as essential that it has:

1. An adequate and flexibly operated budget.
2. Legal entitlement to core grants in a limited list of cases.
3. Greater provision for discretionary grants.
4. A limited role for loans.
5. A more independent system of appeal rights.[30]

The Advisory Committee believes that loans should be restricted to the purchase of relatively minor items such as clothes and single items of bedding and that grants should be given for the purchase, maintenance and replacement of beds, basic furniture, storage units, cookers, heaters, floor covering and curtains.

Berthoud has suggested that, although some discretion is essential, its impact could be reduced if a large proportion of the high-priority loans and community care grants were to become regulated entitlements. Berthoud believes that there may be a place for loans, but only if the regular weekly payments for families with children were considerably increased, and if the loans were subject to lower repayments over a longer period.[31]

However, these and other suggestions for modifying the new social security system have elicited no response from the government. A briefing issuing from the Conservative Central Office and distributed to Conservative MPs claims that the loans system is acting fairly in requiring those living on benefit to budget for 'one-off items just like other people whose incomes may be only a little higher.'[32]

Before the social fund came into operation welfare rights workers encouraged supplementary benefit recipients to apply for exceptional needs payments, and this may partly explain the relatively small number of grants and loans made between 11 April and the end of May 1988. It is not a complete explanation, however, since it appears that a high proportion of applications is being refused. In the first seven weeks of the operation of the social fund 37,000 people – 34.3 per cent of all applicants – were refused help. Of the £8 million paid out during this period only £1.5 million was in the form of grants. Some social workers have complained about the complexity of applying for community care grants.[33]

Research carried out a few months later by the National Association of Citizen's Advice Bureaux revealed that 68 per cent of applications for grants and 64 per cent of applications for loans were turned down. Research by Craig claims that applicants are being rejected because they are too poor to repay the loans, and in one office applicants were being turned down unless they could show written evidence of having been refused a loan by two credit companies and one charitable organisation.[34] In spite of strenuous efforts to rescue the situation, by the end of 1988/9 only £41.5 million of the £60 million grants budget and £125 million of the £143 million loans budget had been spent.

The position has now radically changed. The budgets for 1989/90 remained the same, but in July 1989 the DSS issued new guidelines to social fund officers aimed at greater flexibility. Even before the new guidelines were published, however, there were reports of serious over-spending – by as much as 40 per cent in some offices.[35] By September 1989 some offices were overspent by 50 per cent; the Tottenham office, for example, had spent 71 per cent of its loans budget with six months of the financial year still to run. Worse is to come since the social fund budget for 1990/91 has been increased by only £10 million.[36] The social fund has hardly been a resounding success, and in January 1990 it faced further problems when the High Court ruled that the Secretary of State was acting illegally in forcing local social fund officers to stay within strict cash limits. This action, the high Court ruled, contravened the Social Security Act of 1986 because it prevented the exercise of discretion by local officers.

In response to this ruling the law is to be amended to make more explicit the Secretary of State's powers to give directions on the application of the social fund. At the same time that this amendment was announced yet another set of guidelines was issued to social fund officers requiring them to keep their budgets in mind when making decisions about loans or grants, but not to make this the overriding consideration.

Reducing gender inequality?

The Beveridge Report and the post-war social security system were based on the assumption that the typical unit was a nuclear family with a male breadwinner. Married women were not expected to work outside the home and wives were treated as dependants of their husbands. The following quotation from the Beveridge Report makes this quite explicit:

Most married women have worked at some gainful occupation before marriage; most who have done so give up that occupation on marriage or soon after . . . On marriage a woman gains a legal right to maintenance by her husband as a first line of defence against risks which fall directly on the solitary woman.[17]

Beveridge recognised that this dependence exposed married women to new risks in the event of widowhood, separation and divorce, and he recommended the payment of benefits and allowances to cover these contingencies.

In 1978 the European Community issued a Directive on the equal treatment of men and women in social security, and the government took steps to comply with the directive in 1983 by giving men and women formal equality in the claiming of supplementary benefit and family income supplement. But although either the man or the woman in a couple could now claim, only those who had been in work at some time during the previous six months were eligible, and this obviously discriminated against women who were less likely to have had recent contact with the labour market. The 1986 Social Security Act removed this anomaly, so that couples are now free to decide which of them shall be the claimant.

In 1984 the government made further changes in the direction of greater gender equality when it abolished the non-contributory invalidity pension and the housewives' non-contributory invalidity pension and replaced them with the severe disablement allowance. Under the former arrangements men received an invalidity pension if they could demonstrate incapacity for paid work, but women had to prove both incapacity for work outside the home and incapacity for household tasks. The severe disablement allowance dispensed with the household duties test.

Before 1986 the invalid care allowance, paid to those who are out of work and caring for a disabled person in receipt of attendance allowance, was not available to married or cohabiting women. There is no clearer indication of the assumption that women are the 'natural' carers. In 1985 this regulation was challenged in the European Court which found that the British government was in contravention of the Community directive on equal social security treatment. The day before the Court's judgement was to be announced the government conceded defeat, and in July 1986 invalid care allowance became payable to married and cohabiting women, the number of beneficiaries increasing from 10,000 to

80,000. It is perhaps worth noting that there have been no changes in the two areas in which men are discriminated against: the higher retirement age and the absence of widowers' benefits.

There has undoubtedly been some progress towards greater gender equality in social security in the 1980s. In a purely *formal* sense the social security system treats men and women equally, but indirect discrimination arising from factors outside the system is still a serious problem. For example, because women are often in low paid, part-time occupations with less continuous work records, their pension entitlements will be adversely affected. This will be true of all contributory benefits and the increase from one to two years' contributions to qualify for unemployment benefit very obviously discriminates against women.

Glendinning cites the 'availability for work' test as the clearest example of 'effective indirect discrimination'. The test, which was considerably strengthened in 1986, 'requires all new claimants to be prepared to take *any* full time job immediately, work beyond the normal travelling distance, and make immediate arrangements for family care – requirements which will clearly penalise women claimants seeking part time work or with family responsibilities'.[38] The position has been worsened by the Social Security Act of 1989 which stiffens the 'availability for work test' with a requirement that the claimant must demonstrate that he or she has been actively seeking work.

Glendinning also makes the point that women have been particularly affected by cuts in benefits, because more women than men are dependent upon benefits, and it is women who usually have the task of trying to make ends meet on the reduced amounts.

The government can claim little credit for initiating changes which have brought about a greater degree of gender equality in social security. They did so reluctantly and only after a directive from the EC. In other respects their policies have disadvantaged women, and the ideology is still one that portrays women as dependants. As Alcock says:

It is the ideological notion of dependency within existing benefit structures, rather than the issue of equal treatment in claiming benefits which is the root cause of gender inequality in social security. And in spite of the moves towards more formal equal treatment in the 1980s, the fundamental structuring role of this ideology has not been undermined.[39]

The persistence of poverty

This is not the place to discuss the innumerable competing definitions of poverty.[40] A commonly used method of measuring poverty has been in relation to supplementary benefit (now income support) levels. For some years the Department of Health and Social Security has used the basic supplementary benefit level as a rough poverty line and has published figures of low incomes based upon 140 per cent of the scale rates. In March 1988, however, the government discontinued this method of computing low incomes and replaced it with a rather more complicated calculation involving the aggregation of incomes in households, and the use of 'equivalence scales' to convert actual income into the income of 'standard' households. As might have been anticipated, given that the government denies the existence of widespread poverty, the new series of statistics gives a result showing fewer people in poverty or on its margins. Townsend has said that 'the principal objection to the new series is that it builds in no comparison of real incomes with the rates of benefit actually paid, and in some sense therefore regarded as adequate by successive governments'.[41]

The figures, as now produced, apparently leave some latitude for interpretation. The government claims that the bottom 10 per cent of the income scale did relatively well between 1981 and 1985: the average rise in real income during that period was 6.4 per cent but the incomes of the bottom 10 per cent of the population rose by 8.3 per cent.

These figures have, however, been challenged by several groups and individuals, including the House of Commons Select Committee on Social Services, the Child Poverty Action Group, the Low Pay Unit, Labour Party spokespersons and several academic commentators. David Brindle, social services correspondent for *The Guardian*, has reported that official figures published in 1988 reveal that the number of people on or below the poverty line rose by 55 per cent between 1979 and 1985.[42] The Low Pay Unit, commenting on these figures, claimed that had statistics been produced for 1987 they would have shown an 85 per cent increase as compared with 1979. The Social Services Committee has published figures revealing that nearly one family in five lives on or below the poverty line[43] and Hills has calculated that real incomes among the poorest 20 per cent of the population fell by 6 per cent between 1979 and 1986, whereas the incomes of the richest 20 per cent increased by 26 per cent.[44] Figures appearing in *Economic Trends* also show growing inequality. After tax and benefits are taken into account, the share of income received by the richest 20 per cent increased from 38 per cent in 1979 to 42 per cent in 1986, whereas the poorest 20 per cent experienced a cut from 7.1 per cent to 6.3 per cent.[45] It should be noted that these figures pre-date the inequitable budgets of 1987 and 1988.

One of the problems associated with the use of the supplementary benefit level as a poverty line is that an increase in benefit rates automatically leads to an increase in the number defined as poor. The DSS has estimated that 40 per cent of the increased numbers in or on the margins of poverty can be accounted for by the raising of the poverty line, but this still leaves 60 per cent of the increase attributable to other causes.

The disparities between income groups have become wider as a result of changes in the tax system. Dominic Byrne has analysed the differential benefits derived from tax cuts between 1979 and 1987, showing that of the £8.1 billion given away in tax cuts between 1979 and 1986 nearly half went to the richest 10 per cent. The poorest six million taxpayers, by contrast, received only 8 per cent, most of which disappeared in higher national insurance payments.[46] This pattern of unequal tax cuts was continued in the budget of 1987 and the 1988 budget was even more inequitable than its predecessors. The top 1 per cent of earners benefited by a total reduction of £1,880 million. This exceeded the total gains of the bottom 70 per cent which came to £1,730 million. The total reduction in the tax bill for the bottom 5 per cent was £40 million and for the bottom 10 per cent it was £100 million, as compared with the top 10 per cent who benefited by a total reduction of £3,160 million. The 1989 budget did nothing to reduce inequalities, although adjustments to national insurance contributions marginally benefited the lower paid.

It is interesting to note that 60 per cent of the 1988 tax cuts went to South-East England, thus accentuating the North–South divide even further. The higher tax cuts are, of course, a reflection of the preponderance of higher salaries in the South-East, and Steve Winyard provides evidence that regional pay differentials widened between 1979 and 1986. The areas which suffered the greatest decline in relative pay were also the areas with the highest levels of unemployment and the greatest dependence on social security payments. They are therefore likely to be the hardest hit by cuts in social security benefits.

As Winyard points out, however, the North–South divide, based on regional analysis, is too crude an indicator; and there are also big differences *within* regions. There are pockets of prosperity in the North and pockets of poverty in the South-East.[47] A report by the London Planning Advisory Committee, for example, highlights the growing disparities between the increasingly prosperous west London and the depressed and declining east London.[48]

The combined effect of unequal tax cuts and reduced levels of benefit has been to increase inequalities, and this explains why the Child Poverty Action Group and other organisations have concentrated their criticism of government policies on their divisive impact. There are geographical divisions, the North–South divide being simply the most obvious manifestation of these, and there is the related division between the rich and the poor. There are also divisions along gender and ethnic lines. Women may experience some of the worst effects of poverty, and the distribution of resources *within* families is now receiving more attention. Glendinning writes:

women bear the burden of managing poverty on a day-to-day basis. Whether they live alone or with a partner, on benefits or low earnings, it is usually women who are responsible for making ends meet and for managing the debts which result when they don't . . . As more women and men lose their jobs, and as benefits are cut or decline in value, women are increasingly caught in a daily struggle to feed and clothe their families – usually only at considerable personal sacrifice.[49]

Ethnic minorities are also particularly prone to poverty as are all those who live in the decaying inner cities. Hilary Arnott writes:

Despite the lack of adequate statistics it is clear that many black people, and in particular black women and the 'never employed' black youth, are bearing a large part of the social impact of the government's policies: trapped by unemployment and low incomes in decaying inner-city areas where the very fabric of their surroundings is being eroded by neglect.[50]

ALTERNATIVES

Very few people were happy with the social security scheme as it was before the changes of 1986/88. Equally, though, the new system has not found favour, and indeed there is widespread opposition to it. Once a new system gets underway, however, it takes on a momentum of its own, and change, other than piece-meal change, becomes difficult. Major change, when a system has been in place for only a few years, is regarded as premature and disruptive.

The search for alternative ways of organising post-Beveridge social security began in the 1960s and intensified in the 1970s and the 1980s. One of the problems for current reformers is that any new proposals must take account of the changes brought about by the 1986 Act, and this must be borne in mind as we proceed to examine possible alternatives.

Back to Beveridge

It is difficult to summarise the wide variety of proposals contained within this school of thought. Common to all of them, however, is the belief that the principles enunciated by Beveridge still have some validity, although they may need some re-interpretation to take account of contemporary conditions.

The centrepiece of back-to-Beveridge proposals is a more comprehensive form of insurance and a reduction of means testing. The gender inequalities implicit in Beveridge, however, would not be carried over into the new scheme and benefits might be paid to individuals rather than to couples and families. High child benefits, a disability income scheme and much more generous benefits for carers are usually on the agenda. Contributions, which would be earnings-related and progressive rather than proportional, might be tied in with the tax system but, with the possible exception of pensions, benefits would not be earnings-related.

A greatly expanded insurance scheme with higher benefits would remove most people from means-tested assistance benefits, but a minor role for means testing might, at least in the short term, be retained. The Child Poverty Action Group would go much further than this, however, and in the long term they would like to see a completely non-contributory, non-means-tested system, so that benefits would be paid automatically to anyone out of work for whatever reason. Esam, Good and Middleton also support this idea.[51] Once this stage of the argument is reached, however, one begins to wonder whether 'back to Beveridge' remains an appropriate title.

Taxation

There is a limit to the amount of vertical redistribution which a social security system can achieve. The tax system and the wages structure are much more significant in this respect. Since 1979 the tax burden has been decisively shifted in favour of the better-off, and vertical redistribution in favour of the poor, therefore, can be achieved only if the trends of the last ten years are reversed. A transfer from indirect to direct taxation would also redistribute, since taxes such as the value added tax are less progressive than income tax.

Other possible distributive changes within the present tax system include a wealth tax and the abolition or reduction of tax allowances (for example, mortgage interest tax relief) which favour the better-off. Wilkinson has calculated that between 1979/80 and 1983/84 subsidies paid in respect of public sector housing were reduced by 21.5 per cent, but relief on mortgage interest payments increased by 28.6 per cent.[52] Hills has stated that between 1978/79 and 1986/87 mortgage interest tax relief more than doubled in real terms, despite cuts in the basic rate of tax.[53]

There have been many suggestions for harmonising or integrating the benefit and tax systems. One way of achieving this would be through the introduction of negative income tax – a policy supported by Friedman, Lees, the Institute of Economic Affairs, the Adam Smith Institute and, in a modified form, by the Liberal and Social Democratic party. The idea is a simple one. A guaranteed minimum income is fixed and anyone whose income (wages and/or benefits) falls below that level are paid either the full difference or a proportion of it. Potentially, this would replace the whole of the present benefit system, with the income tax return acting as a generalised means test, and any income above the guaranteed minimum attracting tax.

If the whole of the difference between actual income and the guaranteed minimum is made up, there is the problem of incentives as any increase in wages would be entirely lost until the minimum was reached. On the other hand, if only a proportion of the difference is paid then the effectiveness of the scheme in alleviating poverty is reduced. A fundamental weakness of the scheme is that it encourages employers to pay low wages, and there is also the question as to how far blanket coverage of this kind is able to take account of *individual* needs and *fluctuating* needs.

A rather different system, a tax credit scheme, has been proposed by the Institute for Fiscal Studies,[54] and a watered-down version was published in Green Paper form by the Conservative government in 1972.[55] The Conservative proposal was for a partially integrated tax and benefit system replacing tax allowances, family allowances and family income supplement. Under this scheme everyone would be assigned a tax credit, with a joint one for married couples and one for each child. Credits would then be set off against tax liability. If total credits exceeded tax liability the difference between the two would be paid to the family or individual concerned. If tax liability exceeded credits the person's tax bill would be arrived at by subtracting total credits from tax liability. The Institute for Fiscal Studies proposed a more sophisticated and comprehensive tax credit scheme which would replace the whole of the tax allowance and benefits system.

As with negative income tax there are the problems of high marginal and fluctuating needs. The Institute for Fiscal Studies claim that their scheme is technically simple with recent advances in micro-technology, but whether the general public would find it simple is a matter for conjecture.

Incomes policies

Incomes policies do not enjoy wide support in Britain, being unpopular with both the trade union movement and employers. The Conservative Party claims that it is totally opposed to incomes policies, but as Byrne says, 'since 1979 successive measures have been aimed at driving down the wages of the lower paid', and while there has been a *laissez-faire* attitude towards the middle and upper ranges of the wage structure in the private sector, the wages of manual workers in the public sector have been rigidly controlled.[56] The Labour Party has experimented with incomes policies in the past, but although it supports the introduction of a statutory minimum wage, it balks at the idea of a more general *statutory* incomes policy.

There is much wider support for a statutory minimum wage and equal pay legislation than there is for other aspects of incomes policy: for example, the Child Poverty Action Group and the Low Pay Unit have supported both strategies for some years.[57] Much less is said about a maximum wage, although Michael Meacher has suggested such a development.[58]

A more general incomes policy with flat rate increases, and no increases at all above a certain level, would change differentials if it could be sustained for a number of years. It has to be accepted, however, that there is very little political support for such radical measures, and in a democratic society the cost in terms of loss of public support would be considered by any political party to be too high.

Social dividends

Social dividends were first proposed in Britain by Lady Rhys Williams in 1943. Since then, similar suggestions have re-emerged periodically, with Jordan as their most recent and persuasive proponent. Jordan refers to his proposal as a basic income scheme and says of it:

The basic income principle starts from the idea that, in order to guarantee the basic needs of all citizens, it is necessary to give each individual enough income for subsistence before he or she enters the labour market or the family. This would be the only way of simultaneously preventing poverty and giving all an equal chance to participate and co-operate in the economy and in the household. It would mean . . . that no one could be coerced into a job or domestic responsibility out of dependence on another for his or her basic resources.[59]

The present tax allowances and all existing benefits would be replaced by a social dividend or basic income paid to everyone, whether in or out of work, consisting of 'a tax-free sum sufficient for subsistence' with smaller amounts for children and more for retired or disabled people. There would be no problems of take up, there would be no poverty trap and divisions between those in and out of work and between men and women would disappear. All earnings from paid work would be taxed at the same rate, the product being used to finance the scheme. Jordan claims that his scheme takes account of continued mass unemployment, changing work and household patterns and the impact of new technology.

Jordan concedes that his scheme would require 'a major change in social attitudes'. Wages and salaries would now be thought of as providing *extra* income above the subsistence level. Thus everyone is provided for, but 'wages and salaries become in effect the specific rewards to individual effort, skill and productivity'.[60]

There is an elegant simplicity about this solution, but there would be enormous problems of implementation, and it presupposes a high degree of consensus. There must be some doubt about whether the major change of attitudes can be achieved except in the very long term.

Most schemes for reform stand or fall on the generosity of provision and the cost of providing it. There is little comfort for poor people in having a well designed social security scheme which pays out niggardly benefits. Jordan refers to calculations made by Parker who claims that even a basic income scheme with tax rates of 86 per cent would not eliminate poverty among some groups. Parker therefore suggests a compromise with a much lower basic income and the retention of means-tested housing benefits. Tax rates would then need to vary between 40 per cent and 60 per cent. Unfortunately, however, the level of benefits thus provided would be low;[61] Jordan sees this as possibly providing a starting point with more generous benefits at a later stage.

CONCLUSIONS

What principles should govern the provision of income-maintenance? How should the British social security system be judged?

The Child Poverty Action Group believes that 'Central to the principles which should govern any reform of the social security system is the concept of "social citizenship" '.[62] This implies benefits at a level which does not exclude recipients from full participation in the life of society, recognising people's rights to autonomy. It also implies benefits as of right without stigma or shame.

Jordan sees fairness as the master principle which should govern all welfare provision. Ideas of fairness are related to notions of deserts, needs and abilities, and for a system to be fair it must be concerned with rights, freedom and equality. Jordan also considers the principle of autonomy and claims that the system of basic income would give equal autonomy before people entered the labour market or the family.[63] Weale also supports a comprehensive social security scheme on the grounds of autonomy, arguing that economic deprivation results in a loss of autonomy, because alternatives are absent or strictly limited.[64]

This discussion of principles indicates how far from ideal are the current social security arrangements. They do not enhance citizenship because the poor are treated as second class citizens, excluded from full participation by the low level of benefits and subjected to stigmatising attitudes and procedures. The system is not based on rights, and the notions of equality and fairness are absent. Equal autonomy is not achieved in a system which is based upon dependence and which discriminates against women and ethnic minorities. In a paper published in 1987 Piachaud writes:

Ironically, a government committed to economic independence has overseen a massive increase in economic dependence on the state. Those rendered dependent have received declining shares in national income. The inevitable result has been that the burden of poverty has increased grotesquely over the last eight years of Conservative government.[65]

The social security system before 1986 had serious shortcomings and reform was certainly needed. But the particular reforms initiated by the Conservative government replaced an inadequate system with something much worse. The social security changes are consistent with changes made elsewhere in the welfare system, and they meet some of the aims of Conservative social policy identified in Chapter 2. Increased privatisation, for example, is a feature of the new system, the most obvious manifestation being the encouragement given to private pensions. Increased privatisation also results from the replacement of sickness and maternity benefits by statutory sickness and maternity pay administered by employers. In addition, reduced benefits, and especially the substitution of loans for grants, forces people to rely upon private sources of support and to get deeper into debt.

The social security changes are also consistent with a further aim of Conservative social policy, that of promoting inequality. Benefits have been reduced, the gap between benefits and wages has been widened, there is a greater reliance on means tests and more people find themselves in the poverty trap. The element of discretion is now much greater and rights have been eroded. The combined effect of unequal tax cuts, benefit reductions and a punitive attitude towards the poor, has led to deeper divisions and wider disparities.

NOTES

1. Sir William Beveridge, *Social Insurance and Allied Services*, Cmd 6404, London: HMSO, 1942.

2. *The Times*, 2 December 1942.
3. Sir William Beveridge, *op. cit.*, p. 141.
4. Department of Health and Social Security, *Social Assistance*, London: HMSO, 1978, p. 4.
5. *Ibid.*, p. 3.
6. Department of Health and Social Security, *Reform of Social Security*, Cmnd 9517, London: HMSO, 1985.
7. Department of Health and Social Security, *The Reform of Social Security: Programme for Action*, Cmnd 9691, London: HMSO, 1985.
8. *Ibid.*, p. 1.
9. *The Observer*, 9 June 1985.
10. A. Hadjipateras, *Reform of Social Security: A Checklist of the Responses of 60 Key Organisations to the Government's Green Paper*, London: Child Poverty Action Group, 1985.
11. M. Svenson and S. MacPherson, 'Real losses and unreal figures: The impact of the 1986 Social Security Act', in S. Becker and S. MacPherson (eds.), *Public Issues Private Pain: Poverty, Social Work and Social Policy*, London: Social Services Insight Books, 1988, pp. 41–53.
12. *Ibid.*
13. Social Services Committee, *April 1988 Social Security Changes*, HC 437–1, London: HMSO, 1989.
14. *The Guardian*, 29 March, 1988.
15. J. Bennett, 'What future for social security?', in A. Walker and C. Walker (eds.), *The Growing Divide*, London: Child Poverty Action Group, 1987, pp. 120–8.
16. P. Alcock, *Poverty and State Support*, London: Longman, 1987, p. 94.
17. *The Guardian*, 24 October 1987.
18. Social Services Committee, *Public Expenditure on the Social Services*, HC 548, London: HMSO, 1988.
19. *The Guardian*, 17 December 1985.
20. Social Services Committee, 1989, *op. cit.*
21. D. Byrne, K. MacNeill, C. Pond and R. Smail, 'The 1988 budget and the poor', *Low Pay Review*, no. 33, 1988, pp. 3–12.
22. *The Guardian*, 25 July 1988.
23. Social Security Advisory Committee, *Sixth Report*, London: HMSO, 1988, pp. 26–7.
24. P. Waterhouse, 'Housing benefit', *Community Care*, 28 January 1988.
25. *The Guardian*, 5 August 1988.
26. R. Berthoud and E. Kempson, *Credit and Debt in Britain*, London: Policy Studies Institute, 1990. A good treatment of credit and default can be found in J. Ford, *The indebted society: credit and default in the 1980s*, London: Routledge, 1988.
27. R. Berthoud and T. Hinton, *Credit Unions in the United Kingdom*, London: Policy Studies Institute, 1989, p. 1.

28. R. Berthoud, 'The social fund – will it work?', *Policy Studies*, vol. 8, pt. 1, 1987, pp. 8–26.
29. T. Lunn, 'The social fund', *Community Care*, 28 January 1988.
30. Social Security Advisory Committee, *The Draft Social Fund Manual*, London: HMSO, 1987, p. 20.
31. R. Berthoud. *op. cit.*
32. *The Guardian*, 25 April 1988.
33. S. Becker, *Community Care*, 21 July 1988.
34. *The Observer*, 20 November 1988.
35. *The Guardian*, 17 July 1989.
36. *The Guardian*, 27 March 1990.
37. Sir William Beveridge, *op. cit.*, para. 108.
38. C. Glendinning, 'Improverishing women', in A. Walker and C. Walker (eds.), *op. cit.*, p. 55.
39. P. Alcock, *op. cit.*, p. 42.
40. A very good discussion of the alternative approaches can be found in five articles by P. Townsend, D. Piachaud, J. Bradshaw *et al.*, J. Veit-Wilson and R. Walker in *Journal of Social Policy*, vol. 16, pt. 2, 1987.
41. P. Townsend, letter to *The Guardian*, 30 May 1988.
42. *The Guardian*, 20 May 1988.
43. *The Observer*, 10 July 1988.
44. *The Observer*, 14 May 1989.
45. Central Statistical Office, *Economic Trends*, London: HMSO, 1988.
46. D. Byrne, 'Rich and poor: The growing divide', in A. Walker and C. Walker (eds.), *op. cit.*, pp. 27–38.
47. S. Winyard, 'Divided Britain', in A. Walker and C. Walker (eds.), *op. cit.*, pp. 39–49.
48. *The Guardian*, 18 January 1988.
49. C. Glendinning, *op. cit.*, p. 60.
50. H. Arnott, 'Second-class citizens', in A. Walker and C. Walker (eds.), *op. cit.*, pp. 61–9.
51. P. Esam, R. Good and C. Middleton, *Who's to Benefit? A Radical Review of the Social Security System*, London: Verso, 1985.
52. M. Wilkinson, 'Tax expenditures and public policy in the UK', *Journal of Social Policy*, vol. 15, pt. 1, 1986, pp. 23–49.
53. J. Hills, 'What happened to spending on the welfare state?', in A. Walker and C. Walker (eds.), *op. cit.*, pp. 88–100.
54. A. W. Dilnot, J. A. Kay and C. N. Morris, *The Reform of Social Security*, Oxford: Clarendon, for Institute for Fiscal Studies, 1984.
55. Treasury, *Proposals for a Tax-Credit System*, Cmnd 5116, London: HMSO, 1972.
56. D. Byrne, *op. cit.*, p. 27.
57. C. Pond and S. Winyard, *The Case for a National Minimum Wage*, London: Low Pay Unit, 1983.

58. M. Meacher, 'The good society', *New Socialist*, June 1985.

59. B. Jordan, *Rethinking Welfare*, Oxford: Blackwell, 1987, p. 160.

60. *Ibid.*, p. 161.

61. *Ibid.*, pp. 163–4.

62. R. Lister, 'Conclusion II – there is an alternative', in A. Walker and C. Walker (eds.), *op. cit.*, pp. 139–50.

63. It is impossible to do justice to the complexity of Jordan's argument here. For further details see B. Jordan, *op. cit.*

64. A. Weale, *Political Theory and Social Policy*, London: Macmillan, 1983.

65. D. Piachaud, 'The growth of poverty', in A. Walker and C. Walker (eds.), *op. cit.*, pp. 20–6.

CHAPTER 4

THE NATIONAL HEALTH SERVICE

The National Health Service has a number of characteristics which mark it out from the other areas of social policy analysed in this book.

It is first of all much larger than any of the other services in terms of the number of staff it employs. The National Health Service (NHS) is the biggest employer in Europe with almost 1.1 million people working for it. The structure of employment within the NHS is also unusual in that the medical staff, a very small proportion of the total, are highly professionalised and exert a considerable influence over policy and the use of resources. There is no other professional group in the social services to compare with the doctors – social workers and teachers, for example, are in a very different category.

The NHS is also significant in terms of the proportion of public expenditure devoted to it, accounting for 16 per cent of the total, a proportion exceeded only by social security. More important than these statistics, however, is the place of the NHS in our national life. It has always had a particular significance in Fabian and Labour Party circles as is indicated by Titmuss's description of it as 'the most unsordid act of British social policy in the twentieth century which has allowed and encouraged sentiments of altruism, reciprocity and social duty to express themselves; to be made explicit and identifiable in measurable patterns of behaviour by all social groups and classes'.[1]

The great strength of the NHS, however, is the breadth of its support amongst the general population. Papadakis and Taylor-Gooby maintain that the NHS 'remains the most popular component of the welfare state'.[2] Melanie Phillips puts the point even more strongly:

The NHS . . . rides high in people's affections. Unlike teachers or housing officials, the producers of the service can do little wrong in the eyes of its consumers. The perception is that its faults are caused not by the doctors, nurses or even the hospital administrators but the government. People believe that the health service is not being given enough money. When asked, they even say they would happily pay more in taxes to provide more for the NHS.[3]

No doubt the government is well aware of the underlying support for the NHS within the community. This explains the frequent assertion of the Prime Minister and the minister with responsibility for health that 'the health service is safe with us'. It also explains the government's caution in its dealings with the NHS and the fact that the health service has received more generous funding than other public services.

Nevertheless, the government has managed to change the terms of the debate on health care, through its general approval of the private medical sector. Mrs Thatcher herself uses private medical care saying that she did so because she wished 'to go on the day, at the time, with the doctor I choose'.[4] She received a hostile response when she added that she would use the NHS only if she needed complicated and costly surgery.

A series of changes, each one relatively small when viewed singly, has resulted cumulatively in a considerable shift towards private medicine. Robin Cook, the opposition spokesman on health matters, has described the government's tactics as 'taking a succession of Granny's footsteps tiptoeing away from the universal, publicly-funded comprehensive health service hoping that no one will be sufficiently alarmed by the noise to ask the questions of principle raised by each step'.[5]

THE ENCOURAGEMENT OF PRIVATE PRACTICE

The last Labour government had embarked upon a policy of withdrawing private practice from the NHS with the phasing out of pay beds – a proposal that provoked a very angry response from the medical profession. The dispute between Barbara Castle, the Secretary of State, and the doctors became extremely acrimonious, but eventually a compromise was reached – through the offices of Lord Goodman as mediator – that initially only 1,000 of the 4,400 pay beds would be phased out, and any subsequent reductions would need the approval of the specially-appointed Health Services Board. The Board would sanction the relinquishment of pay beds only where there were adequate alternative facilities within the private sector. The Health Services Board began its work in 1977, and by 1980 a further 981 pay beds had gone.

The Conservative government's determination to reverse this trend was made abundantly clear by the Health Services Act of 1980 which abolished the Health Services Board and empowered the Secretary of State to allow private treatment in NHS establishments. Although the number of pay beds marginally increased as a consequence of this Act, the number of patients treated in them continued to decline because of the rapid growth of private hospitals and nursing homes since 1979.

The biggest boost to private practice came at the beginning of 1980 with changes in consultants' contracts which made it possible to engage in considerable private practice without losing the advantages of working within the NHS. Full time consultants could now earn up to 10 per cent of their gross NHS salary from private practice. Maximum part time consultants could earn an unlimited amount from private practice but forfeited one-eleventh of their NHS salary: prior to 1980 part time consultants had to forego two-elevenths of NHS salary in return for unrestricted opportunities for private practice. Other part-timers receive a pro-rata NHS salary with no restriction on the amount of part time work they can undertake.

These changes had two principal results: first, a big increase in the proportion of consultants accepting full time and maximum part time contracts; and second a considerable increase in the amount of private practice. Joan Higgins writes:

In a situation where there were so few wholly private practitioners and where the service was so firmly consultant-led the potential for the expansion of private practice was dramatically changed. Although the increase in private health insurance and the availability of new private sector facilities were important factors, their contribution to the changing scene would have been marginal were it not for the radical restructuring of consultants' contracts and the consultants' willingness to take on new work.[6]

Higgins claims that there is some evidence that the expansion of private practice was at the expense of the NHS.

A further boost to private medicine came from government concessions in relation to private health insurance. From 1982 people earning less than £8,500 no longer had to pay tax on the value of the premiums paid by their employers, and companies could offset the health insurance premiums paid for their employees against their liability for corporation tax.

THE GROWTH OF PRIVATE MEDICINE

Health insurance

The private medical sector depends heavily upon private health insurance schemes which have expanded rapidly since 1979. In 1988 5.7 million people were covered by private health insurance – just over 10 per cent of the population – double the number who were covered when Mrs Thatcher became Prime Minister. The biggest single increase in the number of contributors occurred in 1980 with a 26 per cent rise. This was preceded by an increase of 16 per cent in 1979 and followed by a further 13 per cent in 1981. Since then the rate has slowed down, with an increase in 1982 of only 3 per cent, in 1985 of 2 per cent, and in 1986 of 5 per cent. Since the late 1970s the proportion of *individual* subscribers has declined, as company schemes and schemes organised by trade unions and professional associations have become more common.

The private insurance market is dominated by three provident associations: the British United Provident Association (BUPA), the Private Patients Plan (PPP) and the Western Provident Association (WPA). BUPA is the biggest single provider with 60 per cent of the market, but more recently a number of profit-seeking companies have entered the field and the competition for business is becoming fiercer. In an effort to attract customers, the insurance companies vie with each other in offering discounts and optional extras.

Of the big three only WPA operates a maximum annual benefit limit (£40,000). Among the smaller companies upper limits are more common. Primecare, for example, has an annual upper limit of £25,000, although this can be avoided if a considerably higher premium is paid. All of the companies have limits on the amounts they are willing to refund for operations, and most of them have maximum amounts for out-patient treatment and home nursing. Debbie Harrison identifies twelve companies that provide health insurance, and makes the following comment:

Consumers face a bewildering array of premium levels, benefits, exclusions and optional extras, making comparisons virtually impossible. Before deciding which policy is best suited to your needs it is important to understand exactly what your money is not buying . . . Private medical scheme documentation seems to specialise in small print and exclusions.[7]

The private insurance market is not intended for the chronically sick and disabled; elderly people are also excluded and those who joined a scheme when they were younger face stiff increases in premiums when they reach sixty-five. It is instructive to note that in the White Paper, *Working for Patients*, the government promises 'legislation to give income tax relief from April 1990 on premiums for those aged 60 and over, whether paid by them or, for example, by their families on their behalf'.[8] Families with a number of young children, unless they are wealthy, will not be able to afford the high premiums. Joan Higgins points out that although membership of private schemes has been extended to lower income groups and some manual workers the main beneficiaries continue to be male professional workers and senior management.[9]

In 1988, as already stated, just over 10 per cent of the population was covered by private medical insurance. The government's declared aim was that 25 per cent of the population should be covered by private insurance by 1990; but this target has not been achieved, and even in the long term a quarter of the population seems to be an over-optimistic aim. According to a report prepared by a leading actuary for the Institute of Health Service Management, private insurance is unlikely to reach more than 20 per cent of the population. If the government gave only limited encouragement to private insurance, the private share might rise to 16 per cent. If there was also a designated NHS tax with 10 per cent relief for those with private insurance, then private schemes might increase their share to 18 per cent. If, in addition, the present NHS structure was replaced by health management units, the proportion of the population taking out private insurance might reach 19.5 per cent and just over 20 per cent would be achieved if the government also limited NHS expenditure.[10]

It should be noted that not all private treatment in hospitals, even in private hospitals, is covered by insurance: some patients pay directly. The UK managing director of American Medical International Healthcare (AMI) claims that in 1987 15 per cent of the treatment provided in the group's thirteen hospitals was paid for by the patients themselves. Ian Moore, a city healthcare analyst, is reported as saying:

AMI is looking for strong growth among the self-paying customers rather than among people who carry health insurance, and surveys suggest that they will get it. They have found that people who are too young or too old, or not insured, are increasingly willing to pay for one-off private therapy.[11]

Private facilities

The number of in-patients treated privately in NHS hospitals has been declining since 1971. In spite of the present government's reversal of Labour's policy of phasing out pay beds and the encouragement given to private insurance, the decline continued after 1979. Between 1979 and 1986 the number of private in-patients treated in NHS hospitals declined by 29 per cent: from just over 92,000 to just over 65,000. It is interesting to note that the number of pay beds did not alter greatly between 1979 and 1986 and this suggests much lower occupancy rates. The most dramatic growth in private practice occurred in the hospital out-patient departments, the number of attendances increasing from 132,400 in 1979 to 261,600 in 1986; an increase of over 97 per cent.[12]

From the very beginning of the NHS some hospitals remained in private hands. Such hospitals, many of them small with a particular clientele and frequently run by charitable or religious bodies, did not really compete with the NHS, and most private patients were treated in NHS hospitals. The Labour government's attempt in 1976/7 to phase out pay beds provided the impetus for the growth of private facilities outside the NHS, and this trend has been accentuated since that time. Griffith, Iliffe and Rayner, writing in 1985, said: 'While in the 1970s around three out of every four private patients were treated in the NHS, the reverse is now the case'.[13]

There are two kinds of hospital falling outside the NHS: commercial hospitals run for profit and those run by non-profit foundations which sometimes, as in the case of the Nuffield hospitals, have a charitable status. In 1987 the non-profit hospitals accounted for about 49 per cent of all private beds as compared with 72 per cent in 1979. In eight years, therefore, the for-profit sector had out-stripped the non-profit sector; a quite remarkable reversal. Rose-mary Collins quotes a survey conducted by the Association of Independent Hospitals which claims that 98 per cent of all new hospital beds in the independent sector since 1983 have been in the for-profit hospitals.[14]

Relationships between the two sectors have been far from har-monious, with BUPA, for example, accusing the commercial companies of pushing up prices and contributing to over-provision of hospital places. Striking a more ethical note Robert Graham, the Chief Executive of BUPA, stated that 'the recent injection of commercialism goes against the grain of tradition in this country where the care of the sick has always transcended commercial interest.'[15]

In 1986 there were just over 65,000 beds in private hospitals and nursing homes in England and Wales; about 10,000 in hospitals and the remainder in nursing homes. This compares with just under 33,000 beds in 1979 with approximately 7,000 in hospitals.

The position of the nursing homes is very different from that of the hospitals. Catering largely for long-stay elderly patients, almost half of nursing home fees are paid by the Social Security Depart-ment. Joan Higgins, quoting Association of Independent Hospitals figures, notes that between 1979 and 1985 there was a net increase of fifty-two private hospitals and 3,577 beds.[16]

The two major British hospital providers, Nuffield and BUPA, expanded steadily if unspectacularly after 1979 and by 1986 provided 1,266 beds and 600 beds respectively. The greatest changes in the hospital sector, however, have come about through what Griffith and his co-writers call an 'American invasion' akin to the incursions of McDonalds in the fast food industry.[17] The American health corporations run chains of hospitals and clinics in the United States, and since 1970 have been gradually extend-ing their operations to Britain. The greatest expansion occurred in the 1980s, and by 1987 they controlled half of the for-profit sector and slightly more than a quarter of the entire independent sector. Joan Higgins describes the 'American invasion' in the following terms:

Although the private market in health care in Britain only began to expand to any significant degree in 1979, the American for-profit companies have wasted no time in procuring a share of the market . . . Typically they have bought out existing or almost completed hospitals and clinics, thus establishing their presence with the minimum of delay. Each of the companies already settled in Britain has sufficient resources to expand further if the opportunities arise, and other US companies not yet a part of the British scene are already poised to enter the market.[18]

The largest of these American commercial enterprises is American Medical International Healthcare (AMI) which has thirteen hospitals with 1,200 beds. Another American company, Hospital Corporation of America, owns nine small hospitals with a total of 452 beds. In contrast Humana Inc. owns one large hospital with 265 beds. AMI has developed extensive facilities for the treatment of mental illness and drug and alcohol addiction, and two other American companies, Charter Medical of England and Community Psychiatric Centers, specialise in these areas of work.

Initially, the American companies were primarily concerned with acute in-patient care, and although this remains their main concern, many of them now have out-patient departments and offer sophisticated screening and diagnostic services. With the opening of a number of health centres, AMI has diversified into primary health care.

A recent trend has been for hospital providers to offer their own healthcare insurance packages. AMI and Nuffield Hospitals have taken a lead in this development. In October 1988 Nuffield joined with Crusader Insurance to offer a cut-price health insurance scheme in which participants will have all hospital costs reimbursed provided that they attend one of Nuffield's thirty-two hospitals or one of fifteen hospitals that have accepted Nuffield's invitation to join the scheme. BUPA, rather sourly, said: 'People may undercut us but there is nothing for nothing in this world. A cut price means a cut something else; a cut service to some extent'.[19]

The private hospitals are obviously in competition with NHS provision. This is also true in the case of diagnostic and some of the screening services such as cervical smear tests. In other instances the private sector has attempted to fill gaps in provision or to make good any shortfalls. The private addiction units and therapeutic abortions provide examples of the private sector moving into areas that are under-provided in the NHS.

The filling of what the private sector perceives as gaps in pro-vision has led to some innovation. For example, the Independent Hospital in Stepney has established a private cardiac ambulance service for people in stressful jobs. The hospital claimed that market research had indicated sufficient demand for such a service to make a worthwhile profit. The ambulance is staffed by highly trained personnel who have all the latest equipment at their disposal. Another example is provided by the ubiquitous AMI who have opened a clinic to help people who suffer head injuries as a result of traffic accidents. An unseemly aspect of this scheme is its cost, £75,000 a patient, and the offer that AMI makes to help patients who wish to do so to sue for damages, presumably in the hope that some of the money will come AMI's way.

The private sector gains considerably from the NHS in three directions. Firstly, the NHS is forced to accept all patients who seek help from it, and in particular the NHS treats those suffering from chronic sickness whose inability to pay for care makes them unattractive to the for-profit corporations. This leaves the private sector free to concentrate on the more 'glamorous' and profitable acute cases.

Secondly, the private hospitals have gained financially from work farmed out to them by health authorities. In 1987 the government made £25 million available for the purpose of reducing waiting lists; in December 1989 the Health Minister announced the allocation of a further £33 million. Much of this money is going to the private sector because Regional and District Health Authorities are paying private hospitals to perform minor operations on patients on the waiting list. For example, the West Middlesex Hospital was given £150,000 in 1987 to reduce its waiting list by contracting out 250–300 operations to the Royal Masonic Hospital. Also in 1987, St Bartholomew's Hospital paid the private Princess Grace Hospital to perform tonsil operations on 175 children. The Princess Grace Hospital charges £190 a night.[20]

At the end of 1987 the West Midlands Regional Health Authority announced that it was going to use £240,000 allocated to it by the DHSS to pay private hospitals for operations on NHS patients. The Health Authority invited BUPA to act as its agent in negotiating contracts with private hospitals. The Trent Regional Health Authority had the same amount available which it planned to use in a similar way.[21]

Another case in 1987 received a good deal of publicity. Pontefract General Infirmary received DHSS funds to enable it to reduce its waiting list. By re-arranging sessions in the operating theatres the Infirmary was able to carry out surgery on an extra 718 patients. The Infirmary had hoped to treat a further 250 patients by using operating theatres on Saturdays, but only one surgeon agreed to this which went beyond consultants' contractual obligations. Pontefract had to spend its allocation of funds within the financial year or lose them altogether, and so it decided to carry out the operations at Methley Park private hospital at a total cost of £52,000. Two of the consultants who had refused to work on Saturdays performed some of the operations but at NHS rather than private rates of pay. There is no suggestion whatsoever of anything at all underhand in this, but some concern was expressed when it was learned that 15 of Pontefract's 46 consultants owned shares in Methley Park.[22]

The 1989 White Paper claims that 'in 1986 contractual arrangements between the NHS and the independent sector led to over 26,000 in-patient treatments at a cost of some £45 million. Many of these are long-term contracts'. These figures are likely to have been exceeded in subsequent years.[23]

Another way in which the NHS encourages private practice is through the use of locum agencies in the case of both doctors and nurses. At the 1987 Annual Conference of the National Association of Health Authorities a delegate from Sandwell said that the rates for locums worked out at between £55,000 and £77,000 a year which was more than double a consultant's salary. A delegate from Wakefield claimed that one agency charged over £400 for a senior house officer for a weekend and that health authorities were facing extra costs of between £100,000 and £500,000 a year.[24] In December 1988, however, the Health Minister announced curbs on the amounts payable to locum agencies for hospital doctors.

The NHS massively subsidises the private sector through the provision of medical and nursing staff trained at the state's expense. The training of medical personnel is shared between universities and associated NHS teaching hospitals, and nurse training is shared between District and Regional Health Authorities, universities and colleges. Nurse training schools are responsible not only for basic nurse training but also for in-service continuing education of both nurses and auxiliaries. Sometimes the private sector makes use of the in-service training courses for their own staff, although they do, of course, pay for this.

The private sector does engage in some staff training, especially of nurses. However, as Higgins points out, only eight private hospitals provide *basic* nurse training 'and the majority mount only brief post-basic courses or study days'.[25] At a time when hospital wards are closing and intensive care beds remain empty because of a shortage of trained staff, it is difficult not to conclude that the private sector is damaging the NHS. The extent of the subsidy is estimated by Griffith, Iliffe and Rayner:

According to official statistics, it costs £9,750 to train a nurse and £100,000 to train a doctor. While it is not possible to make a precise calculation as there are no published figures on consultants' commitment to private practice, we can safely say that the taxpayer has invested well over £100 million in training the personnel of commercial medicine.[26]

These are 1982 figures and the total subsidy must now be very much higher. Griffith *et al.* also refer to the serious disruption which occurs when a new private hospital opens in proximity to an NHS hospital and some vital staff move over in whole or in part, to the private sector. The position in London is particularly acute with 25 per cent of nursing posts unfilled in 1987.

THE NHS IN THE 'ENTERPRISE CULTURE'

Raising funds

In February 1988 the Secretary of State urged health authorities to explore new ways of raising funds, and to this end an Income Generation Unit was set up within the Department of Health to advise health authorities about money-making ventures. The Secretary of State said that he expected health authorities to raise £20 million in 1988/89 rising to £70 million a year by 1991. In addition the sale of land and buildings was expected to realise £400 million between 1988 and 1990.

Among the suggestions made by the Secretary of State was the leasing of space to fast food chains, retail outlets for clothes, newsagents and hairdressers, laundries, dry cleaning and the sale of advertising space. The latest available index of these schemes (1988) lists 828 income-generation projects.[27] Among the projects were a host of retail outlets, shopping arcades, mother and baby photographs, building societies, banks, outside catering, the renting of mortuary space and the sale of ultrasound scan photographs. Two hospitals in South Wales have converted their generators into mini-power stations and are selling electricity to the national grid.

Among the more bizarre schemes is the renting out of land by three authorities for horse grazing. Equally bizarre, and also rather unsavoury, was the sponsorship of a hip replacement operation in a private hospital by the magazine *Retirement World*. Mrs Currie, at that time junior health minister, welcomed this development.[28]

Other health authorities are looking for commercial opportunities to market their services. St Bartholemew's in London, for example, has announced plans to sell its clinical treatment to city firms, overseas governments and insurance companies, and a private wing is to be opened to accommodate fee-paying patients. At the same hospital a stress research unit is setting up a team to sell a service offering counselling to survivors of disasters: several airlines have expressed interest. Merseyside Health Authority has approved the plans of a hospital in Chester to close two geriatric wards and to replace them with a nursing home built in the hospital grounds. The home is to be run by either a charitable organisation or a private firm. There are similar plans in other Merseyside hospitals.

Internal markets
The government is also anxious to develop internal markets in the NHS in the interests of increasing competition. The 'No Turning Back Group' of Conservative MPs argue for internal markets in the following way:

Particular hospitals and particular areas should be able to specialise, with patients being referred to whichever can provide the best or cheapest service. Excess capacity should be traded across district boundaries instead of having empty places in one location accompanied by shortage in another.[29]

The Conservative government favours such a system because it is seen as a way of increasing competition in the NHS with efficient producers securing extra resources at the expense of the less efficient. Cross charging is beginning to develop in a haphazard way at present with some authorities imposing charges and others not. If internal markets are to be developed any further, then greater uniformity of practice is essential, and to this end the White Paper proposes the introduction of a general cross-charging scheme in 1991.

The implementation of the provisions of the NHS and Community Care Act will take the development of internal markets a stage further. Individual hospitals, while remaining in the NHS will be able to become independent of the District Health Authorities by forming self-governing Hospital Trusts controlling their own funds and appointing their own staff, negotiating with them over pay and conditions. NHS Hospital Trusts will be free to enter into contracts with any District Health Authority, not only with the one in whose area they are situated. On the funding of Hospital Trusts, the White Paper has this to say:

An NHS Hospital Trust will earn its revenue from the services it provides. The main source of revenue will be from contracts with health authorities for the provision of services to their residents. Other contracts and revenue will come from GP practices with their own NHS budgets, private patients or their insurance companies, private hospitals, employers and, perhaps, other NHS Hospital Trusts.[30]

General practitioners are also to be given the opportunity to become more entrepreneurial. GP practices above a certain size will be able to apply for practice budgets. The budgets will consist of three elements covering: hospital services, practice staff and improvements, and prescribing costs. GPs are expected to buy treatment for their patients from other health care providers such as hospitals, and it is envisaged that practices will 'negotiate fixed price contracts for each speciality with particular hospitals' although they 'will want to hold some money back, to keep the possibility of obtaining services at marginal cost where hospitals have spare capacity to offer in the course of a year'.[31] Practices may, of course, choose to enter into contracts with private hospitals.

In the White Paper it was proposed that only practices with a minimum of 11,000 patients on their lists would be eligible for the scheme. Something over 1,000 practices would qualify: 9 per cent of all practices, covering between them about a quarter of the population. Participating practices would have annual budgets of £6–700,000. At the end of 1989 the Secretary of State announced the scheme's extension to practices with 9,000 patients and to smaller practices grouped together. At the same time it was revealed that family doctors are to be offered a management allowance of up to £32,000 a year and a 75 per cent discount on computer equipment. It is hoped that these inducements will persuade more practices to agree to run their own budgets.

Internal markets and a more general entrepreneurial approach to health care demands health authorities which more closely resemble boards of directors in private companies. Accordingly, the White Paper proposed a reduction in the size of Regional and District Health Authorities from their present sixteen to nineteen members, to five non-executive members, up to five executive members and a non-executive chairperson, with local authorities losing their right to appoint members to district authorities.

Streamlining will also occur at the apex of the service with a new policy board responsible for general strategy and finances and a new, small NHS management executive which will deal with operational matters, looking for the most cost-effective options.

The government believes that the infusion of market principles will lead to the elimination of waste and better value for money. However, not everything is being left to internal market forces, and in future, health care providers will be subjected to stricter controls.

The government intends to extend the system of medical audit to all hospitals. Medical audit, in which all consultants are expected to participate, is based on peer review and entails 'a systematic, critical analysis of the quality of medical care, including the procedures used for diagnosis and treatment, the use of resources, and the resulting outcome for the patient'.[32] Financial audit will be entrusted to the Audit Commission.

There will also be an attempt to reduce the amount the NHS spends on drugs. The White Paper says that the drugs bill is the largest single element – more than a third – of total expenditure on the family practitioner services. 'The cost of medicines accounted for £1.9 billion in 1987–8, more than the cost of the doctors who prescribed them.'[33] A system of indicative drug budgets will be instituted. Every year the Parliamentary Estimates will allocate to each region a sum of money for expenditure on drugs and the region will then divide the sum among its family practitioner committees which will in turn set indicative drug budgets for each practice. The government is to seek powers to enable family practitioner committees 'to impose financial penalties on GPs who persistently refuse to curb excessive prescribing'.[34]

The White Paper suggested that 'an improved information system will . . . be needed before the new scheme can fully operate'.[35] The same may be said of the whole of the internal market system. If patients are to exercise choice and evaluate the services they receive, if GPs are to prepare packages and purchase services for their patients, and if hospitals and District Health Authorities are to negotiate contracts, then all concerned will need easier access to reliable information. The White Paper included proposals for improving information systems. In the case of general practice the government intends 'to encourage and invest in the development of the information systems which will be needed to support the calculation of budgets, the pricing and costing of hospital services to GPs, and the monitoring of prescribing costs'.[36] In hospitals the existing resource management initiative, providing 'a complete picture of the resources used in treating hospital patients', will be extended and accelerated.

Competitive tendering
Competitive tendering usually refers to putting contracts for the provision of non-medical services out to tender, and although contracting out is not new, it has flourished in the enterprise culture. As Ascher says:

The popularity of contracting out as an alternative means of public sector service delivery grew dramatically between 1980 and 1988 in Britain . . . In 1978, the year before the Conservatives took power, the presence of contractors in both local government and the health service went virtually unnoticed. Very few contractors thought public sector work would grow significantly, and none would have predicted the explosion that was about to occur.[37]

The Conservatives encouraged contracting out in the NHS, using it as a weapon against the public service unions. The strike of ancillary workers in the winter preceding the 1979 General Election had strengthened public support for an anti-union privatisation programme. Although Conservative Party support for competitive tendering is usually stated in terms of increased economic efficiency, the unstated, underlying reasons are ideological.

The first Conservative administration relied mainly on exhortation, but this was not notably successful. Indeed, between 1980 and 1983 contracting out in the NHS declined: in catering, cleaning and laundry, as Ascher demonstrates, there was a partial return to in-house services.[38] These trends persuaded the government to move from exhortation to more coercive measures.

In the autumn of 1983 the government issued a directive in the form of a circular requiring health authorities to invite tenders for cleaning, catering and laundry services. The District Health Authorities were to submit plans to Regional Authorities within five months, and two months later Regional Authorities were to submit proposals for the whole region to the DHSS, all services having been put out to tender by September 1986. Health authorities were also encouraged to consider other areas for contracting out.

Although there was considerable opposition from health authorities, they were forced to at least give the appearance of compliance. Allegations by private contractors of unfairness and irregularities were levelled at health authorities when in-house tenders were successful. Ascher reports that of the 519 contracts completed by the end of 1985, 123 (23.7 per cent) had been awarded to external companies. Outside firms were most successful in gaining cleaning contracts: 30 per cent of these went to outsiders. By contrast, outside catering firms held only 5.5 per cent of the total number of contracts, and about 25 per cent of the laundry contracts went to outsiders.[39] A more recent figure produced by the government indicates that in the first five years of the operation of the scheme '85 per cent of contracts were won in-house, despite the keen competition'.[40]

The relatively small proportion of successful bids from outside contractors is not necessarily a sign of unfair practices. A study conducted by Milne found that there was 'genuine competition' between in-house and private contractors and he notes that 63 per cent of a small sample of thirty-two contracts had no outside submissions when they were put out to tender.[41]

There is ample evidence that competitive tendering is accompanied by a reduction in costs, but estimates of the scale of the savings vary. The Institute for Fiscal Studies claims that hospital domestic services were 20 per cent cheaper after tendering, but the Institute expressed concern that some companies had under-priced their work and others had had their contracts terminated for poor performance.[42] The government claims savings of only 17 per cent – £120 million a year by 1988.[43] Milne identified much bigger savings of between one-third and two-thirds. Milne and the Institute for Fiscal Studies are in complete agreement, however, that the savings occur irrespective of whether the contract is placed in-house or outside.

The interpretation of these statistics needs to be approached with caution. Milne, for example, argues that in a majority of contracts major reductions in total expenditure arose from changes in specification – a reduced amount of work being done and a lower level of service provided. Furthermore, putting contracts out to tender was frequently seen by managers as an opportunity for 'rationalisation': nurses being required to clean their own rooms and the closing down of one of two kitchens are examples quoted by Milne. Under one private contract described by Milne, staff had to work at a faster rate and forego bonuses, amounting to a cut in pay of 25 per cent. Redundancies are also more likely when contracts are awarded to private companies. Milne concludes that most of the differences identified 'favour the in-house tender' which is preferred because it provides a 'more efficient way to monitor contracts and control opportunistic behaviour'.[44]

Government pressure for contracting out has not lessened. As soon as the savings from privatising domestic services began to peter out, the government put forward fresh candidates for competitive tendering. None of the support services is exempt, but particular favourites are hospital transport, sterile supplies, portering, building and engineering, energy maintenance and gardening. It is clear that this list includes some services, such as gardening, which have very little direct impact on patient care, and others, such as hospital transport and sterile supplies, which affect patient care directly. Perhaps it is unwise to search for general principles, and the government has now stated that 'there is scope for much wider use of competitive tendering, beyond the non-clinical support services which have formed the bulk of tendering so far'.[45]

During the ambulance dispute of 1989 the Secretary of State threatened to privatise the non-emergency ambulance service. This was already on the agenda and a confidential document revealed plans to allow London's thirty-two District Health Authorities to buy in non-emergency services.[46]

The Department of Health has vacillated over two other services: nurses' homes and pathology laboratories. Nurses' homes have been considered for privatisation, but the government, following an outcry from the nurses, has shelved its plans for the time being. There have been contradictory statements about pathology laboratories. It is obvious that the government would like to privatise pathology services, but it appears that the political implications have led them to delay their plans.

Individual health authorities can be sure of the warm support of the government should they decide to exceed the Department of Health's requirements. One such authority is Forth Valley which proposes to put financial management, medical records, hospital pharmacy, X-ray services and some laboratory services out to tender.[47]

Among the most radical proposals for contracting out are those relating to management. One idea is for hospitals to remain under the control of health authorities which would contract out the *management* of some or all of its hospitals. Tenders would be invited from companies specialising in hospital management, with successful companies being paid a fixed fee and having all their costs reimbursed. The White Paper made no mention of this idea, but it is by no means incompatible with NHS Hospital Trusts.

Charges

Increasing existing charges or introducing new ones is a form of privatisation. Birch refers to this process as 'backdoor privatisation' and demonstrates that 'patients who are subject to charges are providing an increasing proportion of the cost of their own treatment'.[48]

NHS charges have increased dramatically since 1979. Prescription charges, for example, have been raised on twelve occasions, increasing from 20 pence an item in 1979 to £3.05 an item in 1990. Between 1979 and 1986 dental charges more than doubled in real terms. In 1984 the provision of spectacles under the NHS began to be phased out, and everyone now has to purchase their spectacles privately. Children and people on low incomes receive vouchers.

The White Paper *Promoting Better Health*, published in 1987, introduced a completely new principle into the charging arrangements in the ophthalmic and dental services. In the interest of early diagnosis and preventive treatment, sight testing and dental examinations had always been available without payment under the NHS. *Promoting Better Health* proposed the abolition of free sight and dental checks: sight testing would now cost about £10 and dental examinations £3. At the same time dental treatment charges would also rise and in relation to this the White Paper stated: 'The overall effect of these changes will be to increase the proportion of the cost of the general dental services contributed in charges'.[49]

The Health and Medicines Bill which introduced these charges reached the statute book after a very rough ride through Parliament. On several occasions Conservative MPs voted against the Bill or abstained and the House of Lords completely rejected the charges. In the course of the debate both inside and outside Parliament it was claimed that eyesight tests were an important preventive service since they frequently revealed early signs of glaucoma, diabetes and high blood pressure. It is certainly surprising that these charges were announced in a White Paper which had as 'a major theme . . . the need . . . to shift the emphasis in primary care from the treatment of illness to the promotion of health and the prevention of disease'.[50]

There are categories of patient who are exempt charges: children and young people, pregnant women, nursing mothers and those with low incomes. Three-quarters of all prescriptions are free of charge as are just under half of all courses of dental treatment.

Birch identifies two main arguments used to justify higher patient charges: raising extra revenue and deterring over-utilisation or 'abuse'. He says that extra revenue is generated but that the extra resources are, at least in part, used to replace other sources of public finance rather than to extend provision. On the question of over-utilisation he concludes that 'although the empirical evidence suggests that increases in patient charges do lead to some reduction in utilization, there is no reason to believe that it is the inefficient (and perhaps more importantly only the inefficient) utilization that is deterred'.[51] An investigation by the *Observer* revealed that the number of people having eye tests had fallen by 40 per cent less than three months after the charges had been introduced.[52]

CONCLUSIONS

Since 1979 the Conservative Party has time and time again proclaimed: 'The National Health Service is safe with us'. This claim is backed up with statistics purporting to show vastly increased expenditure on the NHS and an expansion of staff numbers and facilities.

These claims, which will be examined in a little more detail later, seem to fly in the face of common experience and public perception of the state of the NHS. The common perception is that the NHS has been *under*-funded, and there is ample evidence of shortages and shortcomings to support this view.

There is, for example, a chronic shortage of nurses in spite of vigorous recruitment campaigns in 1988 and 1989/90 which cost a total of £6.5 million. The UK Central Council has reported that the number joining the professional register fell by 7.9 per cent in 1988–9 and that there had been a 17 per cent fall over the last four years. Disillusioned nurses are either leaving the profession altogether or moving abroad, while others are moving from the NHS to the private sector. According to Robin Cook, the opposition spokesperson on health matters, the number of nurses moving to the private sector doubled to almost 63,000 between 1982 and 1986. Morale among NHS nurses is low and the pay and regrading dispute certainly did not help matters. There are shortages everywhere, but London and the south-east of England have the most serious problems.

It is the most highly trained nurses who are in particularly short supply. Three examples will serve to indicate the problems arising from shortages of skilled nursing personnel. Birmingham Children's Hospital was much in the news in 1988 and 1989 because of long delays and repeated postponements in the admission of children requiring heart surgery. The reason given for this was a shortage of nurses trained in intensive care. In late 1989 the Royal Manchester Children's Hospital was reported as having only 246 nurses out of its full complement of 270. It, too, was turning patients away and delaying operations. Only four of the eight beds in its bone marrow transplant unit were open.[53] A shortage of nurses also led to the closure of a children's cancer ward at St Bartholomew's in 1988.

In terms of pay, however, some NHS workers have done very much worse than nurses and doctors. There are 450,000 workers whose pay is settled through Whitly Council machinery rather than by pay review boards. The National Association of Health Authorities has complained that the low rates of pay have made it difficult to recruit staff and there are serious shortages in all categories, including pharmaceutics, medical secretaries, management accountants, computer staff, psychologists, physiotherapists and a range of manual workers.

Shortages of staff present health authorities with their most urgent problem; a problem which can only be exacerbated by poor working conditions. Certainly, conditions in some of the older hospitals are less than satisfactory and the Royal College of Nursing has made the following judgement:

Dingy waiting rooms are but the first symptom of the poor standards of hygiene, decoration and repair endemic in the hospital sector. The lack of functioning toilets on wards and the dirty state of many hospital kitchens are serious issues of consumer safety.[54]

The Royal College of Nursing claims that these shortcomings arise from gross under-funding. Hospital doctors, too, complain of an under-funded service and a shortage of places in hospitals for the acutely ill. In the six months ending 31 March 1989 hospital waiting lists increased by 40,000 and reached their highest figure since 1983. A group of Birmingham consultants has claimed that people are dying because of delays in finding hospital places. Ferriman reports that cardiac centres are running short of funds and are having to turn patients away. As many as twelve centres were facing crisis in 1989 and all eighty centres may reach this position in the next two or three years.[55] In 1989 it was reported that Guys Hospital had turned away 450 suspected cancer victims in three months due to lack of funds.[56]

A survey by the National Association of Health Authorities found that one-third of the 190 health authorities had planned cuts in services in 1988 with some of them planning to close beds. If the authorities were to stay within their cash-limited budgets an extra £164 million would have to be found.[57]

In 1989 District Health Authorities were said to be facing a total deficit of £323 million, and although efficiency savings from 'cost improvement programmes' were expected to yield £162 million, this would still leave a net deficit of £161 million. Nine out of ten authorities were attempting to make cash savings: 23 per cent were postponing or cancelling spending plans, 15 per cent were reducing services, 12 per cent were selling land or buildings and 11 per cent were freezing recruitment.[58]

In the Chancellor's Autumn Statement in November 1989 an extra £2.4 billion was allocated to the National Health Service for 1990/91. Health authorities would receive £1.17 billion which was said to represent a 3.5 per cent increase above forecast inflation. This will certainly afford some relief but the Chartered Institute of Public Finance and Accountancy claims that even with this increase there will be a shortfall in 1990/91 of £37 million after clearing deficits which the government says must be cleared by 1991.[59]

Although this picture of shortages and cuts in service ignores some of the successes of the NHS in the last decade, it is certainly difficult to reconcile it with the government's claim to have substantially increased expenditure in real terms since 1979. The government claims that between 1978/79 and 1989/90 gross expenditure on the NHS increased by 37 per cent in real terms. This calculation includes both current and capital expenditure.

However, there are several reasons for treating the government's expenditure figures with extreme caution:

1. In some of the statistics the expenditure figures are made to look higher by adding in 'efficiency savings' derived from 'cost improvement programmes', the sums accruing from the authorities' own income generation schemes and the proceeds from the sale of NHS assets.
2. The NHS is a labour intensive 'industry' and labour costs rise faster than prices. Therefore expenditure has to rise faster than prices for the NHS simply to stand still.
3. When the government talks about increases 'in real terms' it is allowing for increases in the retail price index, but the retail price index is a totally inappropriate measure of inflation within the health service. The rate of inflation within the health service is determined by rises in the prices of such items as drugs and dressings, and since the prices of these items rise faster than prices generally, the rate of inflation in the NHS is higher than that arrived at by using the retail price index. Hills comments:

   Using a specific 'NHS deflator' suggests that the *volume* of health services provided by government rose by only 5 per cent over the period 1978/9 to 1983/4, as opposed to the 16 per cent increase in their real *cost* over the same period . . . Since then there has been little rise in the volume of services provided.[60]

4. Insufficient account is taken of demographic factors, particularly the growing proportion of elderly people in the population. The International Labour Organisation estimates that in 1985 the elderly (65+) were responsible for a little over 41 per cent of health spending in the UK. By the year 2000 this proportion will have risen to 47 per cent and by 2015 it will reach 58 per cent.[61]

The average annual cost to the NHS of someone who is aged 75 and over is about seven times the cost of someone who is aged between 25 and 44. Another factor making for increased costs is that more disabled children are surviving and living for longer.

5. New technology and medical advances exert a considerable upward pressure on costs.

Taken together, these factors help to explain the discrepancy between the government's claim of increasing expenditure and the evidence of declining standards. Subjected to this kind of analysis, the £2.4 billion increase in NHS funds for 1990/91 becomes much less impressive.

An OECD report demonstrates that Britain spends a smaller proportion of its GDP on health (6 per cent) than any other major country. The United States spends almost twice the proportion of its much higher GDP: the OECD average is 7.5 per cent of GDP and Canada, France, Germany, Sweden and the United States spend in excess of 8 per cent.[62]

In the 1989 White Paper the government claimed that 'simply injecting more and more money' into the NHS is not an answer to its problems. The White Paper argued that 'the organisation of the NHS – the way it delivers care to the individual patient – also needs to be reformed'.[63]

There is general agreement that the implementation of the White Paper's proposals for independent audit and peer review should lead to greater efficiency, but the remainder of the proposals have been heavily criticised by the House of Commons Select Committee on Social Services, the Labour Party and organisations representing nurses, GPs and consultants.

The House of Commons Select Committee on Social Services is particularly concerned about the timing of the proposals, saying that in working towards implementation in 1991 the government is trying to go too far too quickly. If GPs are to manage budgets and health authorities are to buy in services, precise and detailed information about hospital costs will be necessary, but it is most unlikely that hospital budgeting will have reached the required level of sophistication by 1991. The Committee would have preferred a small number of local experiments before implementing an untried and untested system in full.

The Committee also criticised the absence of arrangements for local consultation, and opposed the granting of tax relief on private insurance premiums for those aged 60 and over.[63]

Criticisms of the White Paper, principally from the nursing and medical professions but also from other sources, have included the following:

1. GPs may be under pressure to prescribe the *cheapest* treatment rather than the *best*.
2. There will be an incentive to refuse 'expensive' patients such as elderly and chronically sick people who may be seen as a drain on the practice budget. The Nuffield Institute says that 'the new arrangements risk a situation where those most in need of primary health care are least able to obtain it'.[65] The government has promised to stop this happening, but it is not at all clear how easy it will be to force doctors to accept particular categories of patients.
3. Doctors' training does not prepare them for making profit-maximising financial decisions.
4. The White Paper is too much concerned with organisation and too little concerned with patient care – in particular, the needs of dependent elderly, chronically sick and disabled patients are completely ignored.
5. Much is made in the White Paper of patient choice, but it is difficult to see how the new system will enhance this. It is suggested, for example, that GPs may wish to negotiate contracts with hospitals to provide a range of services for all the practice's patients, and such contracts are unlikely to leave much room for choice. The Nuffield Institute Report already referred to states:

   Closer scrutiny of the proposals raises doubts about the extent to which patients can expect to benefit in terms of choice and quality from the major shifts proposed in relationships between consumers, purchasers and providers. The White Paper's approach to consumerism emphasises providing information *to* consumers rather than obtaining it *from* them. As such the approach is firmly paternalistic.[66]

6. Hospitals may find they can maximise their income by concentrating on particular specialities, and general medical cases may suffer as a consequence. The Nuffield Institute expresses the fear that 'competitive behaviour could stimulate the over-provision of high technology medicine of unproven efficacy'.[67] Equally

hospitals, under the pressure of the internal market, may gravitate to those areas with the greatest potential for income generation and some patients may have to travel further afield to find a suitable hospital.

7. Inner city hospitals are likely to be hardest hit by the new funding arrangements. In future the budgets of health authorities will be determined by the size of the resident population rather than by the level of the services they provide. Thus, inner city areas with big hospitals but small resident populations will find their budgets greatly reduced. A Labour Party survey has revealed potential budget reductions as high as 78 per cent, and there are twelve hospitals with losses in excess of 50 per cent. Hospitals in such areas will have to make good these huge deficits by selling services to other districts and Mr Cook, Labour's health spokesperson, has expressed the worry that 'the need to make ends meet will force hospitals to compete on price instead of quality'.[68]

8. The reorganised service will require 4,000 extra administrators and an additional £217 million a year.[69]

9. The Labour Party sees the development of NHS Hospital Trusts as a prelude to complete privatisation.

A Gallup poll conducted in June 1989 revealed widespread public disquiet about the changes. Only 15 per cent of voters approved of the proposals. Three-quarters thought the changes would lead to cuts and 73 per cent saw them as the first stage towards the privatisation of the NHS. Only 23 per cent of respondents believed the NHS to be safe in the hands of the Conservative government.[70]

The volume and vehemence of the criticism took the government by surprise. The Secretary of State for Health has attempted to persuade the critics that their fears are unfounded, and a £2.25 million publicity campaign has been launched. The impression has been given, however, that the government is not prepared to listen to criticisms: the Secretary of State's response to the Gallup poll results was to claim simply that three out of four people were mistaken.[71] The government has re-affirmed its determination to push the changes through, keeping strictly to the timetable set out in the White Paper. Such hasty and ill prepared action carries the risk of a decline in standards of care.

There can be no doubt that the NHS has shortcomings, and in terms of customer relations and communication it has something to learn from the private sector. However, the NHS also has strengths and its contribution to the quality of life in Britain should not be under-estimated. It offers a largely free service of reasonable quality to the whole nation. It deals with both acute and chronic health care and is concerned with both physical and mental ill-health. It is less concerned than it ought to be with the promotion of health, but it does offer a wide range of preventive services. The service that came into being in 1948 was based on the notion that access to health care should not depend upon the ability to pay; the NHS was to respond to need, not demand.

In the changes made to the NHS since 1979, the twin objectives of privatisation and creation of inequality are clearly discernible. The two are closely intertwined, and both aims have been promoted by the increased use of charging and by the encouragement given to the development of private markets in health care. It is true that compared with the NHS private markets are still relatively small, but for-profit health care is no longer simply tolerated, it is given positive approval and welcomed as a partner. At the conclusion of a study of private medicine in Britain Higgins states that:

the growth of for-profit medicine in Britain has weakened the commitment to equal access to health services for all, irrespective of age, gender, race, class or ability to pay. It has . . . rejected the claim that the distribution of health services should take place beyond the play of market forces . . . Moreover, it has created a change in the moral climate of health service provision . . .[72]

The NHS has been forced to become part of the enterprise culture and to adopt some of the attitudes and practices of the private market, and although the White Paper affirms the government's commitment to the NHS, it is plain that in future the public sector will have to embrace even more closely the competitive principles of the private market. Indeed the NHS Hospital Trusts will be in direct competition with each other, with District Authority hospitals, and with private hospitals for funds and contracts. The government has maintained that the NHS and Community Care Act is not the first stage towards NHS privatisation, but once the new arrangements are in place, future privatisation will certainly be easier.

The shortcomings of the NHS are not likely to be overcome by the implementation of the Act: the problems stem from years of under-funding. The Act will do nothing to stop the closure of beds and the curtailment of services. The refurbishment of dilapidated hospitals will proceed no more quickly as a consequence of the changes and shortages of staff, and long waiting lists, will continue. The White Paper did the NHS a disservice by treating its problems as organisational rather than financial, but this is not an unfamiliar story.

NOTES

1. R. M. Titmuss, *The Gift Relationship: From Human Blood to Social Policy*, London: Allen and Unwin, 1970, p. 225.
2. E. Papadakis and P. Taylor-Gooby, *The Private Provision of Public Welfare: State Market and Community*, Brighton: Wheatsheaf, 1987, p. 40.
3. *The Guardian*, 23 October 1987.
4. *The Observer*, 7 June 1987.
5. R. Cook, *Life Begins at 40: In Defence of the NHS*, London: Fabian Society, 1988, p. 6.
6. J. Higgins, *The Business of Medicine: Private Health Care in Britain*, London: Macmillan, 1988, p. 87.
7. *The Guardian*, 13 February 1988.
8. Department of Health, *Working for Patients*, Cm 555, London, HMSO: 1989, p. 69.
9. J. Higgins, *op. cit.*, pp. 94–5.
10. *The Guardian*, 9 May 1988.
11. *The Guardian*, 18 February 1988.
12. Central Statistical Office, *Social Trends 19*, London: HMSO, 1989.
13. B. Griffith, S. Iliffe and G. Rayner, *Banking On Sickness: Commercial Medicine in Britain and the USA*, London: Lawrence and Wishart, 1987, p. 79.
14. *The Guardian*, 18 February 1988.
15. Quoted in B. Griffith *et al.*, *op. cit.*, p. 239.
16. J. Higgins, *op. cit.*, p. 102.
17. B. Griffith *et al.*, *op. cit.*, p. 102.
18. J. Higgins, *op. cit.*, p. 139.
19. *The Guardian*, 26 October 1988.
20. *The Observer*, 7 June 1987.
21. *The Guardian*, 28 November 1987.
22. *The Observer*, 16 August 1987.
23. Department of Health, *op. cit.*, p. 68.
24. *The Guardian*, 19 June 1987.

25. J. Higgins, *op. cit.*, p. 188.
26. B. Griffith *et al.*, *op. cit.*, p. 246.
27. National Association of Health Authorities, *Income Generation in the NHS*, Birmingham: NAHA, 1988.
28. *The Guardian*, 27 April 1988.
29. No Turning Back Group of Conservative MPs, *The NHS: A Suitable Case for Treatment*, London: Conservative Political Centre, 1988, p. 20.
30. Department of Health, *op. cit.*, p. 24.
31. *Ibid.*, p. 52.
32. *Ibid.*, p. 39.
33. *Ibid.*, p. 57.
35. *Ibid.*, p. 58.
36. *Ibid.*, p. 53.
37. K. Ascher, *The Politics of Privatisation: Contracting Out Public Services*, London: Macmillan, 1987, pp. 22 and 25.
38. *Ibid.*, pp. 174–81.
39. *Ibid.*, pp. 190–1.
40. Department of Health, *op. cit.*, p. 69.
41. R. G. Milne, 'Competitive tendering in the NHS: An economic analysis of the early implementation of HC (83) H8', *Public Administration*, vol. 15, no. 2, 1987, pp. 145–60.
42. *The Guardian*, 12 December 1988.
43. Department of Health, *op. cit.*, p. 69.
44. R. G. Milne, *op. cit.*, p. 160.
45. Department of Health, *op. cit.*, p. 70.
46. *The Guardian*, 27 November 1988.
48. S. Birch, 'Increased patient charges in the National Health Service: A method of privatising primary care', *Journal of Social Policy*, vol. 15, pt. 2, 1986, p. 168.
49. Department of Health and Social Security, *Promoting Better Health*, Cm 249, London: HMSO, 1987.
50. *Ibid.*, 'Foreword'.
51. S. Birch, *op. cit.*, p. 180.
52. *The Observer*, 25 June 1989.
53. *The Observer*, 22 October 1989.
54. *The Guardian*, 17 March 1989.
55. *The Observer*, 21 May 1989; and Birmingham Consultants for the Rescue of the NHS, *Counting the Cost of Cost-Cutting*, Birmingham, 1989.
56. *The Guardian*, 7 August 1989.
57. National Association of Health Authorities, *Autumn Survey 1989: The Financial Position of District Health Authorities*, Birmingham: NAHA, 1989.

59. Treasury, *The Government's Expenditure Plans, 1990/91 – 1992/93*, Cm 879, London: HMSO, 1989.
60. J. Hills, 'What happened to spending on the welfare state?', in A. Walker and C. Walker (eds.), *The Growing Divide*, London: Child Poverty Action Group, 1987, p. 95.
61. *The Guardian*, 10 August 1989.
62. Organisation for Economic Co-operation and Development, *Financing and Delivering Health Care*, Paris: OECD, 1987.
63. Department of Health, *op. cit.*, p. 3.
64. Social Services Committee, *Resourcing the NHS: The Government's Plans for the Future of the NHS*, HC 214 – III, London: HMSO, 1989.
65. S. Harrison, *et al.*, *Competing for Health: A Commentary on the NHS Review*, Leeds: Nuffield Institute For Health Service Studies, 1989.
66. *Ibid.*, p. 7.
67. *Ibid.*
68. *The Observer*, 23 July 1989.
69. *The Guardian*, 23 November 1989.
70. *The Guardian*, 5 July 1989.
71. *Ibid.*
72. J. Higgins, *op. cit.*, p. 257.

CHAPTER 5

RESHAPING EDUCATION

The Education Reform Act received the Royal Assent at the end of July, 1988. The Act is of mammoth proportions with profound implications for every sector of education, and it has been the subject of intense discussion both inside and outside Parliament. The professional teaching associations at all levels of the educational system objected to many of the Bill's provisions, and a joint rally and lobby of Parliament was organised. The House of Commons spent over 215 hours on the Bill, including ten days on the floor of the House and twenty-two days in committee, and the House of Lords devoted over 150 hours spread over sixteen days to a discussion of the Bill.

Hundreds of amendments, some on matters of substance but the vast majority on points of detail, were tabled. The House of Lords alone proposed 569 amendments, and the Secretary of State for Education and Science, Kenneth Baker, said: 'I have been unable to find any measure since the war that has been more debated or had more parliamentary time allocated to it'.[1] Some changes were made and a few concessions were wrung from the government. But, although the Act differed in detail from the original Bill, the main principles remained intact and Mr Baker had achieved most of what he wanted. Many of the Act's provisions, at the time of writing, are only beginning to be put into operation, but it is clear that once they have been fully implemented they will completely transform the educational system in Britain.

The Educational Reform Act is to be the main focus of what

follows, but not all of the major changes flow from the Act. These other changes (in levels of funding, the growing role of the Training Agency, and the enterprise culture as it affects higher education, for example) will be incorporated into the discussion. For convenience, the chapter is divided into two main sections, one dealing with schools and the other concentrating on further and higher education.

SCHOOLS

The National Curriculum

In a speech delivered in 1976 when he was Prime Minister, Sir James Callaghan sparked off what became known as the 'great debate' about the quality and role of education in Britain. He referred to the frequent complaints from industry that new recruits from school were ill-equipped with basic skills. He was also disturbed by the relatively small proportion of graduates who chose to work in manufacturing industry. There was a need for more technologically-based science courses and a change in the balance of educational priorities:

The balance was wrong in the past. We have a responsibility now . . . to see that we do not get it wrong in the other direction. There is no virtue in producing socially well-adjusted members of society who are unemployed because they do not have the skills. Nor at the other extreme must they be technically efficient robots. Both of the basic purposes of education require the same essential tools. These are to be basically literate, to be basically numerate, to understand how to live and work together, and have respect for others and respect for the individual.[2]

The speech was followed by a series of meetings throughout the country organised by the Department of Education and Science. Eventually, in 1977, a Green Paper was published which identified four major topics for consideration: the school curriculum, assessment and standards, the education and training of teachers and the relationship between school and working life.[3] The same topics were addressed in a White Paper in 1985,[4] and these issues became a major concern of the Education Reform Act which introduced a national curriculum backed up by standardised tests at the ages of seven, eleven, fourteen and sixteen. The national curriculum is to consist of three core subjects of English, maths and science, and seven other areas: a foreign language (not required in primary schools), technology, history, geography, art, music and physical education. Several working parties were set up to make recommendations on the content of each subject and on the appropriate levels of attainment at each stage. By the beginning of 1990 most of the working parties had reported.

A National Curriculum Council has been set up to advise the Secretary of State on matters relating to the national curriculum and to supervise the introduction of new curricula into schools and review their progress. Within a few months of its establishment the National Curriculum Council had produced reports on the in-service training of maths and science teachers in the operation of the national curriculum and on attainment targets and study programmes in maths and science. A School Examinations and Assessment Council has also been established to advise the Secretary of State on the operation of testing and assessment procedures.

The aims of the national curriculum and its related assessment procedures were set out in a consultative paper published in July 1987[5] in which it was anticipated that standards of educational provision and attainment would be raised by:

1. Ensuring that all children studied a broad range of subjects and did not drop at too early a stage in their school careers subjects which might be useful to them later.
2. Setting clear objectives for what children over the full range of abilities should be able to achieve; this will help all children to reach their full potential.
3. Ensuring that all children irrespective of sex, ethnic origin and geographical location have access to broadly the same, sound curriculum.
4. Checking on progress and making appropriate adjustments.

It was also claimed that a national curriculum would facilitate movement from one area of the country to another with minimum disruption to children's education. Finally, the national curriculum and testing arrangements would make schools more accountable. It should be noted that the national curriculum applies only to maintained schools – private sector schools and the city technology colleges are excluded.

There has been some opposition to the proposals even among the government's own supporters. Lord Joseph, a former Conservative

Secretɔ ry of State for Education and Science, has argued that the plans involve too much central control and that they will lead to a loss of flexibility and a stifling of initiative and innovation. Lord Joseph made two unsuccessful attempts to limit the national curriculum to a purely advisory role and to restrict its operation to the three core subjects.

Some concern has also been expressed by teachers, local authorities, the Labour Party and others that the national curriculum is being implemented with too much haste. The Task Group on Assessment and Testing recommended that assessment arrangements should be phased in over five years, and that an intensive teacher-training programme should be mounted in the meantime. Nevertheless the national curriculum in maths, science and English was introduced in 1989 and the teachers have complained bitterly of the short time available for training and of the meagre resources devoted to it – £47.5 million for training in content and £33.1 million for preparing teachers for the new tests and assessment. By the start of the school year in 1992 the national curriculum will have been introduced in all subjects.

There is a problem of fitting the curriculum into the school day. The maths and science reports imply that together these two subjects should occupy about one-third of the timetable. The science report suggests that in the fourth and fifth years pupils should be devoting 20 per cent of their time to science. Although no specific percentages were mentioned in the Act, the government had originally intended that the *whole* of the national curriculum should occupy 70 per cent of the timetable; but it should also be remembered that religious education has been mandatory since 1944 and remains so. There have even been suggestions that the length of the working week for secondary school pupils may have to be increased.

The greatest controversy has been over the question of assessment and testing. Teachers have expressed concern about the emphasis on testing which they claim will lead to greater stress among pupils and parents and will carry implications of failure. It is possible, too, that tests will distort the curriculum with pupils being coached more than at present for examinations.

The Task Group on Assessment and Testing recommended a mixture of standardised written tests and continuous assessment by treachers, but with the emphasis very definitely on the latter. The

Secretary of State shared this preference for assessment by teachers, but the Conservative leadership was split on this issue with Mrs Thatcher herself favouring nationally standardised pencil and paper tests mainly because they lend themselves to direct comparisons between schools. The government firmly believes in the value of competition among schools as a means of raising standards. The idea is that all results are published and schools are then placed in league tables, so the main purpose of the tests is as much about the stimulation of competition as it is about diagnosing individual children's strengths and weaknesses. The Task Group on Assessment and Testing said that results should be published using average scores, but as part of a more general report on the school together with information about the socio-economic characteristics of the school's catchment area.

Goldstein and Cuttance have argued that the use of average scores as advocated by the Task Group is meaningless and unfair to schools in deprived areas. They claim that a more accurate picture is gained by using attainment data. In this method, the attainment of a child at the time of the test is compared with his or her attainment at time of entry to the school. What is then being measured is the *progress* of the pupil, and putting these together for all the pupils of a particular age in a school gives a far more accurate measure of a school's effectiveness.[6]

At present several attempts are being made to devise performance indicators which would enable schools to be graded, and serve both as a management tool and as a guide to parents in choosing a school.[7] Choice of school is an aspect of 'parent power' which is the subject of the next section.

Parental power

Free parental choice of school was supposedly granted by the 1980 and 1986 Education Acts. Local authorities, however, faced with the need to make the most effective use of school buildings and staff, did not make parental choice the paramount consideration. The matter came to a head in Dewsbury where parents refused to send twenty-six children to a school in which the vast majority of the pupils were Asian. They wished instead to send their children to a school two miles away. As the law stood at that time local authorities could place limits on the number of pupils in each of its schools, and the Secretary of State said that he had no power to intervene in the

Dewsbury case. Eventually the local authority reversed its decision after two parents had instituted a judicial review in the High Court. The 1988 Act allows open enrolment, so that schools are forced to accept children up to the limit of their capacity.

The Dewsbury parents were vehement in their denial of racial prejudice. It is undeniable, however, that the new regulations could easily lead to racially segregated schools. Mr Roy Hattersley, Deputy leader of the Labour Party, said at the 1987 national conference that the new arrangements could lead to 'an apartheid education system'.[8] In November 1987, Baroness Hooper, the Under Secretary of State for Education, stated in the course of a television programme: 'If we are offering freedom of choice to parents we must allow that choice to operate. If it ends up with a segregated system – then so be it'.[9] In the House of Commons Mrs Thatcher refused to disassociate herself from these comments, although she was invited to do so on three occasions. The opting-out arrangements (see below) makes segregation even more likely and racial or religious segregation will be compounded by social segregation. It is interesting to note that some Muslim schools are considering opting out of local authority control and offering separate provision.

In the three Education Acts passed during their first nine years of power, the Conservative government has made parental influence and involvement a central issue. In 1980 it implemented the proposals of the Taylor Committee for representation of parents on governing bodies of schools, and under the 1986 Act, which became operative in September 1988, parent representation on governing bodies was extended. At the same time governing bodies were made accountable to parents for the first time. Governors are now required to produce annual reports and to organise parents' meetings at which the reports and any other matters parents wish to raise may be discussed. Any meeting attended by at least 20 per cent of the parents may pass resolutions which the head teacher, the governors and the local education authority must consider. The 1988 Act has altered the position by giving governing bodies increased powers and greater financial independence while retaining accountability to parents as a whole. The devolution of detailed financial control from local authorities to head teachers and governing bodies means that schools will in future have to manage their own budgets which include an amount for teachers' salaries. There can be no guarantee that head teachers and parent governors have the necessary skills to perform this task effectively.

However, there is some evidence to suggest that parent power may be somewhat illusory. In 1988 the Consumers' Association found that only 25 per cent of parents had attended a parent–teacher association meeting in the past twelve months and only 9 per cent had attended a school governors' annual meeting. Over half of those questioned thought that teachers should be allowed to get on with their jobs free from parental interference. Buckinghamshire is monitoring the process and in 1987 Audrey Simpson reported:

Only a trickle of progress reports have so far found their way back to Buckinghamshire's education department, but they confirm the trend nationally of a poor overall response and turnout confined principally to a hardcore of parents, generally stalwarts of a school parent–teacher association.[10]

The National Confederation of Parent–Teacher Associations cites the example of a secondary school in the Midlands with a roll of 1,100 where the annual meeting was attended by the head teacher and deputy, four governors and seven parents.

Parent representation on governing bodies under the 1986 Act did not have an auspicious beginning. It is evident that in some areas the local political parties were intent on retaining control. In Barnet and Kent (both Conservative) and Manchester (Labour) nominations from opposition groups were refused.[11] A survey carried out by the Labour Party revealed that two-thirds of the authorities questioned were experiencing difficulties in recruiting parent governors, a quarter of them claiming that the problems were serious.

The Labour Party, which supports the idea of parent governors, has identified a number of shortcomings in the present arrangements. It does not believe that all parents have been informed of their rights under the Act and it is critical of the lack of training for parent governors. A number of local authorities, universities and polytechnics are offering courses for governors, but the Labour Party maintains that there should be a properly funded national scheme. Something approaching this may yet emerge through Action for Governors' Information and Training – a co-ordinating agency based in Coventry. The government has allocated £4.9 million to governor training.

As in all participatory schemes, there is a risk of middle class bias in parental representation on governing bodies, with the evidence pointing to the active involvement of relatively few parents.[12] This apparently low level of active parental involvement has important implications for other aspects of current policy – especially the arrangements for schools to opt out of local authority control.

Opting out

The most controversial sections of the Education Reform Act are those which allow secondary schools and primary schools with 300 or more pupils to opt out of local authority control. Such schools, known as grant-maintained schools, become self-managing units funded directly by the Exchequer.

A ballot of parents has to be held before a transfer to grant-maintained status can be accomplished, the decision to hold a ballot being taken either by resolution of the governing body or at the request of a percentage of the parents. A secret postal ballot of parents then determines the fate of the school, and once a decision to opt out of local authority control has been taken it cannot be reversed at a later date, although there is, of course, nothing to stop a new government introducing a legislation to repeal this provision.

The schools were given six weeks in which to draw up a register of parents, but decisions had first to be made about what constituted a parent. This decision is to be left to the governors of the school, but the Department of Education and Science is recommending as wide a definition as possible, to include legal guardians, foster parents and the head of a children's home when the child is in care. In the case of divorced couples who have remarried the vote will go to both natural parents and the spouse of the natural parent who has custody of the child. A substantial number of Conservative MPs argued that parents of prospective pupils should be allowed to vote on the grounds that the parents of prospective pupils have a bigger stake in the future of the school than parents whose children are in their final year and who will not therefore be affected by any changes.

The ballot has been surrounded by considerable controversy. In its original form the Bill made provision for a single ballot, the decision resting on a simple majority *of those voting*. Critics pointed out that this could very well mean a well-organised minority taking an irreversible decision about the future of a school. The Conservative

Education Association strongly urged the government to amend the legislation so that a majority of parents *on the register* would be required to vote for opting out. The House of Lords passed an amendment to this effect, but the government overturned it when the legislation returned to the Commons. The Labour Party argued that a two-thirds majority of those voting, or a simple majority of those on the register, should be required, and the National Union of Teachers went even further with its suggestion that opting out should be allowed only if two-thirds of those on the register approved it. In the end the government was forced to make a minor concession, and the present position is that a second ballot will be held if fewer than 50 per cent of those eligible record a vote on the first occasion. A second ballot will be held within fourteen days and a simple majority of those voting will be sufficient.

Many of those proposing changes to the balloting system were opposed to opting out in principle and were really seeking ways of reducing the number of schools withdrawing from local authority control. The Conservative Education Association, the Labour Party, the National Union of Teachers, the Secondary Heads Association, the National Association of Head Teachers and the Local Education Authorities are all opposed to opting out in principle and the leaders of the Church of England and the Catholic Church have serious reservations. A leader in *The Times Higher Education Supplement* had this to say:

Of course opting-out is a nonsense which will undermine rather than reinforce the Government's professed ambition to raise standards in schools. Moreover, it is an obscure nonsense. Mr Baker seems to see opting-out as the reinvention of the direct-grant schools, while Mrs Thatcher appears to regard it as analogous to selling off council houses or British Gas . . . But opting-out is central to the Bill. It is close to the cold heart of neo-Tory belief.[13]

The Secondary Heads Association claims that opting out will not 'improve good schools but will certainly weaken those that are less strong'.[14] It talks of the problems arising from 'the power of possibly prejudiced and short-term pressure groups and the inexperience and lack of know-how of governors and the undermining of the local education authority.'

The National Union of Teachers fears that, because of its divisive potential, opting out will considerably weaken the educational system: 'What is proposed is really a means of reintroducing in a covert manner an elitist and centrally controlled system of direct grant schools on the lines of the grammar schools under the guise of increasing parental choice'.[15]

The National Union of Teachers has also expressed fears that eventually the opted-out schools will become selective and fee paying. This is expressly ruled out in the Act, but only for five years, although the Conservative Education Association recommended that the period should be ten years. It is interesting to speculate on the likely effect of opting out on the present independent schools. Dr John Roe, former headmaster of Westminster School, has estimated that the private schools could lose one-third of their pupils.[16] A further point made by the teachers is that opting out will jeopardise efforts to adjust to falling school rolls.

Public support for opting out is low and appears to be declining. The low level of public support is demonstrated by the results of two opinion polls published in January and February 1988. A poll conducted on behalf of the National Union of Teachers, published in January, found 36 per cent to be in favour of opting out. A Marplan poll showed a very much smaller proportion of the population in favour – only 18 per cent. In the previous June when Marplan asked the same question, 35 per cent expressed support for opting out.

Obviously the effect of opting out on educational provision will depend upon the number of schools electing to withdraw from local authority control, and Mrs Thatcher and Mr Baker seemed to disagree about what would be an appropriate number: Mrs Thatcher hoped that at least 50 per cent of schools will become grant-maintained, but Mr Baker talked of a trickle.

The government had hoped that left wing councils, especially those in the inner cities, would lose their schools, but the evidence so far does not bear this out. Research by the Calham College Institute suggests that in the primary sector of education Conservative-controlled councils are more likely to lose schools than are councils controlled by Labour.[17]

Schools threatened with closure or with the loss of their sixth forms are among the most likely to seriously consider opting out, and the Grammar School Association expects about one-third of the remaining 150 grammar schools to opt out. Thus, schools opting out will vary considerably in character and resources.

In July 1988 an independent trust was set up to advise schools on how to opt out of local authority control. The Grant Maintained Schools Trust, which has the Secretary of State's blessing, is chaired by a Conservative MP and its director is a former adviser to the government. Its stated aim is to 'advise' schools, but 'active encouragement' might be a more accurate description of its activities. The Trust has sent prospectuses to all secondary schools and explanatory leaflets to primary schools. In the first month of its operation it received 280 inquiries; but commenting on this figure, a spokesman said: 'We expect a dramatic increase in inquiries once head teachers come back from holiday and examine the information we have sent them'.[18]

On 1 September 1989 eighteen schools began their independent existence. Eight of them were grammar schools, nine were comprehensive and there was one middle school. On 1 January 1990 a further two schools, both comprehensive, became grant-maintained. On 1 April four comprehensive schools and one grammar school left local authority control, and a further transfer of a Leicestershire high school took place on 21 August.[19] When it is remembered that there are about 5,000 secondary schools the number opting out is very small.

Abolition of the Inner London Education Authority

The Inner London Education Authority (ILEA) survived the abolition of the Greater London Council, but its control by Labour did not endear it to the Conservative government. It seemed only a matter of time, therefore, before the spending cuts and restrictions already imposed on the ILEA were followed by more drastic action.

The Education Reform Act aimed to allow London boroughs to opt out of ILEA control. The deadline set for this was 1990, a simple majority vote of the borough council being sufficient to ensure separation; neither parents nor governors were to be involved in the decision. The reason for their exclusion, despite the government's professed desire for parent power, was that parents and governing bodies were known to be likely to reject opting out of the ILEA.

The results of allowing boroughs to withdraw would, to say the least, be chaotic. The ILEA was to be killed off by attrition, and the Education Officer of the ILEA, Mr William Stubbs, claimed that the proposals would 'result in a breakdown of the administration of the service in the capital'.[20] The chaos would be compounded by some schools claiming grant-maintained status. The Secretary of State recognised that if a high proportion of the boroughs left the ILEA, then what remained would be unworkable, and he therefore decided that if eight or more of the thirteen boroughs opted out he would force the remainder to follow suit.

At the report stage of the Education Reform Bill, Mr Heseltine and Mr Tebbitt tabled an amendment proposing outright abolition of the ILEA. Even some ILEA officials agreed that abolition was preferable to attrition. Finally the Secretary of State bowed to the inevitable, and agreed to abolish the ILEA in 1990, although he personally had expressed doubts about the ability of some of the boroughs to provide an effective education service.

Abolition may be preferable to a slow death but education in London is bound to suffer, especially in the poorer boroughs. A leader in the *Times Higher Education Supplement* called the plan to abolish the ILEA 'a disgraceful measure that plainly verges on maladministration', and went on to claim that the abolition 'will set back education in London for a generation'.[21] The view of parents lent support to this verdict. A ballot organised by parents found that 94.3 per cent of those who voted were in favour of retaining the ILEA; and 51.6 per cent of those entitled to vote rejected abolition. The Conservative Education Association also condemned the government plan and opposition mounted when it was learned that the government planned to cut education spending in London by 40 per cent following abolition of the ILEA. However, the government continued to stand firm, and no concessions were made. The abolition of the ILEA was not based on educational considerations nor even on economic ones. Its intent was blatantly political.

Aspects of privatisation

Independent schools
In 1987 over 620,000 pupils, 7 per cent of the school population, attended the 2,563 independent schools. The amount spent on school fees is about £2 billion a year, but this is expected to almost double by 1991. In 1987 school fees rose by an average of 11 per cent as compared with an inflation rate of 4.1 per cent, but despite higher fees the independent schools are growing by about 6,000 pupils a

year, and by the end of the century they are expected to account for 8.5 per cent of the school population.[22]

Not all independent schools are of a high standard, but Judith Judd claims that 'independent schools are generally better resourced than their state counterparts and the gap is growing'. This is a view shared by the Educational Publishers' Council which claims that independent schools spend twice as much as state schools on books and equipment per pupil.

Pupil–teacher ratios are much lower in the independent sector than in the public sector, and the disparity widened between 1975–6 and 1985–6. In state primary schools the pupil–teacher ratio went down by 7.5 per cent and in state secondary schools there was a fall of 9.5 per cent, but in the same ten year period the pupil–teacher ratio in independent schools came down by 17.7 per cent.[23]

In 1981 the Conservative government introduced the Assisted Places Scheme which provides help with tuition fees and certain other incidental expenses. Schools participating in the scheme have a set quota of assisted places, and make their own selection of the pupils to be admitted. The financial assistance is paid on a sliding scale according to family income. In theory, the scheme is meant to help pupils who would otherwise be unable to do so to benefit from education at an independent school, but Janet Finch argues that past experience of the direct grant system 'would lead one to suppose that many beneficiaries of such a scheme will be middle-class children'.[24] In 1986–7 about 24,500 pupils attended independent schools under the Assisted Places Scheme in England alone, and this transferred £43 million of taxpayers' money to independent schools.

Opting out may also serve to encourage the development of private education. Under the Education Reform Act opted-out schools are prevented from charging fees for a period of five years. After that period has elapsed, however, shortage of funds may make the charging of fees an attractive proposition, and there will be a double incentive if fee paying permits a reduction of government expenditure.

Fee paying may be related to the frequently recurring proposals for education vouchers. Proposals differ in detail, but the most usual one is to give vouchers, which would pay for basic education, to everyone. People could then 'cash' their vouchers at any school of their choice, and they could top them up by paying out of their own pockets for a more expensive school. Such a scheme would be of considerable help to private suppliers of education. Blaug writes:

The concept of education vouchers fits remarkably well into the Tory programme of 'privatisation' of the social services and one might have expected the Conservative Party to move quickly towards a practical scheme of education vouchers . . . Nevertheless, the idea of education vouchers is . . . regarded as so politically explosive that even the Tory government has moved very cautiously.[25]

City Technology Colleges
City Technology Colleges are modelled on examples to be found in the United States, especially in New York. As with their counterparts in the United States, the City Technology Colleges were originally intended as a contribution to inner city programmes.

The government plans to establish twenty City Technology Colleges with private industry footing a substantial proportion of the bill and being involved in college policy-making. Among the distinctive features of the colleges are their highly selective nature and their specialisation, with about 50 per cent of the timetable devoted to maths, science and technology and the remaining 50 per cent of the time occupied by subjects found in the usual school curriculum, including art, music and drama. In order to fit everything in, the school day may be lengthened. The first City Technology College, in Solihull, opened its doors in September 1988.

The scheme has run into some difficulties in finding both sites and sponsors, although the City Technology Colleges Trust, set up to promote the scheme, claims that the programme is on course to meet its target. By September 1989, however, only £44 million had been pledged by industrial sponsors, and since this £44 million can be offset against tax, industry's share is actually £26.4 million; the Treasury has committed £140 million. Contrary to the original plans, therefore, over 80 per cent of the capital is coming out of public funds.[26] Mr Straw, the shadow Secretary of State for Education, says that the programme is 'morally degenerate and educationally divisive',[27] and claims that most of the big companies are shunning the scheme: although 1,800 firms had been approached by July 1988, only twenty had promised contributions.

A leader in *The Guardian* in September 1988 confirmed this gloomy picture and reported that seventy-seven of the 100 biggest firms approached had refused to help. The big tobacco companies, which offered financial support, caused some embarrassment by suggesting that anti-smoking campaigns should not be brought into the classroom. The same leader outlined some of the criticisms of the scheme:

1. The 'pure irrelevance' of the scheme as a response to a national shortage of scientifically and technologically trained personnel. When set against the scale of the problem, the contribution of the City Technology Colleges is of negligible significance.
2. The City Technology Colleges divert valuable resources of staff and equipment away from other schools where the need for them is great and they also cream off some of the more able pupils.
3. The scheme interferes with the rational implementation of school closure plans and some local authorities have refused to sell their unwanted schools to the Trust.[28]

By October 1989 only three City Technology Colleges had actually opened, although eleven more were at the planning stage.

Charges and parental contributions
The whole area of charges in education is filled with inconsistencies and variations between one local authority and another. The present Conservative government found it much more difficult to introduce and regulate charges than it had anticipated, an indication of the difficulty being the long delay in issuing a promised consultative document on charges and the further delay before guidelines were produced.

One of the problems lay in the wording of section 61 of the 1944 Education Act which says that 'no fees shall be charged in respect of the education provided in any maintained school'. This could, of course, have been repealed, but to do so would have breached the general principle of free education, and the resulting expansion of charges would have risked a public outcry.

In several cases brought by parents, both the local government ombudsmen and the courts have ruled that charges (for field trips and music lessons, for example) are illegal. Nevertheless, the Secretary of State has the power to draw up regulations about what can be charged for and what cannot and the Education Reform Act required local authorities and school governors to draw up policies on charging parents for their children's out-of-school activities.

The consultative document published in 1987 followed the

principle that had been acknowledged for some time, drawing a distinction between essential items which were to remain free, and desirable but not essential items for which charges could be made, a distinction not in practice very easy to make.

The guidelines issued in 1988 distinguished between activities within school hours and out-of-school activities. The lunch break was defined as being outside school hours, and so any activities held during that time could be charged for. Essential field trips could be charged for if more than half the time spent on the visit was outside school hours, and 'optional extras' such as *individual* music lessons might also incur a charge. In addition, parents could be asked for voluntary contributions towards non-chargeable activities and the proceeds could be used to subsidise activities for children from poor families.[29]

Irrespective of charges, there is a discernible trend towards higher parental contributions to state education. Judith Judd reports one estimate of £70 million a year. She also cites evidence from school inspectors which says that in almost 40 per cent of primary schools parents were topping up the capitation allowance for books and equipment by more than 30 per cent. A survey by the National Association of Head Teachers conducted in 1987 found that half of the schools questioned were using voluntary funds to supplement their spending on materials and equipment which in previous years had been provided entirely out of local authority funds. Some state schools have followed the example of the independent schools in asking parents to give covenanted sums. Judd states:

So protests about the Government's proposals to charge parents for 'extras' such as swimming lessons and cooking materials fall wide of the mark. Money donated by parents is already paying not only for extras and luxuries but also for such basic tools of education as books, art materials and computers.[30]

One of the problems arising from reliance on parental contributions is that it produces wide disparities between the resources available to schools with different catchment areas. In middle-class areas there is obviously much more spare cash to give to schools. Hertfordshire County Council has revealed that primary schools with the greatest additional funds had fourteen times the extra amounts available to the poorest schools. In the secondary sector the disparities were even wider with the richest schools having thirty-seven times as much additional income as the poorest.[31]

Some charges are particularly burdensome for poor parents. The charge made for school meals is a good example, and in recent years the burden has grown as the price of a school meal has increased dramatically. A Labour Party survey found that in the year up to August 1987 the price of a school meal in primary schools had risen at twice the rate of inflation, and this had resulted in a reduction in the number of children taking school meals.[32] In 1987 33 per cent of children were having packed lunches as compared with 13 per cent in 1979. In September 1988 the situation worsened with the phasing out of free school meals for 500,000 children whose parents were in receipt of family credit. An allowance is made as compensation in the rates for family credit, but the amount allowed varies from 45 pence to 60 pence a day, whereas the average price of a meal in primary schools is 65 pence.[33]

The school meals service is a prime target in the government's plans for bringing in outside contractors. Local authorities are obliged under the Local Government Act 1988 to invite tenders for the provision of school meals and for school cleaning.

As far as the school meals service is concerned, there are reports of lack of interest on the part of catering contractors. Three major catering firms are being 'highly selective about tendering for council contracts'.[34] Indeed, two of the three are offering a consultancy service to local authorities to help them to retain control of the service. Two factors have influenced the contractors – one is the size of the school meals service with 2.5 billion main meals a year, and the second is the loyalty of the school meals staff to their present employers.

HIGHER EDUCATION

The Education Reform Act

One of the most important changes brought about in higher education by the Education Reform Act was the removal of polytechnics from local authority control and their conversion into independent institutions in much the same position as the universities. Although one or two polytechnics had misgivings about the break with local government, the vast majority welcomed the greater independence of action implied by the separation.

There were some difficulties in achieving a smooth transition to independence. For example, having lost the institutional support of local government, polytechnics had to strengthen their management structures very rapidly. The government allocated £6.5 million to ease the transition but this was totally inadequate when set against the costs associated with reorganisation. Another financial penalty was the loss of local authority 'topping up' money. Prior to independence many local authorities topped up the amounts the polytechnics received from central government and from fees: the total addition to resources from topping up was between £60 million and £70 million a year.

The Education Reform Act established two new funding bodies: The Polytechnics and Colleges Funding Council and the Universities Funding Council. Many people argued that, as the polytechnics had moved out of local government, two separate funding bodies made little sense and hindered the development of an integrated system of higher education. Although there is little sign of it at present, the two funding bodies may eventually merge. This was certainly the view of a leader in *The Times Higher Education Supplement* which talked of 'the expectation, and for many the hope, that the bipartite structure to be established by the Bill will not endure for long'.[35]

The universities complained that the replacement of the University Grants Committee by the Universities Funding Council posed a threat to their independence, arguing that whereas the University Grants Committee represented the universities to the government, the Universities Funding Council represents the government to the universities. The Universities Funding Council was merely a creature of the Secretary of State, and the Committee of Vice-Chancellors and Principals saw this as a step towards central government control of the universities. In an attempt to allay some of these fears, the government made a number of concessions during the report stage of the Bill:

1. The funding councils were given the right to advise the Secretary of State.
2. Any directions to the funding councils by the Secretary of State were made subject to negative resolution by both Houses of Parliament.
3. The funding councils no longer have the power, as they had in

the original Bill, to direct institutions about how they should spend funds derived from private sources.

An issue related to the independence of the universities and their fears about central control is the whole question of academic freedom and the importance attached to tenure. For many years university academic staff have enjoyed the unique position of having tenure for their working lives, the argument in support of this being that it protected academic staff from political pressure and avoided the possibility of someone being dismissed for expressing unpopular or unconventional views.

In the face of protests from the Association of University Teachers, the Education Reform Act abolished tenure for all staff appointed or promoted after 20 November 1987. There was nothing in the original Bill about academic freedom and universities were to be permitted to dismiss senior staff in order to replace them with younger and cheaper people. It was clear from the beginning that the government was going to remain firm on the question of tenure, but a concerted campaign secured two concessions: the clause relating to the dismissal of senior staff was withdrawn and a statement guaranteeing academic freedom was written into the Bill.

Funding of higher education

In 1963 the Robbins Report on Higher Education enunciated the following principle: 'Throughout our Report we have assumed as an axiom that courses of higher education should be available for all those who are qualified by ability and attainment to pursue them and who wish to do so.'[36] This remained the guiding principle in higher education throughout the 1960s and the 1970s when higher education experienced an unprecedented expansion. New universities were established and existing ones were expanded; between 1969 and 1973 thirty polytechnics came into being; and during the 1970s a third tier, colleges and institutes of higher education, was added. Between 1965/6 and 1976/6 the number of students in higher education increased by 71 per cent: an 89 per cent increase in the universities and a 58 per cent increase in the polytechnics and colleges.

However, rapid growth came to an end in 1981 when, with very little warning, universities were told to cut costs by 18 per cent over three years. This entailed the loss of about 3,000 posts with some universities shedding 25 per cent of their staff; some departments were closed and a number of institutions came close to bankruptcy. The cuts were not made evenly; Salford, for example, suffered a 44 per cent cut and Hull's grant fell by 31 per cent.

Further cuts were made in 1985 – 2 per cent in real terms – and subsequent years showed similar reductions so that the universities were forced to cut staff by any means they could. The University Grants Committee made funds available for what it called re-structuring, and universities began encouraging staff to take voluntary severance payments or enhanced early retirement. Between 1980 and 1987 the number of academic staff in British universities declined by 12 per cent. One of the problems with these job losses is that they were almost entirely unplanned: anyone who wanted to take severance or early retirement was allowed to do so irrespective of its effects on the department concerned and on the shape of the university. Many of the more senior academics have left university employment and the Committee of Vice-Chancellors and Principals has spoken of the threat this poses to academic leadership.

The polytechnics have been under a similar financial strain. The unit of resource (the yearly cost per full time student) has always been lower in the polytechnics than in the universities and recent downward pressure has widened the gap from £1,425 in 1982 to £2,315 in 1986/87. In 1979/80 the expenditure per student in polytechnics was 82 per cent of that in the universities: by 1987/88 per capita expenditure in the polytechnics had fallen to 58 per cent of the university figure and by 1989/90 it stood at a little over 50 per cent.[37] While the number of students in universities remained virtually unchanged between 1982 and 1986, the polytechnics accepted the equivalent of 34,000 extra full time students. Polytechnics have been pushed towards marginal funding, and this cannot continue for very long without the service to students suffering in terms of overcrowded facilities and over-stretched resources.

In the years since 1986 both sectors have increased their intakes. In 1989/90 there was an increase of 12,000 students and the projected increase for 1990/91 is 20,000. In January 1989 the Secretary of State for Education and Science said that he was expecting a doubling of student numbers during the next twenty-five years. Elaborating on this statement, he said that some of the increase would come from widening access, with more women, more older people and more people from ethnic minorities entering higher education, but he also anticipated a doubling of the participation rates among young people of the relevant age, from the present 15 per cent to 30 per cent. He was careful to point out that not all of this increase would be funded by the government. Eleven months later the new Secretary of State said that he was equally committed to a very substantial expansion in student numbers, and stated that the government's plans were for an increase of 50,000 by 1993.

In the government's statement of its expenditure plans, published in November 1989, higher education was allocated an extra £750 million between 1990/91 and 1992/93.[38] This is said to represent an increase in real terms of 5 per cent, but this assumes an inflation rate of 5.75 per cent by the fourth quarter of 1990/91 and a rate of 3 per cent in 1992/93. At the time of the statement inflation was 7.3 per cent, and the government has consistently under-estimated future inflation.

Auriol Stevens, Director of the Universities Information Unit, said that there appeared to be no extra money to cover the projected increase in students:

It doesn't look at this moment as if there is any real increase and any money for the extra students. When you do all the sums and move all the money from pocket to pocket it looks as if there is an increase of between 2 to 2.5 per cent and that is almost the difference between the previous inflation forecast of 3.5 per cent and the present inflation forecast of 5.75 per cent.[39]

Even the most generous interpretation of the figures reveals a very modest increase in funding and it most certainly does not even begin to compensate for ten years of cuts. In addition, both of the teaching unions in higher education have substantial pay claims awaiting settlement.

From 1981 onwards, the University Grants Committee attempted to introduce a greater degree of selectivity into its allocation of funds to the universities. It undertook to grade all departments accord, ng to the quality of their research and it inaugurated a series of subject reviews. Some of the reviews recommended the closure of departments and the restriction of others to undergraduate teaching.

However, the Universities Funding Council which replaced the University Grants Committee in 1989 has now announced that no further subject reviews will be carried out, and that the recommendations of reports not yet implemented will not be enforced. The universities may treat them as advisory and act upon them only if they so wish.

The Committee of Vice-Chancellors and Principals co-operated with the University Grants Committee, before its demise in 1989, in drawing up a list of 'performance indicators'. Much more attention has also been paid to formal staff appraisal, and every university now has such a system, some institutions employing outside consultants to train the appraisers. Polytechnics have had appraisal systems for some years.

Institutions in higher education have responded to the harsher financial climate in several ways. They have, for example, made strenuous efforts to attract overseas students from outside the European Community because they pay full cost fees. There is fierce competition in this lucrative market, with polytechnics and universities mounting recruitment drives in the middle and far east using high-powered sales techniques, some of which are not wholly appropriate and may lead to unrealistic expectations on the part of prospective students.

Polytechnics and universities are also competing to secure funds from non-government sources: research trusts and foundations, industry, special appeals to the community at large or to former alumni. Industry provides funds in a variety of ways: financing doctoral or post-doctoral fellowships, contracting research or entering into joint research agreements, setting up business in one of the increasing number of science parks, funding lectureships and professorships, the provision of equipment. Research by *The Guardian* in 1989 indicated that universities receive just under £200 million a year from industry and commerce and the polytechnics receive about £60 million – taken together, these sums represent about 6 per cent of total funding. As the author of the article says: 'While a relatively small amount, this money nevertheless represents a significant statement of industry's commitment to higher education . . .'[40]

There are, of course, dangers to be guarded against. Too heavy a reliance on a particular firm or industry might lead to lack of balance in research output – fundamental research without an immediate pay-off may be pushed out, and there is also a danger that commercial pressures may begin to dictate the courses on offer. There are problems, too, if firms withdraw their sponsorship.

In 1986/87 universities alone raised £630 million from all non-governmental sources: an increase of 18 per cent on the preceding year. There was also an increase of 9 per cent in the number of posts dependent upon outside funding, and posts of this kind now constitute one-third of all appointments.

Institutions engaged in higher education are now expected to be much more aggressively entrepreneurial, and they are also being invited to help their students to acquire marketing and business skills through the Enterprise in Higher Education Initiative. Under this scheme the Training Agency is empowered to offer individual institutions up to £1 million to enable them to give every undergraduate the opportunity to learn the skills and acquire the attitudes that he or she will need in industry and commerce. Just over 100 institutions submitted bids for 'enterprise money' in 1988.

This competitive, entrepreneurial spirit is reflected in the new funding arrangements in higher education. Both of the funding councils are committed to a system of competitive bidding for students, but each council will have its own separate arrangements. The bidding process began in the polytechnics in 1989, coming into operation in 1990, but the system will not be used in the universities until 1991/92.

The system is one in which the institutions compete for students on the basis of prices, and the Universities Funding Council has produced a detailed list of guide prices, banded to take account of the varying costs of providing courses in different subject areas. The prices published in 1990 vary from £2,200 for politics, law and social sciences (other than economics, sociology and social work) to £5,400 for metallurgy: some high-cost subjects, notably medicine, dentistry and veterinary science, are excluded from the competitive bidding. The prices quoted by the Universities Funding Council are meant to represent the maximum they are prepared to pay for student places in each subject group.

Rosalind Yarde describes the new system as 'a radical shift away from the traditional method of formula funding and towards a reliance on market forces',[41] but a great deal will depend upon how the system works out in practice. However, institutions will be tempted to try to undercut one another in bids to attract funding and this may very well result in reductions in the unit of resource.

The early experience of the polytechnics and colleges has not been encouraging, with complaints from the Directors of Polytechnics that fierce competition was leading to the under-funding of courses and falling standards; they also claimed that the Polytechnic and Colleges Funding Council was favouring diploma courses over degree work.

In the first year of its operation only 5 per cent of polytechnic and college funding was allocated on the basis of competitive bidding, but the proportion is expected to be increased to 10 per cent in 1991 and further increases in subsequent years can be anticipated.

In the universities competitive bidding is to apply to all student places, although the Council has said that institutions will be protected from sudden and drastic cuts in funding as a result of unsuccessful bidding.

In spite of the problems associated with the new system of funding, the universities are busily making plans for expansion. Fees are set to rise substantially. In 1990 they considerably more than doubled and further increases are planned for 1991 and subsequent years until they approach the full cost of providing courses. Polytechnics are also expanding rapidly – more rapidly at present than the universities – and it now looks as though government targets will be met. Whether quality can be maintained in the face of such rapid expansion is a matter for conjecture.

Student funding

For more than a decade the real value of student maintenance grants has been continuously eroded. A government survey of student expenditure, published in April 1988, showed that since 1982 alone the real value of the grant had fallen by 6.2 per cent. Barr has claimed that 'today's grant would have to be increased by 12 per cent to restore its purchasing power to its level in 1978/79, and by nearly 25 per cent to restore it to its 1962/63 peak'.[42] A survey conducted by the Committee of Vice-Chancellors and Principals in 1988 found that students outside London, after paying for board and lodgings, had £380 a year left for all other expenses, and students in London were even worse off with only £109 a year. The only way in which students can make ends meet is by getting into debt. The simplest solution would be to raise grants to a civilised level and then to peg them to the movement of wages or prices, but this was not among the options considered by the government when it began to look at student funding. There was instead considerable support for a system of loans.

The case for loans has been most strongly argued by a group at the London School of Economics[43] whose main criticism of an entirely grant-based approach is that it favours better-off families, and as it is currently operated it leaves many students in poverty. The system of parental contributions is unfair and unacceptable in that it expects students to remain dependent on parents into adulthood. Furthermore, 35 per cent of parents pay less than their full contribution.

The government promised a White Paper on student finance, but the very long delay before it finally appeared in November 1988 suggests that there were problems in devising a suitable alternative to grants. The government has long favoured a system of loans, but recognising that the complete replacement of grants by loans would arouse considerable opposition, they are introducing a mixed system.

From the academic year 1990/91 grants will be frozen, housing benefits for students will cease and top-up loans of up to £420 will be available to all students. Each year the loan element will increase, until by 2001 loans will constitute 50 per cent of student finance. The loans will be interest free but the amount outstanding each year will be increased in line with inflation. It is intended that loans will replace parental contributions and that repayments will be similar to mortgage repayments.

At one stage it seemed as though the government would decide on a scheme operated by banks as the lenders, but the financial institutions were unenthusiastic. Consequently, both the loans and the starting up costs will come entirely from the Treasury. The loans were to be administered by a specially formed company under contract to the government; but the government has been unable to secure the co-operation of the major banks, who were to be the chief participants in the new company, and the loans scheme is in disarray.

To say the least of it, this scheme is clumsy and over-complicated. Nick Barr, a keen supporter of loans, is of the opinion that the government has chosen the worst possible option, claiming that the scheme is inordinately expensive and that it will accentuate the middle class bias in access to higher education.[44] Kenneth Baker, formerly Secretary of State for Education, claimed that the normal repayment period would be five years. Barr says that this will mean repayments of about £88 a month for a London student and that many, finding themselves unable to afford this, will have to extend the repayment period.

Barr and Barnes and their colleagues favour a scheme based on bank loans repayable through an additional national insurance contribution. The additional contributions would be channelled back to the lending institutions by the Department of Social Security.[45]

Barr and Barnes are among an increasing number who favour vouchers or bursaries topped up by loans. The idea is supported by several Vice-chancellors and Directors of polytechnics, and the government is attracted to vouchers because such a system would encourage competition among higher education institutions, making them more responsive to the demands of students.

The polytechnics support vouchers because they believe that the system will give them parity of resources with the universities by allowing them to compete for students on equal terms. The universities' support for vouchers is less whole-hearted, but those committed to the system see it as a means of increasing university independence from government. This may be illusory since the government will decide the value of vouchers and can alter them at will. Vouchers make planning more difficult, and there is also the problem that students following the more expensive courses, in science or engineering for example, or those with exceptional educational needs, may find the vouchers inadequate. It would be possible to vary the value represented by a voucher according to the course, but this would open up the possibility of governments manipulating the voucher system to encourage some courses and discourage others.

The schemes currently being canvassed allow for variations in the amount of the voucher according to the subject studied. Among the more sophisticated proposals are those put forward by Barnes and Barr that make provision for tied bursaries to protect shortage subjects and for positive discrimination by means of 'bonuses' on top of the standard bursary for particularly disadvantaged students.[46]

CONCLUSIONS

Education under the Conservatives has been under-resourced. It is true that between 1980/81 and 1988/89 expenditure on education in real terms increased by 7.4 per cent but this compares unfavourably with defence and law and order. Furthermore, expenditure on education as a percentage of GDP has fallen, In 1975/76 educational expenditure represented 6.3 per cent of GDP but in 1986/87 it represented only 4.9 per cent.[47]

There are chronic shortages of teachers at every level of the school system. The government admitted to 3,500 full time vacancies at the start of the 1989/90 school year, but the six teachers' unions reported an extensive survey which showed total vacancies of more than 8,000 affecting at least 250,000 children.[48]

There are particular shortages in certain subjects: notably maths, science, technology and languages. The inner cities – especially London – are very badly hit and some children have had to be sent home for lack of teachers. In an attempt to overcome these problems, London and some other authorities are recruiting foreign teachers.

In February 1990 Her Majesty's Inspectors reported that 30 per cent of school lessons and 20 per cent in colleges were poor or very poor. Not all of the shortcomings stem from inadequate resources, but problems arising from the lack of books and equipment, the poor state of some of the buildings and shortages of staff would be considerably eased if extra resources were made available. Certainly, the Education Reform Act does nothing to solve the resource problems.

The reshaping of education incorporates all three of the main aims of Conservative social policy: privatisation (including promotion of the enterprise culture), curbing local government and the creation of inequality.

Education, seen by the Conservative government as an integral part of the enterprise culture, is expected to adopt the principles of the market-place. The clearest manifestation of this is that institutions at all levels have to compete with one another. Thus schools compete for pupils and, to this end, they must produce annual reports, publish examination results and operate a system of open enrolment. An extra element of competition is the creation of grant maintained schools and city technology colleges.

City technology colleges illustrate another aspect of privatisation in their attempts to attract resources from industry and commerce. Higher education is also expected to rely more heavily on private sources of finance with polytechnics and universities competing for commercial, foundation and research council contracts and building up relationships with industry through consultancy and science parks.

The new system of funding is also intended to foster competition as institutions attempt to outbid one another for student places; and should a voucher system be introduced, competition will intensify.

Higher education is also affected indirectly by the enterprise culture in that education is treated as a commodity like any other, and study and education for their own sake is no longer respectable. Consequently, business management, economics, computer science and accountancy courses are increasingly popular, while subjects such as philosophy and classics are in decline. There is a strong anti-intellectual element in the present government which appears to believe that the greatest achievement is making money as fast as possible. Mary Warnock provides a scathing analysis of the government's attitude to higher education when she writes of the contempt that the government has for universities and their staff:

We are piously told the function of the universities is cultural and educational in the widest sense, yet at the same time all departments, even the most abstract and theoretical, are in practice required to show their cost-effectiveness, output measured against input in the manner of a commercial company.[49]

The changes made to the educational system have also helped the government to achieve one of its other policy aims – reducing the role of local government. A particularly disturbing feature of educational change since 1979, especially since the Education Reform Act, has been the greatly increased centralisation and the concentration of power in the hands of the Secretary of State. Opted-out schools will receive their finance direct from central government. The polytechnics have moved out of local government control and are now funded by the Polytechnics and Colleges Funding Council acting on behalf of the Secretry of State.

Jack Straw, Labour Party spokesman on education, claims that in the first instance the Education Reform Bill gave the Secretary of State 175 new powers, but that these increased to 415 during the Bill's passage through Parliament. Mr Straw comments:

How ironical that, as the Soviet Union moves away from bureaucratic control of its national life, the British educational system is being systematically nationalised by Mr Kenneth Baker. His bill gives new meaning to the idea of the 'nanny state'.[50]

Among the most resented of the new powers acquired by the

Secretary of State is his right to veto senior appointments to the education departments of the London boroughs, following the abolition of the Inner London Education Authority. The leader of the Authority, Mr Neil Fletcher, claims that up to twelve senior appointments in each of the thirteen boroughs could be made subject to the Secretary of State's veto.[51]

The national curriculum puts considerable power in the hands of the Secretary of State and provides a good example of centralisation. The subject working groups were given very detailed 'guidance'. What was expected of them was made very clear and Mrs Thatcher has been very quick to criticise their findings.

Finally, since 1979 the educational system in Britain has become less concerned with equality. At the Conservative Party annual conference in 1987 Mr Baker stated that 'the pursuit of egalitarianism in education is over'.[52] This serves as an explanation of changes already made and as a warning of those still to come.

The considerable expansion of the assisted places scheme is one of the factors contributing to greater inequality, entailing the use of taxpayers' money to swell the profits of private schools. The greater use of charges and the use of parental contributions to purchase quite basic school equipment discriminates against poor children and schools in poor areas. Poor families have also suffered from the withdrawal of free school meals for 500,000 children in 1988/89, following a tightening of the eligibility criteria.

The introduction of grant-maintained schools and city technology colleges is without question divisive, leaving local authority schools as poor relations. It will be even more divisive if religious and ethnic minorities establish their own grant-maintained schools and if opted-out schools introduce fees.

Since 1944 the education service has been singularly unsuccessful in achieving greater equality of opportunity, use or outcome. Perhaps too much has been expected of it: education policy is too weak an instrument for counteracting the great weight of inequality in British society. But the policies of the Conservative government since 1979 have changed the nature of the debate in that equality in any of its forms is not to be pursued; it is not only unachievable but also undesirable. An aggressively competitive market economy *requires* inequality.

NOTES

1. *The Guardian*, 19 July 1988.
2. Quoted in J. Finch, *Education as Social Policy*, London: Longman, 1984, p. 222.
3. *Ibid.*
4. Department of Education and Science, *Better Schools*, Cmnd 9469, London: HMSO, 1985.
5. Department of Education and Science, *The National Curriculum 5–16*, London: HMSO, 1987.
6. *The Guardian*, 1 March 1988.
7. For the details of one such attempt see *The Guardian*, 4 July 1988.
8. *The Guardian*, 11 October 1987.
9. *The Guardian*, 14 November 1987.
10. *The Observer*, 5 July 1987.
11. *The Guardian*, 5 August 1988.
12. For evidence confirming middle class bias see research carried out by the Education Department of Exeter University – reported in *The Observer*, 18 September 1988.
13. *The Times Higher Education Supplement*, 15 April 1988.
14. *The Guardian*, 9 September 1987.
15. *The Guardian*, 21 November 1987.
16. *The Guardian*, 12 November 1987.
17. *The Guardian*, 14 January 1988.
18. *The Guardian*, 31 August 1988.
19. *The Guardian*, 29 August 1989.
20. Letter to *The Guardian*, 12 October 1987.
21. *The Times Higher Education Supplement*, 15 April 1988.
22. *The Independent*, 3 September 1988.
23. *The Observer*, 20 September 1987.
24. J. Finch, *op. cit.*, p. 48.
25. M. Blaug, 'Education vouchers – it all depends on what you mean', in J. Le Grand and R. Robinson (eds.), *Privatisation and the Welfare State*, London: Allen and Unwin, 1984, pp. 160–76.
26. *The Guardian*, 7 October 1989.
27. *The Guardian*, 20 July 1988.
28. *The Guardian*, 10 September 1988.
29. *The Guardian*, 12 September 1989.
30. *The Observer*, 18 October 1987.
31. *Ibid.*
32. *The Guardian*, 26 August 1987.
33. See Child Poverty Action Group, *School Meals – Not Suitable in All Respects*, London, CPAG, 1987; F. Dobson, *School Meals Price*

Survey, Autumn 1987, London: Labour Party, 1987; S. McEvaddy, *One Good School Meal*, London: CPAG, 1988.

34. *The Guardian*, 3 August 1988.
35. *Times Higher Education Supplement*, 19 February 1988.
36. Ministry of Education, *Higher Education*, Cmnd 2154 (The Robbins Report), London: HMSO, 1963.
37. *Times Higher Education Supplement*, 4 February 1990.
38. Treasury, *The Government's Expenditure Plans, 1990/91–1992/93*, Cm 879, London: HMSO, 1989.
39. *Times Higher Education Supplement*, 17 November 1989.
40. *The Guardian*, 11 July 1989.
41. *Times Higher Education Supplement*, 15 December 1989.
42. *Times Higher Education Supplement*, 13 May 1988.
43. The group includes Nicholas Barr, John Barnes, Iain Crawford, Mervyn King and William Low.
44. N. A. Barr, 'Review article: The White Paper on Student Loans', *Journal of Social Policy*, vol. 18, pt. 3, 1989, pp. 409–17.
45. *Ibid*. See also A. J. L. Barnes and N. A. Barr, *Strategies for Higher Education: The Alternative White Paper*, Aberdeen: Aberdeen University Press, 1988; N. A. Barr, *Student Loans: The Next Steps*, Aberdeen: Aberdeen University Press, 1989.
46. See *Times Higher Education Supplement*, 30 September 1988.
47. Central Statistical Office, *Social Trends*, nos. 17 and 19, London: HMSO, 1987 and 1989.
48. *The Guardian*, 22 September 1989 and 7 November 1989.
49. M. Warnock, *Universities: Knowing our Minds*, London: Chatto and Windus, 1989 and *The Observer*, 5 November 1989.
50. Quoted in *The Guardian*, 18 July 1988.
51. *The Guardian*, 28 June 1988.
52. *The Guardian*, 7 October 1987.

CHAPTER 6

HOUSING AND INNER CITY POLICY

Housing differs from the other services we have loo'.ed at in three ways: first, it is a durable asset and this gives exclusive rights of use; second, housing is the biggest single item of expenditure in the budgets of most households; and third, the housing market is dominated by an extensive and powerful private sector (cf. education and health services).

Housing is an important component of welfare: it is difficult to imagine anything more damaging to an individual's welfare than the lack of somewhere to live, and this is especially so in the case of families with young children and elderly people. Furthermore, housing difficulties frequently give rise to other problems. For example, there is growing evidence showing the relationship between poor housing conditions and poor health, both physical and mental,[1] and it is also known that poor housing adversely affects educational attainment, and that overcrowded conditions can lead to domestic tension and perhaps violence.

Differences in housing must be included in any account of inequality and there is evidence in Britain of a wide gap between the majority of the population who are well housed and the poor who occupy the worst accommodation. According to Willmot and Murie the housing market has become increasingly polarised in the 1980s.[6]

One of the problems in evaluating the changes brought about by the Conservative government since 1979 is that of disentangling long term trends from the direct effects of policy initiatives. The changing pattern of housing tenure might be taken as an example. A very

Table 6.1 Changes of tenure, 1970–87

United Kingdom				
Tenure	1970 %	1978 %	1979 %	1987 %
Owner-occupation	49.9	53.9	54.5	64.0
Rented from local authority or new town	30.5	32.2	33.1	26.0
Privately rented and other	19.6	13.9	13.4	10.0

Source: Social Trends, nos. 10, 12 and 19, Central Statistical Office.

marked long-term trend since the end of the second world war has been a growth in the proportion of dwellings in owner-occupation. Nevertheless, as Table 6.1 shows, the rate of growth has quickened since 1979.

Between 1970 and 1978 the proportion of dwellings in owner-occupation increased by 4 per cent whereas the increase between 1979 and 1987 was 9.5 per cent. Table 6.1 shows that another long term trend – a steady growth in the proportion of households renting from local authorities or new town corporations – has now been reversed. This is a direct result of the right to buy policies introduced in 1980.

SALE OF COUNCIL HOUSES

Local authorities had the power to build houses for sale and to sell houses originally built for renting before 1980, but the proportion of dwellings sold was relatively slight until the Conservative government of 1970–4 presided over a substantial upsurge in sales. However, the antipathy of Labour controlled local authorities towards the large-scale selling of council houses pushed the Conservative Party in the direction of compulsion.

The arguments used by the Conservatives in support of council house sales were a mixture of the pragmatic and the ideological. They stressed the virtues of a property-owning democracy, encouraging thrift and prudence and leading to greater security and stability (and increasing the proportion of the electorate inclined to vote Conservative). A property-owning democracy, it was argued, also leads to the improvement of the housing stock since people take a greater pride in homes they own. There were the usual arguments about freedom of choice and to these were added the less usual one about equity, allowing local authority tenants to share in the economic benefits of owner-occupation. The sale of council houses is part of the general movement towards privatisation, reducing the role of the state, and curbing public expenditure.

The Housing Act of 1980 extended the rights of tenants in a number of areas but, as Malpass and Murie say, 'the centrepiece of the Tory version of the tenants' charter is the right not to be a tenant'.[3] The Act converted the permissive policy, *allowing* local authorities to sell their houses, into a mandatory one which compelled local authorities to sell houses to tenants who expressed a wish to purchase the houses they were occupying. Generous discounts were available: 33 per cent off the market value for tenants of three years' standing, rising by 1 per cent a year up to a maximum of 50 per cent after a total of twenty years as a tenant. Furthermore, local authorities were obliged to offer mortgages to prospective purchasers who could include up to another four members of their households as joint mortgagors.

Between 1980 and 1982 twenty-seven councils were said by the Secretary of State to be either failing to implement the Act or employing tactics of delay. Sheffield City Council simply refused to implement the Act and employed two officers to persuade tenants to withdraw applications to purchase. The Secretary of State threatened the recalcitrant authorities that unless they met specific targets he would use his power under the Act to appoint an agent to take over the sale of a council's houses.

In the event, the power was invoked only in the case of Norwich City Council, the Secretary of State appointing a solicitor, aided by a team of civil servants, to organise the sale of houses. Norwich City Council sought an injunction to prevent the intervention of the Secretary of State, but both the High Court and the Court of Appeal upheld the Secretary of State's decision, and permission to take the case to the House of Lords was refused. This case had the desired effect of persuading other recalcitrant authorities to proceed more quickly.

The rules pertaining to the right to buy have been modified on several occasions. One such change arose because, although in general it was the better houses that were sold, some tenants bought houses, without survey, that were in poor structural condition (especially prefabricated buildings) and were soon experiencing difficulties paying for repairs and maintenance. In September 1982 the Secretary of State announced that grants of up to 90 per cent of the cost of remedying structural defects would be available to those who had bought their houses under the 1980 Act.

In 1984 the Housing and Building Control Act reduced the qualifying period of tenancy from three years to two and increased the maximum discount from 50 per cent to 60 per cent, and this was followed by the Housing and Planning Act of 1986 which increased the discounts available on flats to 70 per cent.

Between 1980 and the end of 1987 approximately 1.1 million local authority and new town houses were sold in the United Kingdom. The annual number sold rose from 92,660 in 1980 to a peak of 228,455 in 1982. There was then a steady decline in the numbers sold until 1986 when sales reached 109,020. There was a sharp upturn in 1987 when 141,530 houses were sold.[4] In January 1989 the government said it expected a further 361,000 sales over the next three years.

The winding up of the New Town Development Corporations began in the mid-1980s, and in December 1986 the Minister for Housing said that all of the New Town Development Corporations would have gone by 1992. As the corporations were wound up some of the houses passed into private ownership.

A study carried out by Kerr for the Department of the Environment found that it was the better properties with gardens that were most likely to be bought (especially three-bedroomed, semi-detached houses) while the number of flats purchased remained small.[5] The Department of the Environment survey confirmed the results of earlier work carried out by Bristol University School for Advanced Urban Studies; that it was predominantly the better-off and middle-aged tenants who bought, usually with more than one wage-earner in the household. As could be anticipated, those who had been tenants for several years, and therefore qualified for bigger discounts, were over-represented among the purchasers. Elderly people, single person households and households with pre-school children were significantly under-represented among those purchasing.[6] As the better-off tenants buy their houses, the proportion of poor, unemployed people in local authority housing increases and polarisation occurs.[7]

Another possible route to home ownership for local authority tenants has met with less success. In a number of areas local authorities have sold blocks of flats to private developers who then refurbish them prior to sale. A Department of the Environment report on eleven such schemes found that there was often little or no consultation with tenants over the future of their homes and only a small proportion of the purchasers were local authority tenants or people on the council waiting list.[8]

The rapid increase in home ownership has not been without its problems. First-time buyers – especially in the South-east – frequently borrow to the very limit of their capacity to repay, and if there is a change for the worse in their circumstances, or if interest rates rise steeply, then they may find themselves in great difficulty. Similar problems occur when local authority tenants buy their homes and then become unemployed or sick. Even if they remain in employment, the combined costs of mortgage payments and maintenance may be difficult to meet.

The number of people more than six months in arrears with their mortgage payments rose from 8,420 in 1979 to 41,900 in 1984 and to 45,840 at the beginning of 1988. It then fell to 37,440 by the beginning of the following year, but in the first six months of 1989 it rose by 20 per cent to 45,100 and by a further 29 per cent to over 58,000 in the second half of the year.

These figures, emanating from the Council of Mortgage Lenders, are challenged by Janet Ford who claims that they underestimate the number of people in arrears because they rely upon cross-sectional data, drawn from the experience of only the largest mortgage lenders. She also questions the usefulness of looking only at those who are six months or more in arrears. She produces figures of those who are two months or more behind in their mortgage repayments. Between March and July 1989 the number of people in this position increased by 25 per cent. Taking a longer view, in 1985 295,000 mortgagors, 4.6 per cent of the total, were two months or more behind in their payments. By the end of 1989 the proportion had risen to an estimated 6 or 7 per cent, representing 450,000 to 600,000 mortgagors. In 1978 the repayment of home loans absorbed about 23 per cent of take-home pay whereas the 1989 figure may be as high as 40 per cent.[9]

In these circumstances it is not surprising that the number of repossessions has also increased sharply, from 2,530 in 1979 to

10,950 in 1984 and to over 24,000 in the twelve months ending in March 1988, and that some local authorities who sold houses under the right to buy scheme are now reporting mortgage repayment problems among the new homeowners. In some instances local authorities have approached housing associations suggesting that the problem might be remedied if an association were to buy the properties and convert them into assured tenancies or into shared ownership.

The sale of council houses has produced an accumulated total of £8 billion in local authority housing accounts. Until March 1990 the authorities were allowed to spend only 20 per cent a year of the receipts from the sale of council houses, and the purposes to which the money could be put were circumscribed. From April 1990 local authorities were allowed to spend 25 per cent of the proceeds as and when they choose, but the remaining 75 per cent must go towards paying off council debts.

It is obvious that in future very few council houses will be built, and in 1987 sales exceeded total completions by local authorities, new town corporations, and housing associations by more than four to one. The sale of council houses, as Malpass and Murie argue, 'reduces the housing opportunities of those who must rent – of those who cannot buy on grounds of means, age and eligibility for borrowing – and who rely on becoming council tenants and on transfers and exchanges to satisfy their housing need.'[10]

RENTED HOUSING

The government has consistently maintained that market rents should prevail in the private sector and that local authority rents should more nearly approach those obtaining in the private sector. The higher local authority rents rise, of course, the more attractive purchase becomes, and this has no doubt influenced the government's determination to push up local authority rent levels. However, in its first two terms the Conservative government was more interested in the sale of council houses, and it was only when this policy was fully established that they could turn their whole attention to the rented sector.

The government's proposals for rented housing, outlined in a White Paper in 1987, were given legislative form in the Housing Act 1988.[11] This Act may be divided into four main sections:

1. The private rented sector.
2. Housing associations.
3. Housing action trusts.
4. Changing landlords.

These four sections provide a convenient framework for an examination of the Act.

The private rented sector

One of the long term trends identified in the introduction to this chapter was the decline of the privately rented sector. The Conservative government, which seeks to reverse this trend, blames the decline on over-regulation and rent controls, although it allows that the relative attractiveness of owner-occupation has been a contributory factor. Freely negotiated market rents and deregulation, the government believes, will be sufficient to revive the private rented sector, and the White Paper promised 'to put new life into the independent rented sector' claiming that 'the letting of private property will again become an economic proposition'.[12] The main strategy was to be 'the deregulation of new lettings by private landlords'.[13]

The Act introduced revised forms of tenancy for new lets: assured tenancies and assured shorthold tenancies, which became available to landlords after 15 January 1989. Without becoming enmeshed in too much technical detail, the Act took one step further the policy changes initiated by the 1980 Act which created assured tenancies and shorthold tenancies. The revised tenancies and those they replaced differ from the regulated tenancies under the 1977 Rent Act in that there is a weakening of security of tenure and other rights, and most rents will be set at market level.

Assured tenants can be evicted only on the authority of a court order, and the landlord has to give the tenant a notice of proceedings for possession, which will include a statement of the grounds for possession the landlord is using. There are altogether sixteen grounds for possession that the landlord may use. Assured shorthold tenancies have no security of tenure. Burrows says that in general the Act:

has meant a general weakening of tenancy rights, and a corresponding weakening of landlord responsibilities. And it is not all a question of which policy will provide homes for the future. There is also a strong element of brimstone in the legislation. The Government really does believe that tenants have fallen victim to what William Waldegrave, who ceased to be Minister of Housing halfway through the Bill, called the dread drug of dependency.'[14]

As a result of the 1988 Act private sector rents will rise. The White Paper referred to 'a more diverse pattern of rents' which appears to mean higher rents for all new tenancies. In new assured tenancies fair rents will give way to market rents freely negotiated between the landlord and the tenant, and neither assured nor assured shorthold tenants will have access to a Rent Officer under the fair rent procedures. There is limited access to a Rent Assessment Committee, but it will set what it judges to be a market rent.

Whether these changes will achieve the government's aims of reviving the private rented sector is open to question. Burrows argues that the reverse will happen:

The Government cannot avoid the simple truth – the rents demanded by landlords to persuade them to stay in letting are far beyond the means of the great majority of potential tenants . . . the 1988 Act will lead to a smaller not a larger sector. Six months assured shortholds will be the dominant face of new letting – with eviction and homelessness at the end.[15]

The Institute of Housing, in more moderate tones, claims that the replacement of fair rents by market rents will slow down the decline of the private rented sector rather than revive it.

Existing tenants are unaffected by the changes, except that their mobility may be reduced. The White Paper recognised that unscrupulous landlords might be tempted to harass existing tenants to force them out of the property, which could then be let to new tenants at the higher market rent, and in an effort to prevent this, the harassment provisions of the 1977 Protection from Eviction Act were strengthened and a new right of compensation – civil law damages – was introduced in cases of unlawful eviction. Damages are equal to the difference in the value of the house when vacant and when occupied. The Act also gives local authorities stronger powers to force landlords to carry out repairs. If a landlord refuses to comply with a repair notice the local authority now has increased powers to carry out the repairs itself and recover the costs through sequestration of rents.

The extension of assured tenancies and the deregulation of rents have been important contributory factors in the increased use of the

Business Expansion Scheme (BES) in the private rented sector. BES was first introduced in 1983 to give tax incentives to investment in high-risk new technology, but the government extended BES to assured tenancies in the budget of 1988.

In 1988 the Nationwide Anglia Building Society, already involved in rented housing, was the first to launch a BES fund linked to the rented housing market. Since then other building societies and financial institutions have followed Nationwide's lead. Those who buy shares in BES funds receive tax relief on their investment, and after five years the houses are sold.

Housing associations have begun to take an interest in BES projects. An interesting example is a scheme initiated in 1989 by Assured Tenancies Ltd and the Bradford and Northern and the North British Housing Associations. Under these arrangements the housing associations undertake to buy the BES houses at the end of the five year period at a pre-agreed price. The associations manage the properties and nominate tenants from their own lists.[16]

A report published at about the same time as this scheme was being inaugurated suggests, however, that BES competition for limited funds may damage housing associations by raising the cost of borrowing. The report, by researchers at Glasgow University's Centre for Housing Research, was based on a study of nineteen BES companies in Scotland and the authors conclude that BES entails a misdirection of public resources which would be better employed as direct payments to housing associations.[17]

Housing associations
Housing associations, supervised by the state-funded Housing Corporation, are non-profit-making organisations whose main purpose is to provide good quality homes at rents which are affordable by people on low incomes. There are about 2,600 housing associations in England and Wales with a total stock of over 600,000 dwellings,[18] and although this represents only about 3 per cent of all dwellings, the associations' share of the total stock will increase substantially as the full impact of the 1988 Act begins to be felt. In 1988/89 the Housing Corporation invested more than £1 billion – an increase of £80 million over the previous year – and approved 25,000 dwellings: 22 per cent more than in 1987/88.

It is clear from ministerial statements and the White Paper that the government is pinning great hopes on housing associations.

The use of associations adds a degree of respectability to the 'pick a landlord' scheme, and the government clearly expects housing associations to become the main providers of 'social housing' – housing for those in need. Addressing the Institute of Housing in 1989, the Junior Minister of Housing said of housing associations: 'We have given them a vital job to do. We have done so because we think they can do it better than anyone else. Let them go out and show us and the world that we are right'.[19] Given the government's enthusiasm for housing associations, it is curious that recent changes have made the associations' task more difficult.

Most of the provisions of the Housing Act 1988 relating to private sector renting apply equally to housing associations, but the most important change relating to housing associations came not in the Act but by ministerial decision. In 1988 it was announced that in future government grants in support of housing association projects would fall from 100 per cent to an average of 75 per cent, the balance having to be provided from private sources. Private financiers will, of course, require a return on their investment, and this will almost inevitably mean rent rises.

The National Federation of Housing Associations (NFHA), which monitors all new lettings, has produced figures showing that only 25 per cent of association tenants work full time, that 98 per cent have lower than national average incomes and 66 per cent have incomes derived wholly or partly from state benefits.[20] These statistics indicate that even slight rent increases would cause considerable hardship among housing association tenants. The government continues to stress affordable rents, but does not say what it understands by the term. In the past, the Housing Corporation has always regarded no more than 20 per cent of net income as an affordable rent, but in July 1989 the Chief Executive of the Housing Corporation, David Edmonds, suggested one-third of net income as an affordable rent. The NFHA reported that in 1989 the rents of tenants in work had already reached 21 per cent of disposable income and single elderly people were paying up to 35 per cent of their incomes in rents.

Between April 1988 and March 1989 average rents in housing association properties rose by 24 per cent with most of the increases occurring in the first four months of 1989. An editorial in *Housing Associations Weekly* says:

The period of greatest rent increases, during the first four months of this year, corresponds with the scrapping, on 15 January, of fair rents and the introduction of assured tenancies for all new lettings. This appears to validate the NFHA's prediction that the abolition of fair rents would fuel rental inflation.[21]

It appears from another NFHA report that single adults are the most seriously affected by increasing housing association rents. Single adults constitute 30 per cent of total lettings, with 13,000 of the group moving into association homes each year, most of them in poorly paid jobs or unemployed, whose rents amount to about 38 per cent of net income. Some tenants would be better off or only slightly worse off when unemployed, because housing benefit would then cover their rents in full. The report anticipates increasing rent arrears.[22]

Housing associations have been thrown off-balance by the combination of increased responsibilities, the reduction in the proportion of funding coming from government, and changed tenures. The voluntary movement seems determined to retain its traditional role, and the government is apparently relying upon it to do so. If the upward shift in rents continues, however, the poorer members of the community may be excluded from housing association provision.

One welcome step is the clearer duty placed on the Housing Corporation to adopt anti-racist policies, to promote racial harmony and to ensure equality of access. Both the Housing Corporation and the NFHA have produced guidelines on how anti-racist policies are to be effected.

The public sector

Housing Action Trusts
Housing Action Trusts (HATs) are set up to take over run-down estates from local authorities. The HAT becomes responsible for managing the estates and particularly for improving both the housing and the environment.

Originally the Housing Bill allowed the Secretary of State to impose HATs against the wishes of tenants who simply had the right to be informed, but the opposition to this proposal was widespread and sustained. After a defeat in the House of Lords the government agreed that transfer to HATs would be preceded by a ballot among the tenants concerned. The opposition had wanted HAT takeovers to depend upon a majority of those eligible to vote, but the government insisted upon only a simple majority of those voting.

Cnce a positive vote has been recorded by a designated estate, the Secretary of State appoints a board of between seven and thirteen members to manage its affairs.

Occupants of houses taken over by HATs will be secure tenants, but during the passage of the Bill fears were expressed about the possibility of much higher rents. The government has said, however, that rents will rise only after improvements have been made, and any increase following improvement will be in line with council house rents. It should be noted, though, that the government is making efforts to push up council house rents.

The improvements to estates should have been completed in five years when the HATs will be wound up and the houses disposed of to new landlords who could be the local council, a private individual or company, a housing association or a co-operative. If the houses are bought by the council then the occupants remain secure tenants, but if a private landlord or a housing association becomes the new owner then occupants become assured tenants.

Initially the government proposed establishing HATs in twenty estates but by March 1989, because of financial constraints, they had decided to proceed with only nine. Although the government has always maintained that HATs will be restricted to the worst estates, it is by no means clear what criteria have been applied in the selection of these nine. Between 1989 and 1991 £180 million will be spent on the programme.

Changing landlords
The most controversial section of the 1988 Housing Act allows for the transfer of council and new town property to either private landlords, housing associations or tenants' co-operatives. The initiative for a change of landlord may come from prospective landlords, the local authority or from tenants themselves. The government expressed the hope that most applications would stem from tenants, but the Housing Corporation has described the tenants' response as lack-lustre. A small number of tenants' co-operatives have been formed, but if Burrows is correct in his assertion that the scheme was 'structured around landlord applications', then an unenthusiastic response from tenants is hardly

surprising.[23] Most of the applications, then, have come from prospective landlords; most but by no means all of them being housing associations. In many cases local authorities have taken the initial steps and some have gone so far as to form housing associations for the specific purpose of transfer.

Landlords who wish to take over public sector dwellings have first to seek the approval of the Housing Corporation which has set out the criteria for approval in some detail. Among the more important requirements are: the demonstration of management skills and financial viability; commitment to equal opportunities policies; the provision of full information to tenants and the Corporation; an agreement to retain dwellings acquired as a Tenants' Choice landlord for letting at rents within the reach of those in low-paid employment; compliance with the terms of the Housing Corporation's guidance on the management of Tenants' Choice dwellings.[24]

The first stage in the transfer is a preselection process, involving informal discussions with tenants where they may make their own alternative suggestions, which eventually produces a single applicant to go forward to the final stages. The present landlord and the alternative landlord then enter into lengthy and quite complex negotiations at the end of which a price is agreed.

The next step is to ascertain the views of the tenants about the proposed takeover by means of a ballot of all those affected. The ballot is organised by an independent teller – usually the Electoral Reform Society – and takes place over several weeks. All those who have not voted will be visited by the teller who will try to persuade them to vote.

The ballot has been the subject of much hostile comment. Particular anger has been caused by the treatment of abstentions as votes in favour of the proposal. If the 'yes' votes and the abstentions add up to 50 per cent or more of those eligible to vote, then all those who voted 'yes' and all those who abstained will become tenants of the new landlord, their tenancies changing from secure to assured. Those who recorded a 'no' vote will stay with their present landlord.

When the Bill went to the House of Lords this system was rejected on the grounds that it was undemocratic. The government overruled the Lords' amendment, but made one small concession: if less than 50 per cent of the eligible voters recorded their vote then the election was to be declared null and void.

The change of landlord scheme is another example of the government's drive towards privatisation. It is also indicative of the antipathy of the Conservative Party leadership towards local government. Burrows says:

The essential aim of the scheme is the dismantling of council housing – an adjunct to the Right to Buy. It is notable that private tenants are not given the right to choose a council landlord. It is yet another part of the Government's overall policy of transferring the means of housing provision from the public to the private sector.[25]

Higher council house rents

The 1987 White Paper said that public sector landlords 'should seek an adequate return on investment'.[26] Wherever possible rents should be at 'full economic levels', but the government recognised that in some areas this would put rents beyond the means of many tenants and some degree of subsidy might be necessary.

Ministerial statements have talked about raising council house rents to 'more realistic levels' or so that they more nearly approach rents in the private sector. In its most recent statements the government's main concern has been to try to ensure that council house rents reflect more closely the values of the houses.

The Local Government and Housing Act, which came into force in April 1990, prevents local authorities from subsidising their rents and insists that 75 per cent of the product of sales goes to pay off housing revenue account debts. Central government subsidies are to be calculated according to a complicated formula that takes into account house prices in each area. Using this formula, the Department of the Environment issues 'guidelines' on local authorities' rent levels, and since levels are meant to relate to local house prices, they will vary considerably from one part of the country to another. The guidelines published in July 1989 indicated average rent increases for 1990 of 10 per cent, the amounts varying from 95p to £4.50 a week. The Labour Party claims that this represents the first stage in a policy of full market rents.

Using government subsidies to increase local authority rents is not a new ploy. Murie says that this was also happening under the previous system: 'As the new subsidy scheme under the Housing Act 1980 had been operated to increase council rents (which in 1982–3 accounted for a higher proportion of average earnings than at any time since 1945), so exchequer subsidies have fallen'.[27]

Council housing is becoming more and more marginalised as the better off tenants move out and higher rents encourage others to exercise their right to buy. This means that the higher rents are being imposed on some of the poorest members of the community, including a high proportion of elderly and unemployed people and a preponderance of semi-skilled and unskilled manual workers. It is, of course, true that housing benefits are available and, as rents in all sectors rise, total expenditure on housing benefit increases; but the amounts paid to many individuals were drastically cut in 1988, and the consequence may be rent arrears, eviction and homelessness.

HOMELESSNESS

In 1979 local authorities in England and Wales accepted 57,000 households as homeless under the homeless persons legislation. By 1987 the number accepted as homeless had more than doubled to 118,000. At the end of 1987 25,000 homeless households were in temporary accommodation; double the number at the end of 1984.[28] By June 1989 the number of households in temporary accommodation had increased to 33,750 – the highest figure ever recorded: some 14,800 were in short-life dwellings (including properties leased from private landlords), 11,720 were in bed and breakfast accommodation and 7,230 were in hostels and women's refuges.[29]

In 1987 there were 236,000 enquiries in England and Wales from people claiming to be homeless; 62,000 were found not to be homeless within the definition used in the legislation and 57,000 were found not to be in priority need and were given advice and assistance only. But these are official figures which do not include what are referred to as the hidden homeless – those sharing households and those living rough.[30]

Bed and breakfast accommodation for homeless people is usually overcrowded and insanitary, and yet some London boroughs have been paying £250 a week for a single room. In 1987 the average cost of accommodating people in bed and breakfast hotels was over £11,000 in London and about £8,000 elsewhere, and in 1987/88 English and Welsh local authorities spent a total of £92 million on bed and breakfast.[31] This must be one of the most objectionable forms of privatisation with public funds being used to line the pockets of sometimes unscrupulous owners of bed and breakfast establishments. A report produced jointly by the British Medical Association and the Health Visitors Association in 1989 warned that bed and breakfast accommodation constituted a serious risk to health, and many homeless families receive little or no health care.[32]

In 1987 the Department of the Environment set up a national review of homelessness to look at the implementation of the law relating to homelessness and to consider whether it needed changing. Plans to change the definition of homelessless to rooflessness were reported to be under consideration, but when the review body reported in November 1989 no changes in either the definition or the law were recommended.

Some of the statements of Mrs Thatcher and some of her ministers have not been at all helpful. In 1988 the Secretary of State for the Environment suggested that people were becoming homeless simply to jump the housing waiting list queue. The Social Security Minister suggested that unmarried women were deliberately getting themselves pregnant in order to be housed and Mrs Thatcher has endorsed this view saying that the problem arises from family instability and unrealistic expectations. The government shows an increasing tendency to blame the victim.

In view of these attitudes, it came as something of a surprise when the Chancellor's 1989 Autumn statement included an extra £250 million over two years to tackle the problem of homelessness. However, although any extra funds are to be welcomed, this is a very small sum when set against ten years of inaction and a massive increase in the scale of the problem.

The £250 million is to be spent mainly in London and South-east England, its main purpose being to bring empty houses back into use. Some of the money will be used to revive a flagging scheme, introduced in January 1989, which allowed local authorities to award grants to those of their tenants who wished to purchase private sector houses. Grants of up to £20,000 have been offered in London. The measure was principally designed to tackle homelessness by freeing council houses for homeless people. Two pilot schemes had demonstrated the potential effectiveness of the strategy, but a report in August 1989 claimed that the government had failed to attract much local authority support. In Scotland not one local authority had taken up the scheme and only twenty-five councils in England and Wales had responded. Councils were reported as being reluctant to participate partly because grants had to be funded from their existing budgets. Caroline McLaughlin of the Convention of Scottish Local Authorities said: 'We warned the impact of the scheme on homelessness would be negligible . . . paying council tenants to vacate their homes does very little. What we need are more homes and more resources.'[33] It remains to be seen whether the extra £250 million will put new life into the scheme.

The main reason for the rapid growth in homelessness is a shortage of homes to let at rents which the poorer sections of the population can afford. This has been brought about by two main factors: the sale of council houses and a decline in public sector investment in housing. Between 1961 and 1970 local authorities and new town corporations in the United Kingdom built on average 161,000 dwellings a year, and in 1967 the public sector (including a small contribution from housing associations) completed 211,000 dwellings – 51 per cent of all housebuilding completions. Between 1971 and 1980 local authority and new town completions averaged 143,000 dwellings a year, but in 1981 the figure plummeted to 68,000 and in 1987 it reached an all-time low of 22,000.[34] It is worth recalling that in 1987 141,500 council houses were sold.

Inadequate funds for maintenance, repairs and improvement was also a feature of the 1980s. Thus housing in a poor state of repair cannot be brought back into use and marginal property is in danger of deteriorating to the point where it ceases to be habitable. A Department of the Environment report on the condition of local authority housing in 1985 said that in England alone almost £19 billion needed to be spent to restore it to good condition.[35] This gloomy picture was confirmed by an Audit Commission report, published in 1986, which found that 85 per cent of council houses needed repairs.[36]

Another aspect of government policy that has contributed to the growth of homelessness has been the combined effect of reduced entitlement to housing benefit and higher rents. According to the Association of Metropolitan Authorities there was a massive 37.5 per cent increase in rent arrears in the six months immediately following the benefit changes in April 1988.[37] Other benefit changes may have contributed to this increase in arrears: the change from supplementary benefit to income support; the insistence that everyone should be required to pay at least 20 per cent of their rates (community charge) and all of their water rates; and the replacement of urgent needs payments by social fund loans. In 1987 rent arrears and mortgage default accounted for 13 per cent of homelessness.

One problem has been the payment of income support two weeks in arrears. Owners of bed and breakfast establishments nearly always require payment in advance and they are now refusing to take people on social security benefits who are not actually placed and paid for by the local authority.[38] The government has also extended the role of the rent officer who is now responsible for setting the maximum market rent in the area for which she or he is responsible, and any local authority paying housing benefit above the limits set will receive no subsidy from central government for the excess.

The rent officer is also responsible for monitoring the rents which voluntary hostels can claim back in the form of housing benefits, and there are fears that the limits for hostels will be set at too low a level creating difficulties for both residents and the hostel management. Nigel Duerdoth of the National Federation of Housing Associations thinks that the new payment system for hostels is 'most likely to break down in the inner cities – the areas where stress is greatest and hostels are most concentrated and needed'.[39] It is the problems of the inner cities to which we now turn.

INNER CITIES

The problems

At least since the early 1970s successive governments have expressed concern about the decline of our inner cities, but no government has been prepared to devote the massive resources which are now required to overcome decades of neglect. In the 1970s scheme after scheme was launched, but there seemed little sense of direction or coherence.

When the Conservatives came to power in 1979, a series of inner area studies, commissioned by the government, had been completed and a White Paper, *Policy for the Inner Cities*, had been issued two years previously.[40] The Inner Urban Areas Act reached the statute book before the Conservatives took office.

The problems of the inner cities were by now well documented. The Archbishop of Canterbury's report on urban priority areas (UPAs) comes to much the same conclusion as the inner area studies and the Scarman Report: 'We can put forward a confident and melancholy generalisation – that the UPAs are places of severe and increasing deprivation. Economic decline, physical decay and social disintegration are the three afflictions which denote the poverty of people and places.'[41]

The economic decline of the cities is by no means a recent phenomenon. The industries which used to provide employment for inner city residents have either died or long since gone to the new towns or to green field sites and industrial estates on the outskirts of the towns. Consequently, the highest rates of unemployment occur in the inner urban areas – in some cases almost 40 per cent at a time when general unemployment levels, according to the official figures, are about 6 per cent.

Physical decay extends across whole areas of cities like Birmingham, Glasgow, Leeds, Liverpool, London, Manchester, Newcastle and Sheffield. It includes derelict factories and some of the poorest housing in the country. Much of the housing is unfit for human habitation, and the proportion of dwellings which are overcrowded or lack basic amenities is much higher in these areas than elsewhere. The planning blight of the 1960s is apparent everywhere in the poorly designed, poorly constructed high rise blocks, most in a state of disrepair, which replaced terrace houses when whole areas were cleared.

Inner cities have more than a proportionate share of social problems. Homelessness, unemployment, poverty and debt form the background to many people's lives, and ill-health, single parenthood, drug and alcohol abuse, crime, vandalism, outbreaks of civil disorder and poor community relations, especially between the police and ethnic minorities, are more prevalent in the inner urban areas than in other parts of Britain.

It is possible, of course, that some people with social and psychological problems gravitate towards the inner cities. But this simply adds to the concentration of problems; it is not their original cause. There can be little doubt that the problems of the inner city are rooted in unfair and inadequate access to economic and political resources.

In the discussion which follows it must be remembered that not all those who live in inner cities have problems or are poor. Equally, many poor people live outside the inner cities. This is one of the drawbacks of all area-based policies. Nor are the inner cities the only areas suffering from economic decline and physical decay – the coalfields of County Durham and South Wales come to mind, and the problems in some of the overspill estates on the outskirts of the cities may be as great as those in the centre. Nevertheless the policy initiatives have focused on the inner cities and attention will now be directed towards the impact of Conservative policies upon the allocation and utilisation of resources in these areas.

The inner cities, 1980–1986

The Conservative government inherited the Labour Party's inner city initiatives. In particular, the Inner Urban Areas Act of 1978 had initiated, according to Laurence and Hall, 'the biggest single policy shift since inner urban policies were introduced':

Though area-based positive discrimination measures with a primarily social service orientation continued, the new emphasis was strongly on 'economic revival'. Henceforth, inner cities would have first place, after Assisted Areas (with which in part they coincided), in the grant of industrial development certificates, and would thus take precedence over the new towns.[42]

An adjustment of the rate support grant gave inner urban areas more resources and the urban programme was expanded, introducing central/local partnerships for the largest cities and more limited programmes for smaller towns.

When the Conservatives came to power they continued these policies, but with the crucial difference that efforts to control local government expenditure reduced the resources available to inner urban areas. Even more significant, perhaps, was an intensification of the philosophy which promoted wealth generating activities at the expense of social programmes.

The first two Conservative initiatives were announced in 1980:

1. The establishment of two Urban Development Corporations (UDCs) to take over and plan the development of the derelict dockland areas of Liverpool and London. The UDCs were made up of representatives of financial institutions, private developers, construction firms and manufacturing industry. This was a pattern to be followed when UDCs were set up in other areas in

succeeding years. The UDCs were to plan, co-ordinate and supervise the development of the docklands by private contractors.

2. The designation of certain economically stagnant and often derelict areas as 'Enterprise Zones'. The idea was to attract new industry to these areas by offering rent, rates and tax concessions and relaxing planning and other controls. By the end of 1981 eleven Enterprise Zones had been established.

Together, these two initiatives exhibit most of the features which were to characterise Conservative policies towards the inner cities for the rest of the decade:

1. The emphasis on private capital and private sector initiatives. Mrs Thatcher sees the government's role as one of pump-priming, but much more than pump-priming is required to create the conditions that would encourage private investment in the inner cities.
2. The concentration on wealth-generating activities rather than social programmes; this was most apparent in the creation of enterprise zones.
3. The bypassing of local government. This was particularly blatant in the case of the UDCs which to all intents and purposes supplanted local authorities as planning authorities. Local authorities were totally excluded from the activities of the UDCs and some of the government finance which might otherwise have gone to the local authorities was diverted to UDCs. The replacement of directly elected councils by appointed bodies is a quite extraordinary repudiation of democracy. Mrs Thatcher attempted to justify the exclusion of local authorities on the grounds that left-wing city councils persistently refused to co-operate with private industry. The local councils in Birmingham, Bristol, Liverpool, Manchester and Sheffield, among others, denied this charge and pointed to several joint ventures with business, arguing that had they not been denied the resources, more co-operation would have been possible.

Between 1981 and 1985, more stringent controls were placed upon local government finance, and from time to time the government renewed its efforts to interest the private sector in the inner cities. In 1985 there were two developments. The first was the establishment of five City Action Teams: in Birmingham, Liverpool, Manchester–Salford, Newcastle–Gateshead and Hackney–Islington–Lambeth. The object of the teams was to co-ordinate the regional activities of the Manpower Services Commission (now the Training Agency), the Department of Employment, the Department of the Environment and the Department of Trade and Industry, each of which was represented on the teams.

The second development in 1985 was the setting up of the Urban Housing Renewal Unit within the Department of the Environment. The purpose of the Unit was to deal with the problem of run down council estates in urban areas, offering technical advice and assistance on the management of such estates. The Unit also provides additional resources for housing investment in local authority estates where large numbers of houses remain empty because of insufficient funds for renovation.

In the following year Task Forces, intended to maximise the effectiveness of existing programmes, were introduced. Their main concern is to improve training and employment opportunities, especially for young people and particularly those belonging to ethnic minorities; indeed, the size of the ethnic population is the main criterion for the selection of areas. Also in 1986, the Metropolitan County Councils were abolished making strategic planning in the six conurbations more difficult.

The inner cities, 1987–1990

In 1987 the Conservative Party was returned for a third term. The Party was very conscious of the fact that in spite of its large majority it had fared very badly in the inner urban areas, and it was without question this result which prompted Mrs Thatcher to state immediately after the election that policies for the inner city were to have top priority. The rejection of the Conservative Party in the inner cities simply increased Mrs Thatcher's distrust of left-wing local councils and strengthened her determination to reduce their influence.

Although there were six central government departments concerned in one way or another with inner cities, the Prime Minister made it plain that she was to spearhead the inner city campaign and in 1987, to demonstrate the seriousness of the government's intent, a cabinet committee on the inner cities was established with Mrs Thatcher as its chairperson. In addition a cabinet office unit was formed to advise on and co-ordinate inner city policies, and the

Prime Minister drafted specialist advisers into her own policy unit in Downing Street.

Many senior Conservatives, believing that the policies needed greater co-ordination, pressed Mrs Thatcher to appoint a minister with special responsibility for the inner cities. She resisted this for several months, not wishing to loosen her control of urban policy, but eventually she capitulated giving the responsibility to Mr Kenneth Clarke, Minister for Trade and Industry. The Prime Minister made it clear, however, that she would still control the direction of policy.

In the new government's first year of office three policy developments occurred. First, an urban regeneration grant, designed to attract private investment, was introduced. Under this scheme private sector owners or developers could receive a grant or a loan, or a combination of the two, for the redevelopment of derelict or disused sites or buildings in urban areas suffering from economic decline. By 1988 five major schemes had been approved.

Second, four more UDCs were set up along the lines of those in Liverpool and London. The four UDCs would each receive government budgets of up to £160 million over six years. In addition four 'mini-UDCs' were established with much smaller budgets and with more limited objectives.

At the same time as these developments were being implemented, the new town corporations were being disbanded and a massive privatisation programme was well underway as industrial and domestic property in the new towns was sold. Between 1980 and 1988 these sales yielded £800 million and a further £850 million was anticipated by 1991. Some of the money was to be used to finance the new UDCs.

The third policy development in 1987 was the emergence of a curious body, English Estates, as an important government agency in urban regeneration. English Estates had been in existence for some years, but its traditional role had been factory building and commercial development on green field sites with 5,000 factories and offices on 508 estates. In 1987 it began to turn its attention to the inner urban areas, with the idea of opening small factories, workshops and offices in the hope that private industry would then follow suit.[43] As the third example shows, the government continued to pin its hope upon private sector industrial and commercial investment in the inner cities, the Prime Minister and her colleagues constantly urging industry and the financial institutions to do more.

Among the first to respond to these urgings was an organisation known as Business in the Community, led by Sir Hector Laing of United Biscuits. Business in the Community set up six national teams to 'promote the training and recruitment of the young unemployed, encourage partnership between schools and business, help in the formation of new, small enterprises, while promoting new loan funds to emerging entrepreneurs'.[44]

The Confederation of Brtitish Industry responded by setting up its own task force, made up of leading industrialists, to encourage its members to invest in the inner cities. The task force published its first report in September 1988. It suggested small teams of business people in each city to provide leadership and to encourage private sector investment. The CBI report estimated that £50 billion was needed for inner city reconstruction.[45] It is interesting to note that the CBI, not for the first time, was critical of attempts to bypass local councils, and it called for partnership between business, central government and local authorities. This was a view endorsed by the Audit Commission report published in 1989.[46]

The government had promised a White Paper on inner cities, but in March 1988 it produced instead a thirty-two page glossy colour brochure, *Action for Cities*, and twelve separate press releases. The documents were launched at a press conference by Mrs Thatcher flanked by six of her ministers. Of this conference, Hugo Young writes:

So this was an obvious sales pitch, a shameless hype, designed to remind the world that the famous inner cities, which have now received the ultimate accolade of being received into cliche, enjoy the attentions of six ministers as well as the Prime Minister herself. Appropriately, it was one of those news conferences where the journalists are substantially outnumbered by PR men, consultants and the rest of the hucksters' fraternity.[47]

There was precious little that was new in the Paper. There was, for example, the usual emphasis on the private sector. On this occasion we had the formation of a new company, British Urban Development (BUD) backed by eleven property, engineering and construction companies which have each contributed £5 million of initial share capital. The firms participating in this new company are among the main contributors to Conservative Party funds. Between 1988 and 1989 six to eight major projects were planned based on parcels of land of up to 1,000 acres. Local authorities will be obliged to sell derelict and unused land to BUD which will work through the UDCs. Having acquired the land BUD will part-develop the sites by clearing, and by the provision of transport and services, and the sites will then be sold to private developers.

The other initiatives announced in the paper were also 'more of the same'. There was a new UDC for Sheffield and a doubling of the area covered by the Merseyside Development Corporation. The addition of Sheffield brought the total number of UDCs to eleven and the government has stated that there will be no other UDCs before 1992. Two new City Action Teams have been formed in Leeds and Nottingham, bringing the total up to seven. English Estates was given increased funds for extending its workshop programme, and a simpler government grant system was introduced: the three existing grants have been replaced by a single 'city grant' with simpler application procedures.

In education two new city technology colleges were announced and attempts were to be made to extend the system of 'compacts' between business, schools and colleges under which all pupils/ students are guaranteed jobs with local firms when they leave school.

Two major road schemes for London and the Black Country were approved and the Home Secretary announced special crime prevention programmes in twenty areas. Some of these developments were already in the pipeline before the publication of the government plans. *The Guardian* leader quoted earlier said of the proposals: 'There was no major initiative on inner cities yesterday. There was no white paper. No new strategy. No new programme. No major new investment of funds. Instead, there were some useful but modest extensions to the present piecemeal programmes.'[48]

Inner city riots
Civil disorder occurred in 1981 in Brixton and Southall in London; in the St Paul's area of Bristol; in Toxteth in Liverpool; and in the Moss Side district of Manchester. There was considerable damage to property, burning of buildings, looting and violent clashes with the police in which petrol bombs were used and injuries were sustained by both rioters and police. In 1985 further riots of a similar nature occurred in Handsworth (Birmingham) and Tottenham (London). In the Tottenham riot a policeman was killed.

The Scarman report on the 1981 riots has become something of a classic of its kind. Scarman was in no doubt that the root cause of the rioting was unemployment and deprivation:

Whatever the special employment problems of black people, and of young black people in particular, unemployment remains nevertheless an evil that touches all of the community. There can be no doubt that it was a major factor in the complex pattern of conditions which lies at the heart of the disorders in Brixton and elsewhere. In a materialistic society, the relative deprivation . . . it entails is keenly felt and idleness gives time for resentment and envy to grow.[49]

This view was endorsed four years later by *Faith in the City*.[50]

While the underlying cause of the riots was multi-faceted deprivation some of the incidents were sparked off by police action. Scarman was critical of some of the methods employed by police forces, especially the use of special patrol groups in 'saturation swamp 81' which involved considerable police presence and the operation of what were known as the 'sus laws' under which people can be stopped and searched simply on suspicion of misdemeanours. There were complaints by black youths of police harassment, the sus laws merely being used as an excuse for this.

Lord Scarman found no evidence of a *policy* of racial discrimination and prejudice, although there was no doubt that some individual officers were racially prejudiced. Equally, individual officers had over reacted to the disturbances with the over zealous use of dogs, truncheons and a number of unlawful weapons. In most of the areas in which riots occurred there had been a breakdown in community/police relations; the public distrusted the police and they had no confidence in the police complaints machinery. In Brixton consultative machinery involving the police and community leaders had ceased to function.

However, Lord Scarman concluded that:

The police do not create social deprivation, though unimaginative, inflexible policing can make the tensions which deprivation engenders greatly worse. Conversely, while good policing can help diminish tension and avoid disorder, it cannot remove the causes of social stress where these are to be found, as those in Brixton and elsewhere are, deeply embedded in fundamental economic and social conditions.[51]

The riots were unquestionably a blow to the government's law and order policies and to the Conservative's claim to be the party of law and order. Mrs Thatcher, however, claimed that the riots had nothing to do with unemployment and deprivation, but arose as a direct consequence of a lack of discipline within the family and in the schools. She also talked of naked greed, although it takes a curious kind of logic to see the deprived as greedy while company directors were awarding themselves large pay increases and the 'yuppies' in the city were making a great deal of money and spending it as conspicuously as possible.

The government's response to the riots, apart from the setting up of the Scarman Inquiry, was to devote more resources to law and order and to renew its efforts to persuade business people to invest in the inner cities. To this latter end Mr Heseltine accompanied a busload of businessmen on a conducted tour of Liverpool.

Inner city resources
The impression given by political commentators is that it is Mrs Thatcher who controls inner city expenditure – as she controls just about every item of government spending. Mr Heseltine, when Secretary of State for the Environment, constantly argued for extra resources which were withheld by Mrs Thatcher and the Treasury, and succeeding ministers have been no more successful.

The government claims to spend £3.5 billion on urban policies; the Audit Commission puts the figure at £1.9 billion. But even if the government's figure of £3.5 billion is accurate it is still only a fraction of what is required: as has been noted, the CBI estimates that £50 billion is needed. Clearly, there is no possibility of any government achieving this level of expenditure which equals the total spent on the whole of social security and is over double the amount devoted to the NHS and the personal social services.

Inner city resources will be adversely affected by changes in the system of local government finance. The community charge will entail massive increases in the bills to be paid by inner city residents or a substantial reduction in services. However, the full effect of this will not be felt for four years since the government has provided resources to cushion the transfer from rates to the community charge.

Another change in local government finance is that the rate support grant has been replaced by the revenue support grant. The allocation of the rate support grant took account of both variations in need and variations in resources among local authorities. Although the new grant takes account of variations in need, it takes no account of variations in resources, and this will disadvantage inner cities who were the main beneficiaries of resource equalisation. The revenue support grant will be phased in over four years to prevent sharp falls in grant, but this will simply soften the impact.

It is difficult to obtain precise figures of private sector investment in the inner cities, but there may be reasons to doubt industry's willingness to commit billions of pounds to inner city developments. So far the response of the private sector has been a very cautious one. In spite of their support of the Conservative Party, the leaders of British industry have made it plain that there are limits to the extent to which they are prepared to sacrifice profitability in giving support to the government's inner city policies. In the short term some sacrifices may be made, but eventually there must be a reasonable return on investments.

For the government strategy to work, therefore, it must create the conditions which will enable the private sector to make profits in the inner urban areas. This implies massive investment in education and training, in low cost housing and in general environmental improvement; good transport links will have to be established and sites will have to be fully prepared with all the necessary services on hand. There is little evidence that the government is willing to commit funds in quantities designed to bring about substantial improvements of this kind.

CONCLUSIONS

The ideology of the three Thatcher governments is more clearly demonstrated in housing than in any other area of social policy. The policies involve privatisation on a considerable scale. There have been drastic cuts in public investment in housing, both absolutely and relatively, and local authority stocks have been depleted. Between 1978/79 and 1989/90 government expenditure on housing in real terms declined by 79 per cent.

The 1987 White Paper said that the 'provision of housing by local authorities as landlords should gradually be diminished'.[52] But when the reduction in building, the sale of council houses, the introduction of HATs and the transfer of tenancies are taken into account, the diminution does not seem particularly gradual. Flynn makes the connection between retrenchment and privatisation:

'Here lies the key to Thatcherite housing and social welfare policies – within a general programme of retrenchment, the essential and fundamental element is the goal of "privatisation".'[53] Flynn argues that housing policy exemplifies the shift from collective to individualised welfare provision.

The encouragement and support of home ownership, as Hills shows, is obviously the top priority:

the value of mortgage interest tax relief had risen to £4,500 million by 1986/7, more than twice its real level of eight years before, despite the cut in the basic rate of tax. *The increase in the real cost of mortgage interest tax relief over the period – £2.4 billion at 1986/7 prices – was the same size as the real fall in net public capital spending on housing.*[54]

Another feature of Conservative social policy – a distrust of local authorities – is particularly obvious in housing. The sale of council houses, the appointment of HATs and the transfer of council housing to alternative landlords all reduce the role of local authorities. Inner city initiatives exhibit a similar bias against local government. Most inner city councils have a long socialist tradition which makes them even less popular with the government, and despite some recent softening of the government's attitude, local authorities are still largely excluded from inner city initiatives.

Conservative policies intensify housing inequalities. Council tenants become more and more marginalised as the better-off tenants are encouraged, by generous discounts, to buy their homes. Council estates become ghettos for the very poor, the unemployed, elderly people, single person households and young adults with young children. As Forrest and Murie say:

Even the most ardent critics of council housing would find it difficult to conjure up images of featherbedded, oversubsidised council tenants driving expensive cars. The public housing sector is well on the way to becoming an unambiguously residual, second class form of housing provision serving some of the poorest sections of the population.[55]

The right to buy policy and the alternative landlord scheme are presented as extensions of tenants' choice, and for some this is undoubtedly the case. A corollary of this, though, is that the choice for others is curtailed. Those who wish to become local authority tenants find that the best houses have been sold and, as the stock diminishes and fewer council houses are built, waiting lists and waiting times lengthen, and exchanges for those already in council housing and remaining in it become more difficult.

In addition, people are going to find themselves paying higher rents, irrespective of whether they live in privately rented, housing association or local authority property. A report from the Policy Studies Institute, published in 1990, indicated that in the Summer and Autumn of 1989 16 per cent of tenants (more than a million households) were in arrears with their rents. The average amount owed by individual tenants was about £270.[56]

However, the most damning indictment of the Conservative government's record in housing is that it has presided over a massive increase in homelessness. Most of this increase stems directly from government policies and, although some extra resources have been allocated for 1990/91 and 1991/92, little has been done to remedy the situation. For the homeless the right to buy and the provisions of the 1988 Act are an irrelevance.

NOTES

1. See Health Visitors' Association and General Medical Services Committee, *Homeless Families and Their Health*, London, HVA and GMSC, 1989; D. Byrne, *et al.*, *Housing and Health: The Relationship Between Housing Conditions and the Health of Council Tenants*, Aldershot: Gower, 1986; T. Blackman, *et al.*, 'Housing and health: A case study of two areas in West Belfast', *Journal of Social Policy*, vol. 18, pt. 1, 1989, pp. 1–26; P. Townsend, N. Davidson and M. Whitehead, *Inequalities in Health* and *The Health Divide*, Harmondsworth: Penguin, 1988.
2. P. Willmott and A. Murie, *Polarisation and Social Housing*, London: Policy Studies Institute, 1988.
3. P. Malpass and A. Murie, *Housing Policy and Practice*, London: Macmillan, 1982, p. 69.
4. Central Statistical Office, *Social Trends*, no. 19, London: HMSO, 1989.
5 M. Kerr, *The Right to Buy: A National Survey of Tenants and Buyers of Council Homes*, London, HMSO, 1988.
6. R. Forrest and A. Murie, *The Right to Buy? Need, Equity and Polarisation in the Sale of Council Houses*, Bristol: School for Advanced Urban Studies, 1984.
7. P. Willmott and A. Murie, *op. cit.*
8. S. Duncan, *Public Problems, Private Solutions*, London: HMSO, 1988.

9. I am indebted to Janet Ford for the information on mortgage arrears. See J. Ford, *The Indebted Society: Credit and Default in the 1980s*, London: Routledge, 1988; J. Doling, J. Ford and B. Stafford, *The Property Owing Democracy*, Aldershot: Avebury, 1988; J. Ford 'Problematic statistics? The case of mortgage default', *Journal of the Chartered Building Societies Institute*, March 1989; J. Ford, 'Pity the poor home owners – again', *Roof*, November 1989.

10. P. Malpass and A. Murie, *op cit.*, p. 172.

11. Department of the Environment, *Housing: The Government's Proposals*, Cm 214, London: HMSO, 1987.

12. *Ibid.*, p. 3.

13. *Ibid.*, p. 18.

14. L. Burrows, *The Housing Act of 1988*, London: Shelter, 1989, p. 7.

15. *Ibid.*, p. 10.

16. *Inside Housing*, vol. 6, no. 30, 1989.

17. K. Gibb and A. Kearns, 'The assured tenancy business expansion scheme: A framework for research', reported in *Inside Housing*, vol. 6, no. 32, 1989.

18. Private communication from the National Federation of Housing Associations.

19. *The Guardian*, 25 January 1989.

20. *Housing Associations Weekly*, no. 129, 1989.

21. *Ibid.*

22. *Housing Associations Weekly*, no, 130, 1989.

23. L. Burrows, *op cit.*, p. 47.

24. The Housing Corporation, *Tenants' Choice: Criteria for Landlord Approval and Guidance Notes for Applicants*, London: The Housing Corporation, 1989.

25. L. Burrows, *op. cit.*, p. 47.

26. Department of the Environment, *op cit.*, p. 4.

27. A. Murie, 'Housing', in P. Wilding (ed.), *In Defence of the Welfare State*, Manchester: Manchester University Press, 1986, pp. 65–6.

28. Central Statistical Office, *Social Trends*, no. 19, London: HMSO, 1989.

29. Private communication, Department of the Environment.

30. Central Statistical office, *Social Trends*, no. 19, London: HMSO, 1989.

31. *The Observer*, 13 September 1987.

32. Health Visitors' Association and General Medical Services Committee, *op cit.*

33. *Housing Associations Weekly*, no. 129, 1989.

34. Central Statistical Office, *Social Trends*, no. 19, London: HMSO, 1989.

35. Department of the Environment, *An Inquiry into the Condition of Local Authority Housing Stock in England*, London: HMSO, 1986.

36. Audit Commission, *Managing the Crisis in Council Housing*, London: HMSO, 1986.
37. *The Observer*, 18 December 1988.
38. See Central London Social Security Advisers' Forum, *Beyond the Limit*, London, 1989.
39. *Housing Associations Weekly*, no. 129, 1989.
40. Department of the Environment, *Policy for the Inner Cities*, Cmnd 6845, London: HMSO, 1977.
41. Archbishop of Canterbury's Commission on Urban Priority Areas, *Faith in the City*, London: Church House Publishing, 1985, p. 10. See also *Living Faith in the City*, London: Church House Publishing, 1990.
42. S. Laurence and P. Hall, 'British policy responses' in P. Hall (ed.), *The Inner City in Context*, London: Heinemann, 1981, pp. 88–111.
43. *The Guardian*, 30 July 1987.
44. *The Guardian*, 27 November 1987.
45. *The Guardian*, 23 September 1988.
46. Audit Commission, *Urban Regeneration and Economic Development: The Local Government Dimension*, London: HMSO, 1989, p. 2.
47. *The Guardian*, 8 March 1988.
48. *Ibid.*
49. Lord Scarman, *The Brixton Disorders 10–12 April 1981*, London: HMSO, 1981, p. 107.
50. Archbishop of Canterbury, *op. cit.*
51. Lord Scarman, *op. cit.*, p. 100.
52. Department of the Environment, 1987, *op. cit.*, p. 3.
53. R. Flynn, 'Political acquiescence, privatisation and residualisation in British housing policy', *Journal of Social Policy*, vol. 17, pt, 3, 1988, pp. 289–312.
54. J. Hills, 'What happened to spending on the welfare state?', in A. Walker and C. Walker (eds.), *The Growing Divide*, London: Child Poverty Action Group, 1987, pp. 88–100.
55. R. Forrest and A. Murie, 'The social division of housing subsidies', *Critical Social Policy*, vol. 8, no. 2, 1988, pp. 83–93.
56. R. Berthoud and E. Kempson, *Credit and Debt in Britain*, London: Policy Studies Institute, 1990.

CHAPTER 7

THE PERSONAL SOCIAL SERVICES

The personal social services are concerned with a range of services for children and for elderly, mentally disordered and physically disabled people. Local authority social services departments, the principal providers of these services, are the main employers of social workers, but they also employ care assistants and home helps.

Many of the tasks performed by social services departments (SSDs) are statutory duties, although the interpretation of these varies from authority to authority. Statutory duties now cover a wider range of special needs groups than was formerly the case. For example, both the Disabled Persons Act of 1986 and the Children Act of 1989 impose extra duties on local authorities. Statutory duties invariably take precedence over other aspects of the work and because of the publicity surrounding cases of child abuse, and the tendency to blame social workers when things go wrong, a disproportionate share of the energies and resources of SSDs is devoted to work with children.

SOCIAL WORK

After the Seebohm Report of 1968[1] and the Social Services Act of 1970, there was a trend towards genericism in social work practice and training. Specialism never entirely disappeared, but in the 1980s there was a quite definite return to specialisation,[2] especially in mental health and child care.

The 1983 Mental Health Act stipulated that only approved social workers should be allowed to deal with mental health cases. Approved social workers under the Act would require specialist training and an appraisal of their competence, and the central council for education and training in Social Work (CCETSW) insists upon a minimum of sixty days' training culminating in formal examinations. Between 1983 and 1987 just over 2,000 underwent specialist training with 82 per cent completing the courses successfully.

In child care the movement towards specialisation has been even more marked, and child protection teams, for example, are now the norm in local authorities. This development came about in response to an increase in the number of child abuse cases being uncovered and the sensitivity of the issues involved, combined with a widely held view that social workers were ill-prepared to deal with complex cases of this kind. In 1989 the government launched a £10 million training programme in child protection. Most of the money went to local authorities who developed in-service courses and co-operated with educational institutions in establishing post-qualifying courses in child protection. The funds available for child protection were continued into 1990/91 and further money has been made available for training in relation to the new Children Act.

The Department of Health has established a Training Support Programme for training in other areas of work, and in 1988/89, its first year of operation, the programme contributed £10 million to the cost of training 70,000 social care staff working with elderly people. The programme will continue in 1990/91. Also in 1990/91 the programme will provide £2 million for training in social services management.

While the government was willing to set aside very limited funds for specialised and principally in-service training, it rejected a £40 million proposal from CCETSW to replace the two-year Certificate of Qualification in Social Work (CQSW) with a three-year programme leading to the award of the Qualifying Diploma in Social Work. This rejection discounted the recommendations of three separate reports between 1985 and 1987 that social work training should be lengthened.[3] In most EC countries training courses for social workers already last for three years and the Commission has suggested an extension to four years.

CCETSW has had to rethink its training strategy. It now proposes to replace both the Certificate in Social Service and the CQSW with a Diploma in Social Work. The Council is also proposing an Advanced Award in Social Work which will be based on a system of credits taking into account both post-qualifying training and practice.

A review of recent developments in social work, especially in the context of Conservative Party policy, would not be complete without some reference to the development of private practice. The most obvious growth has been in consultancies in child abuse – especially sexual abuse – but there are also consultancies in psychotherapy, stress management and group work. The most far-reaching changes in social work, however, are likely to result from the implementation of the government's proposals on community care.[4]

THE GRIFFITHS REPORT AND COMMUNITY CARE

In discussions of community care a distinction is frequently made between care *by* the community and care *in* the community. Abrams defines care by the community as 'provision of help, support and protection to others by lay members of societies acting in everyday domestic and occupational settings'.[5] Walker, on the other hand, takes a different approach: 'We are concerned . . . with the concept of care *in* the community, which may be provided "informally", through kinship networks, by friends, neighbours and volunteers, or "formally" by statutory social services'.[6]

The mid-1980s saw an intensification of interest in community care, as witnessed by the publication since 1985 of four major reports on the topic.[7] All four reports are agreed that there is a discrepancy between sentiments of support for community care and practical action to implement it. The Griffiths Report, for example, says:

At the centre, community care has been talked of for thirty years and in few areas can the gap between political rhetoric and policy on the one hand, or between policy and reality in the field on the other hand, have been so great. To talk of policy in matters of care except in the context of available resources and timescales for action owes more to theology than to the purposeful delivery of a caring service.[8]

A report from the King's Fund Institute expresses concern that 'there is clearly no articulated national policy on community care',[9] and the Audit Commission found the progress towards community care to be slow and uneven.[10]

It was the indictments of the Audit Commission that led the Secretary of State for Social Services to ask Sir Roy Griffiths 'to review the way in which public funds are used to support community care policy and to advise . . . on the options for action that would improve the use of these funds as a contribution to more effective community care'.[11]

Griffiths follows the orthodox welfare pluralist approach in which the state's role (local authorities in this case) as a direct provider of welfare is diminished, and the roles of the informal, voluntary and private sectors are increased. This approach is clearly expressed in the following passage:

The primary function of the public services is to design and arrange the provision of care and support . . . There is value in a multiplicity of provision, not least from the consumer's point of view, because of the widening choice, flexibility, innovation and competition it should stimulate. The proposals are therefore aimed at stimulating the further development of the 'mixed economy' of care. It is vital that social services authorities should see themselves as the arrangers and purchasers of care services – not as monopolistic providers.[12]

Local authorities are thus seen as 'enablers' – designing, organising and purchasing non-health care services rather than providing them directly. In greater detail, local authority social services departments would be responsible for:

1. Assessing community care needs in their localities, setting objectives and priorities and formulating community care plans.
2. The financial management of community care funds to be transferred from both social security and health authorities.
3. Monitoring and regulating performance.
4. The provision of information to both consumers and providers of care.
5. The assessment of individuals' needs and the design of packages of care to meet them.

Under these arrangements, social workers would become case managers, designing packages aimed at achieving the most effective combination of services within the resources available. Responsibility for the administration of community care grants, at present administered by the Department of Social Security as part of the social fund, should be transferred to local authorities. In its response to Griffiths, the government is non-committal about this transfer, simply saying that the position will have to be reviewed.[13]

The report emphasises the importance of the private sector: a central aim is to secure the expansion of for-profit welfare. In what is described as 'a key statement', the report claims that: 'the onus in all cases should be on the social services authorities to show that the private sector is being fully stimulated and encouraged and that competitive tenders or other means of testing the market, are being taken'.[14] Later in the report local authorities are enjoined to 'maximise choice and competition by encouraging the further development of private services'.[15] However, Griffiths also envisages greater support and encouragement of the voluntary and informal sectors.

The report recommended that local authorities should be given the leading role in planning and co-ordinating community care. This placed the government in something of a quandary. It was attracted to the Griffiths proposals because of their potential for promoting private services, but it went against the grain to leave local authorities with so much power, and it was this dilemma which caused the considerable delay in the government's response to Griffiths. Mrs Thatcher wanted to explore every other possible alternative to local authority leadership of the community care programme. The matter was discussed in Cabinet and a special cabinet committee was established onto which Sir Roy was co-opted. Eventually Mrs Thatcher's reluctance was overcome, and in July 1989 it was announced that responsibility for community care would be given to local authorities. This decision was confirmed in the White Paper, published in November 1989, which outlined the government's plans.[16]

The Griffiths proposals were based on the further development of a mixed economy of welfare. The relevance of this concept is not restricted to domiciliary care, and we will return to it once we have looked at residential services.

RESIDENTIAL CARE

Private residential homes – especially for elderly people – have constituted one of the growth industries during the 1980s. Between 1979 and 1986 the number of private residential homes in Great

Britain increased by an average of 18.1 per cent a year. The number of private homes more than tripled in that period, so that by 1986 over 52 per cent of all residential homes were in private hands. During the same period the number of places in private residential homes increased by an average of over 17 per cent a year. By 1986 there were three times the number of places in private homes than there had been in 1979. The number of places in local authority and voluntary homes remained virtually unchanged. In 1979 almost 65 per cent of places in residential homes were in local authority establishments, but by 1986 the proportion had fallen to just below 50 per cent.[17] Since 1986 the proportion will have fallen even further, as some Conservative local authorities have sold their old people's homes to either private operators or housing associations. Private companies are also heavily involved in the provision of sheltered housing.

This enormous expansion of private residential care was financed in part by the taxpayer. Without an infusion of funds from the DHSS (now DSS), fewer private homes would have been established and many more would have proved to be unprofitable. Phillips *et al.* identify the other factors making for the expansion of private residential care, but give primacy to public finance:

The movement into private care has been accentuated by tight control of local authority expenditure at a time when numbers of people have been 'deinstitutionalised' from psychiatric and psycho-geriatric units, and when people from an ageing population have been seeking residential care for the first time. Most importantly, though, these sources of potential demand coincided with higher levels of DHSS benefits to support residents in private residential homes.[18]

Between 1979/80 and 1986/87 the DHSS subsidy to private homes increased from £10 million a year to £489 million.[19] Estimates for 1989/90 put this figure at £1 billion – a one hundredfold increase in ten years. In 1989 the board and lodging allowance varied from £140 to £230 a week depending upon the category of resident. Both Griffiths and the Audit Commission were critical of this expenditure which, they argued, cut across the declared policy of promoting community care, and in 1991, in accordance with the Griffiths proposals, responsibility for board and lodging allowances will pass from the DSS to local authorities.

Serious allegations have been made about the running of some private homes. A study by Harriet and Sarah Harman, for example, documents appalling and degrading treatment of elderly people in private homes. In some cases homes were being run by convicted criminals. It is not suggested that any but a small proportion of private homes are like this, but where such conditions do occur, it indicates that the vetting, registration and monitoring procedures are failing.

The Harman study looked at the ninety-six cases which had been decided by the Registered Homes Tribunal between 1985 and 1989. The Tribunal hears appeals by prospective residential home owners against local authorities' refusal to register.[20]

The study found inconsistencies in the rulings of the Tribunal and wide variations in the registration practices of local authorities and in the criteria applied by them. The report claimed that the Code of Guidance[21] which accompanied the Registered Homes Act of 1984 was not being applied, partly because of lack of resources and partly because of the restricted power of local authorities. The Code of Guidance, the authors maintain, should be given the force of legislation. Furthermore, the original intention of the 1984 Act was that the burden of proof should rest on potential proprietors to demonstrate suitability, and Harman and Harman claim that the reverse of this is happening with local authorities having to prove unsuitability.

A report by the West Yorkshire Low Pay Unit demonstrated that it was not only residents who ran the risk of exploitation, but also the staff. Rates of pay for what is a stressful job were extremely low, starting at £1.20 an hour: three-quarters of the unqualified workforce received £2.00 an hour or less and the highest rates of pay were well below £3.00 an hour.[22] A forty hour week at £2.00 an hour would produce a weekly income of £80.00 which compares with an average weekly wage for full time female workers in 1987 of £148.00. The average weekly earnings of female manual workers amounted to £115.00 in 1987.

Private residential homes are frequently small family businesses and, as such, they are in tune with Conservative Party ideology and with the government's economic strategy. Residential care is very labour intensive, and fundamental to the viability of private homes is the heavy involvement of the owners and their families, often working very long hours. Reliance upon family labour means that the proprietors need very few employees, and the low wages paid to these employees contributes further to the profitability of the home. Keeping staff to a minimum and paying them very little obviously reduces costs, but it does not necessarily lead to good quality care.

Although private residential homes are typically independent family businesses, if the same happens in Britain as happened in the United States, then large companies may come to occupy a bigger share of the market. Several hotel and leisure groups are already beginning to diversify into this field: they are aiming at the top and more lucrative end of the market, charging fees well above the DSS limits.

In a House of Commons debate on the Griffiths proposals, the Health Minister, Mr David Mellor, said that a commitment to care in the community meant ending the incentives to residential care in the social security system.[23] Such a change is likely to affect the smaller businesses rather than the large companies.

In the same debate Mr Mellor restated the government's intention of encouraging local authorities to make greater use of the private and voluntary sectors and to see themselves as enablers rather than providers. The White Paper, while not excluding local authority provision, stresses the need for actively supporting the private and voluntary sectors: 'The statutory sector will continue to play an important role in backing up, developing and monitoring private and voluntary care facilities, and providing services where this remains the best way of meeting those needs.'[24] The local authority, the White Paper concedes, may have to provide for people 'with high levels of dependency or particularly challenging patterns of behaviour . . .'[25]

The White Paper clearly indicates the government's intention of shifting the balance of provision away from local authorities, and this brings us back to the mixed economy of welfare or welfare pluralism.

WELFARE PLURALISM

The term welfare pluralism became part of the vocabulary of social policy after its use in 1978 by the Wolfenden Report on *The Future of Voluntary Organisations*.[26] Hatch and Mocroft, two prominent welfare pluralists, offer the following definition:

In one sense welfare pluralism can be used to convey the fact that social and health care may be obtained from four different sectors – the statutory, the voluntary, the commercial and the informal. More prescriptively, welfare pluralism implies a less dominant role for the state, seeing it as not the only possible instrument for the collective provision of welfare services.[27]

The shift from description to prescription in this formulation is interesting. The welfare state in Britain has always been pluralistic in that there have always been several sources of welfare provision. But the present government's preference for a mixed system of welfare is based on a desire to reduce the role of the state and correspondingly increase the role of the informal, voluntary and commercial sectors.

This position is clearly stated in the White Paper, *Growing Older*, which appeared in 1981:

Whatever level of public expenditure proves practicable, and however it is distributed, the primary source of support and care for the elderly people are informal and voluntary . . . It is the role of public authorities to sustain and, where necessary develop – but never displace – such support and care. Care *in* the community must increasingly mean care *by* the community.[28]

This view was given even greater prominence in the Griffiths report which, as we have seen, also advocated an enhanced role for the commercial sector.

The government believes that the informal, voluntary and commercial sectors should substitute for the state in welfare provision. The local authorities' functions would be in the planning, co-ordination, regulation and finance of community care, rather than its direct provision.

If local authorities are to provide less, then the informal, voluntary and commercial sectors will need to provide more. It is assumed, on very little evidence, that the other three sectors have the capacity to expand their activities and that there are no countervailing drawbacks to their doing so. There are persuasive reasons for doubting this.

Phillipson, for example, argues that the Griffiths perspective 'conveniently ignores some difficult questions relating to the provision of informal care'. He continues:

Indeed, by failing to acknowledge what applied research has to say on this matter, the Griffiths report proceeds from a false premise (that care by the community – in its present form – is desirable and will continue) to a false conclusion (that publicly provided services can be increasingly restricted to an enabling and facilitating role). By ignoring a substantial body of research produced in the 1970s and 1980s, the report presents . . . a misleading picture of the tasks facing the statutory sector.[29]

Those pursuing a reduction in the welfare role of the state have, in their eagerness, paid insufficient attention to the problems facing the mixed economy of welfare. Some of these problems will now be examined, beginning with those facing the informal sector.

The informal sector

More often than not community care means care by families – especially nuclear families. Within the informal sector, bonds of kinship support the strongest reciprocal obligations, as Bulmer argues:

Kin ties remain the most important source of informal care for the majority of the population . . . Within the web of kinship relations, the nuclear family is central and the source of most caring relationships. Ties with extended kin are very much a matter of personal choice; those with members of one's nuclear family are more enduring and more likely to lead to responsibility for care.[30]

To deny the importance of the family as a source of care would be to ignore the accumulated evidence of several decades. Nevertheless, informal care by families faces considerable pressure at present and this is likely to intensify during the 1990s. Population projections indicate that between 1986 and 2001 the number of people aged 85 and over will increase by 70 per cent.[31] A report from the Office of Population Censuses and Surveys in 1988 revealed that the number of disabled people in Britain stood at six million; twice the number estimated in 1971. Two-thirds of disabled people were at or below the poverty line.[32]

These figures indicate that the number of potential dependants in the population is increasing and likely to go on increasing. At the same time the number of potential carers is declining. Three factors have been particularly significant in bringing about this decline: reduced family size, the increasing participation of women in the labour market, and rising divorce rates.

Between 1971 and 1987 total period fertility rates declined by almost 22 per cent in the United Kingdom. One obvious consequence of this is smaller families, which means that there will be fewer potential carers when the present generation of parents reaches old age or when a sibling becomes disabled.

Traditionally the burden of long-term domiciliary care has fallen on women. It is usually women who have left work, or moved from full time to part time employment, to care for a sick or frail elderly relative. However, one of the most significant trends of the last three decades has been a steady growth in the number of women in the labour force. Between 1971 and 1987 the total labour force increased by 2.3 million, and almost the whole of this was attributable to increased employment among women. Furthermore, while male activity rates are likely to remain constant between 1987 and 1995, women's activity rates will go on rising. The proportion of married women in employment increased from 47 per cent in 1971 to 60 per cent in 1987.[33]

The government's policy on community care ignores the significance of this change, and assumes that women 'will continue to accept their cultural designation as carers' and that they will always be willing to sacrifice work opportunities in the interests of caring for dependent relatives. None of this can be guaranteed.[34]

Divorce rates in England and Wales have risen from 2.1 per thousand married people in 1961 to 6.0 in 1971 and 12.6 in 1987. Rising divorce rates affect the family's capacity for caring by adding to the number of lone parents. Divorce is easily the most common cause of lone parenthood. Lone parents, 91 per cent of whom are women, have fewer resources than other families, and the lack of a partner with whom one can share child-rearing responsibilities leaves little time and energy for other forms of care.

Phillipson identifies another set of problems for the government's family care policies. He challenges the orthodox view that elderly people turn to formal agencies for help only when informal support is absent or inadequate. In relation to Britain this proposition can be neither proved nor disproved. He says that it would be unfortunate if this perspective were used 'as a rationale for distributing resources, particularly when a contrary position stressing a preference for community-based professional support could just as easily be advanced'.[35]

Phillipson summarises American research which indicates that elderly people may be turning away from informal care based on kinship towards formal professional support. A British study by West *et al.* showed low levels of support for informal care packages and a preference for professional support in the community,[36] and this suggests that dependence on state services may be preferred to dependence upon kin. Phillipson writes:

> This is not to say that people will not give the support (as we know they do and invariably at great sacrifice); but it does suggest that care by the community is seen as a less attractive option than care from professionals, but with the support and involvement of the family.[37]

If this view is correct it means that the whole approach suggested by Griffiths, and accepted by the government, is flawed. Falling standards of care may well result from a transfer of responsibility from professional agencies to family care. This in no way underestimates the contribution of families to the welfare of their members: nor does it diminish the importance of care in the community. But the government is committed to the notion of care *by* the community and wants families to take on greater responsibilities.

From the problems identified it would appear that we should be asking not whether the family can provide more care in the future but whether it will be even able to maintain its current level of provision. There are obvious limits to the extra work that families can be expected to absorb and these limits may already have been reached.

Families and people needing care in the community may, of course, receive support from friends and neighbours, and the government's proposals also anticipate a substantial contribution from this source. However, although friendship is an important source of mutual support and companionship, it does not provide a sound basis for long term care. Allan observes that friendship depends upon a degree of equality between the participants, and that a one-sided caring relationship denies the essential element of reciprocity. If caring is unlikely to lead to friendship, the reverse is also true:

> While part of friendship is caring about each other to a greater or lesser degree, caring for one another is not an element inherent in the routine organization of friendship . . . the majority of routine friendships are not particulary well suited for providing the sort of caring community care entails, notwithstanding the friendship ideals that might make one think they would be.[38]

Friends may be spread geographically. Neighbours, by definition, have the advantage of proximity and are in a better position to keep an eye on elderly or infirm people living nearby. Neighbours are useful in emergencies and they provide help in countless small ways, such as shopping, taking in deliveries, admitting tradesmen, providing transport and looking after each other's children for short periods.

Thus, friends and neighbours are usually concerned with short term help of a fairly straightforward nature. Care of a personal kind and care which is long term and continuous is almost always provided by kin.[39] The contribution of friends and neighbours, therefore, is important but limited. It supplements care by kin, but families continue to provide the bulk of domiciliary care.

There is no possibility of the family, even with help from neighbours and friends, substituting for state provision. Indeed, if present levels of family care are to be sustained, the state will have to do more to support families in terms of both services and cash benefits.

Let us now turn our attention to the voluntary sector to see if it is in any better position than the informal sector to compensate for reductions in local authority provision.

The voluntary sector

The voluntary sector is an essential feature of a welfare pluralist system of personal social services. If local authorities are going to withdraw from direct service provision – even if only in part – the voluntary sector will have to be extended, and this will entail increased funding by local authorities. Griffiths makes this clear:

To develop the potential contribution of the voluntary sector further, financial support for its role needs to be provided on a clear basis, fully understood by all concerned. I therefore see a need for clear agreements to be made between public agencies and not-for-profit bodies on the basis of public agency funding. This may be, for example, on a fee per client basis, or a contract providing that the not-for-profit body should provide a given level of service. In either case, this should allow the social services authority to hold the not-for-profit body to account for the proper use of public funds.[40]

In recognition of a role which goes beyond the direct provision of services (e.g. developmental work, advocacy, campaigning and education), Griffiths also recommends a general core grant payable by local authorities to voluntary organisations. This view of the role of voluntary organisations and of their relationships with local authorities is endorsed in the White Paper which states that the government 'will expect public funding agencies to develop an increasingly contractual relationship with the voluntary bodies they fund'.[41]

If substantial public funds are to be made over to voluntary associations then, as Griffiths intimates, some form of audit becomes essential: and this raises the question of the independence of voluntary organisations, which is said to be one of their great virtues. The problem of retaining independence will become more acute as voluntary bodies are drawn increasingly into service provision as the agents of local authorities, as *Caring for People* suggests. The distinction between public bodies and voluntary agencies will be blurred, and the independence of action of voluntary bodies will be hampered as some of their resources and energies are absorbed in winning and fulfilling local authority contracts. Furthermore, if the local authority is known to favour particular kinds of programmes, voluntary organisations applying for funds may feel obliged to tailor their applications accordingly. Billis and Harris have identified the conflicting goals of funders and agencies as a major concern in the voluntary sector.[42]

At present local authority procedures for regulation and control are rudimentary, and the criteria to be applied to funding decisions are less than clear. The call by Griffiths for 'clear agreements' is obviously justified, but their achievement may prove to be a bigger problem than either Griffiths or the government anticipate. Matters may become a little clearer when the results of the efficiency review of government funding of voluntary agencies, begun in 1989, become available.

There is a more general issue of accountability in the voluntary sector. Leat has identified four forms of accountability applicable to voluntary organisations:

1. Fiscal accountability – accountability for the proper use of public money.
2. Process accountability – accountability for following proper procedures.
3. Programme accountability – accountability for quality of work.
4. Accountability for priorities – accountability for the relevance or appropriateness of the agency's work.[43]

The enforcement of these different forms of accountability may not be easy, and voluntary organisations are not subject to direct accountability to the electorate, as are local authorities. It is true that contractual accountability may be viewed as an alternative to political accountability, but much of what the voluntary sector does is not capable of precise measurement for inclusion in a contract.

There are, then, considerable difficulties in attempting to ensure accountability and Leat comments that 'problems are likely to increase if a policy of pluralism and closer relationships between the voluntary and statutory sectors is pursued'.[44] Another problem of the voluntary sector is the unevenness in its provision. In some areas of the country, where voluntary services are well developed, substitution of voluntary for local provision would be easier than in areas where the voluntary sector is weak. Even within a single local authority variations are likely to be considerable.

It is true that local authorities do not achieve uniformity of provision, but usually an attempt is made to match resources to need. The problem with voluntary agencies is that their number and strength is inversely related to need. Although their research was done some years ago, the conclusions of Hatch and Mocroft still hold: 'On the whole, towns low in voluntary organisations tended to be the ones that were low in terms of social class'.[45] If low social class is related to greater need, then voluntary organisations are least active where the needs are greatest. Brenton, in a study looking at the feasibility of the voluntary sector replacing the statutory sector *to some degree* in the provision of personal services, concludes:

Asking what is the capacity for such an expansion, in practical terms, we must conclude that the available evidence suggests that it would require a transformation that would be nothing short of miraculous. Voluntary organisations are thinly and unevenly distributed, and where the need is greatest, they do not exist.[46]

Voluntary agencies are also unevenly distributed among different client groups. Children and physically disabled and elderly people tend to be well served by voluntary agencies, whereas the mentally disordered, alcohol and drug abusers and the single homeless are poorly served.

The voluntary sector is characterised by fragmentation and poor co-ordination, leading to overlapping and gaps, with ample facilities in some areas and shortages in others. Transfer from local authorities to voluntary organisations would result in a less equitable distribution of resources, and it is difficult to see how the shortcomings of the voluntary sector could be sufficiently modified to make voluntary organisations an acceptable alternative to local authorities as providers of community care services. Brenton comments:

> To devolve responsibility for the kind of social services we currently enjoy to a mass of informal, ill-organised groups and organisations would constitute so great a dismantling of the personal social services system as to leave its functions solely to hidden providers of informal care.[47]

The dismantling of the personal social services would also open the way for commercial providers.

The commercial sector

Commercial suppliers are already well established in the personal social services. As we have seen, the residential care of elderly people is predominantly in the hands of private companies. We have also seen how dependent these private companies are on public finance and how difficult they are to regulate.

One of the aims of Griffiths, already noted, is to promote the private sector and encourage competition. The White Paper takes the same approach: 'Local authorities will be expected to make maximum use of the independent sector. The Government will ensure that they have acceptable plans for achieving this'.[48] The 'independent sector' includes voluntary agencies but it also implies private market provision of luncheon clubs, meals-on-wheels, home helps, care attendants, community nurses and day centres. Equally, there would be nothing to prevent private social work companies setting up in opposition to local authority and voluntary agency workers; private training companies are already emerging.

One of the problems is that once the commercial sector has been legitimated, it is difficult to limit its growth. Beresford and Croft voice this fear:

> The problem is that welfare pluralists seem to overestimate the capacity of the state to regulate the slice of the welfare market the commercial sector takes . . . More fundamentally . . . welfare pluralists cannot escape opening wider the door to privatisation by the support for the commercial sector inherent in their advocacy of a plurality of sources of welfare.[49]

The changes envisaged in the White Paper could lead to a personal social service system dominated by commercial suppliers. It might be thought of as over-reacting but the development of local monopolies and cartels is just conceivable.

Full-scale commercial provision by big companies is one possible model of market-based welfare. At the other extreme is the introduction of market principles into local authority practice by means of paid care schemes. An interesting study of ten such schemes by Leat and Gay refers to 'the growing practice within social services departments of paying "ordinary people" to provide various forms of care for a wide range of client groups'.[50] It should be stressed that no payment is made by the client.

Two important distinctions are made: first, between care provided in the carer's home and that provided in the client's home; and second, between substitute care, in which the 'normal' carer (or the local authority) is replaced, and supplementary care, where the paid carer supplements the care of others or the client's capacity for self-care.[51]

According to Leat and Gay: 'Payment for care schemes attempt to overcome the weaknesses of bureaucratically organised statutory care by buying in the strengths of care in the private domain whilst at the same time overcoming the weaknesses of informal sector care'.[52] In this way these schemes form a bridge between the formal and informal sectors. Other schemes, to which we now turn, attempt to interweave statutory, voluntary, informal and, less often, commercial care.

INITIATIVES IN COMMUNITY CARE

The government launched two community care initiatives in the 1980s. In 1983 the DHSS issued the 'Care in the Community' circular which sought to bring about the transfer of long-stay hospital patients into the community: this would allow the closure of long-stay wards and hospitals.

The circular also contained the following statement: 'Ministers wish to encourage a programme of pilot projects, to explore and evaluate different approaches to community care. It will be important to demonstrate methods which are both beneficial to the people concerned and cost-effective'.[53]

A demonstration programme of twenty-eight pilot projects was begun in 1983 with government funding of £19 million until 1988. The Personal Social Services Research Unit of the University of Kent was commissioned to promote, monitor and evaluate the programme. Their results can be seen in *Demonstrating Successful Care in the Community* which describes all twenty-eight projects and looks in some detail at five of them.[54] The projects were small scale, covering only 857 clients between them. Two of the projects were each concerned with only three people.

In 1986 the government launched a second scheme under the title of 'Helping the Community to Care'. There is a strong element of self help in the programme. In October 1986, the Secretary of State for Health announced the setting up of a project in which ten voluntary agencies would be responsible for self-help family centres. Playgroups, mother and toddler groups and the teaching of parenting skills to families at risk would all feature in the family centres, but a subsidiary aim would be to explore different models of self help.

However, most community care schemes have developed quite independently of central government initiatives. Some schemes have been consumer-led; others have been initiated by local authority or health service managers or by local councillors; for others the impetus has come from social researchers; and still others have come about through joint action by social workers and their managers.

It would be impossible to describe all the schemes, and difficult to select a handful as representative of the rest. The most satisfactory approach is to try to identify features which are replicated in most of the schemes. These will be grouped under four heads: decentralisation, consumerism and participation, self help and joint action.

Decentralisation

Almost all schemes involve some element of decentralisation. For example, much publicity has been given to the patch or neighbourhood system of social work which entails a small integrated team of social workers dealing ideally with small communities of between 5,000 and 10,000 people.[55] In fact, many of those authorities operating a patch system have much bigger areas. The average population served by a social work team in East Sussex, for example, is 16,000, but varying from 4,000 to 25,000.[56] Islington operates a decentralised system based on neighbourhoods with populations between 10,000 and 20,000.[57] The notion of neighbourhood social work received something of a boost from the Barclay report of 1982 which endorsed the patch system and community social work as a possible way forward and recommended the 'development of flexible decentralised patterns of organisation'.[58]

Many commentators share the Barclay report's view that decentralisation is crucial to any plans for community care. The Audit Commission, the King's Fund Institute, Hadley, Hatch and Willmott are among those supporting this view.[59] Nevertheless, decentralisation is not without its problems. Glennerster, for example, while supporting the general aims of decentralisation, warns of the dangers of damaging inter-agency co-ordination and planning; he is particularly concerned about links with health services and the fate of specialist teams concerned with mental handicap, mental illness and geriatric assessment.[60] There is also the danger of spreading resources too thinly and separating teams from local authority power structures.[61]

Challis draws a distinction between geographical decentralisation and resource decentralisation where 'decisions over the precise allocation of resources are formally pushed to a lower level than is usual, at times to the individual field worker, to ensure more appropriate allocation of resources'.[62]

Resource decentralisation is practised in the Kent Community Care Scheme which attempts to provide care at home for frail elderly people as a means of avoiding institutional care. Social workers design co-ordinated packages of care for individually assessed elderly people. This scheme, which has now spread to other areas, obviously influenced the Griffiths proposals.[63]

Consumerism and participation

Decentralisation is often regarded as a prerequisite of participation and the effective expression of consumer views. Cambridge and Knapp make very clear the relationship of consumerism to community care:

In the 1980s we have seen greater emphasis than heretofore on the voice of the consumer. Consumerism has been enshrined in most recent government statements about community care . . . Consumerism is now more likely to play a part in individual programme planning and case management. It is clear that consumerism – including self-advocacy and citizen-advocacy – is going to be an important component of community care in the future.[64]

If consumerism is to be as important as this suggests, then the definition of consumer needs to be wide: it must include the 'hidden consumers' who do not have much contact with social services departments, and it needs to include both clients and their carers.

Beresford identifies three models or approaches to hearing the voice of the consumer. The first is the market research model in which clients and potential clients are asked what services they would find helpful and what they think is wrong with current provision and how they think it might be improved. The second model is the consumerist approach which Beresford claims has emerged in response to the expansion of commercial provision. It implies a less passive consumer than the market research model with the emphasis on market preferences and consumers' rights. The third model – the democratic – is much the most difficult to achieve: it is also the most radical, resting as it does on the direct involvement of clients in the planning, management and provision of services. Democratic consumerism is what used to be called participation before the term consumerism became fashionable.[65]

A great deal depends upon how successfully all sections of the community can be persuaded to participate. To date, there has always been a middle class bias in participation in formal organisations. Much more attention needs to be paid to examining how poor and disadvantaged people might be enabled to participate, and particular efforts should be made to find out if there are any factors inhibiting participation by Afro-Caribbean and Asian members of the community.[66] We know that black elderly people, for example, have very little contact with formal social services but we know far too little about the reasons for this.

There are also problems in securing participation for people with mental disorder and for people in institutions. The full implementation of the substance and spirit of the Wagner Committee's proposals might go some way towards giving people in institutions a greater say.[67]

Information is of central importance in a consumer-oriented service. Providers must be fully informed of consumers' needs and consumers must be fully informed of the services available and the options open to them. All information must, of course, be made available in several languages.

It must not be assumed that everyone wishes to participate –

'active citizenship' (to use one of the Conservative Party's catch-phrases) is not for everyone. Many people wish to be left alone to get on with their own lives and they must be allowed to do so, and there must also be opportunities for different degrees and different kinds of involvement. One particular kind of involvement is self help.

Self help

Many community care schemes have elements of self help built into them. The Audit Commission makes the following comment:

The change to a community-based service . . . involves much more than a change to the pattern of service provision. It involves a change of approach, with emphasis and priority placed on encouraging patients and clients to do as much for themselves as possible. . . .[68]

Self help, one of the fastest growing areas of the voluntary sector in recent decades, fits in well with Conservative Party notions of self reliance, individual responsibility and active citizenship. Self help is undoubtedly double-edged. On the one hand, it has the following merits:

1. It may be seen as a challenge to the dominance of bureaucrats and professionals characteristic of both statutory agencies and the more traditional voluntary organisations.
2. It enables groups to identify their own needs and to do something about meeting them.
3. It has the potential for achieving change through political militancy (see, for example, the women's movement, the civil rights movement and consumer groups).
4. It enables people to develop new skills which may enhance confidence and self esteem.

On the other hand, while self help by its very nature is participatory, it has a strong middle class bias. Finch, in a study of preschool playgroups, found that for working class women self help was illusory, because taking turns in looking after other people's children did not fit in with their life styles or with their aspirations. Finch argues that the setting up and running of self help groups is essentially a middle class activity, and she concludes that the promotion of self help is deceitful for three reasons:

First, encouraging the women to run their own preschool facilities rather than seek an extension of statutory resources is deceitful because it promotes a form of provision which such women cannot supply for themselves. Second, the idea of self help obscures the fact that what is being sought are facilities on the cheap, incorporating the unpaid labour of mothers themselves . . . Third, as a form of preschool provision, playgroups make no contribution whatsoever to the needs of parents in paid work, since they both assume and encourage full-time mothering.[69]

Self help, if it can overcome its middle class bias, has considerable potential, but government support for the principle is conditional upon self help groups not threatening the *status quo*. Self help groups may also be used as an excuse for lack of government support, and a general philosophy of self help may lead to deprived people being blamed for their plight.

Joint action

Joint consultative committees and joint care planning teams have been in place since the 1974 reorganisation of the NHS, but joint finance of community care projects on any significant scale dates from 1976. The recent drive towards community care has increased the need for joint planning and joint action, as the Griffiths report stresses:

The proposals mean that joint local planning and action will continue to be essential, but that responsibilities and accountability for the plans and action will be clearer than they are now . . . it must be emphasised that effective co-operation at the local level will be essential, both to the success of individual projects and, more broadly, if the whole range of community care services is to be delivered effectively.[70]

Some research carried out by the Centre for Research in Social Policy at Loughborough University (in collaboration with the Centre for Health Economics at the University of York) has produced some interesting material on joint action. The research was concerned to examine joint finance and joint planning following the restructuring of the NHS in 1982 and the 'community care circular' of 1983.

Five sites were chosen for detailed case studies, but the Loughborough team also undertook a number of issue-based studies to assess the effectiveness of inter-agency collaboration. Among the issues examined were: the success of joint planning in involving a wide range of agencies and personnel; the comprehensiveness and coherence of the joint arrangements and their effectiveness in securing particular outputs; the efforts made to devise systematic procedures for the control, appraisal, selection and monitoring of joint finance schemes. It was hoped to establish what factors were associated with good practice in collaboration.

The results of the survey indicated a number of problems and shortcomings in joint planning and finance, and these will have to receive some attention if the new community care scheme is to succeed.[71]

The achievement of what the Audit Commission calls 'locally integrated community care' depends upon the successful interweaving of statutory, voluntary and informal services.[72] In describing the Dinnington project, Bayley and Tennant say that 'the main aim was to interweave the help and resources of the formal health and welfare services with the informal support and help and services given by family, friends and neighbours, together with the contribution of the voluntary sector'.[73] Judging from its White Paper, the government would be unhappy with Bayley and Tennant's failure to consider the interweaving of commercial services.

If social workers become case managers, as is suggested in both the Griffiths report and the White Paper, then they will assume responsibility for interweaving services at fieldwork level. They will be devising packages of care which draw upon a variety of sources of support.

CONCLUSIONS

When the provisions of the NHS and Community Care Act are fully implemented in 1991 local authority social services departments will be changed out of all recognition.

The government has so far been equivocal about the resources to be made available, but it is significant that the Griffiths proposal for a specific grant has been rejected, except in the case of the mentally ill. If there are insufficient resources, the changes will result in more commercial provision, greater use of charges and greater reliance on informal carers. Wicks maintains that the costs of community care 'tend to lie where they fall – on the family concerned and, in particular, on the female carer within the family'. This tendency is further emphasised by 'a conscious attempt to shift costs from the governmental to the private, family sector'.[74]

Even before the community care changes, the resources of local authority social services departments are stretched to their limit. At the end of 1988 there were 2,200 social work vacancies, the position being most serious in the inner cities.[75] In London alone there are 600 children at risk who are unsupervised because of staff shortages, and there are over 4,000 vacancies in social services departments, including 700 social work posts. A report in October 1989 said that many people were leaving the social work profession: low morale, increased pressure and poor pay all contributed to this exodus. Many workers were also worried that the community care proposals would lead to de-skilling, partly because of the increased use of non-professional helpers and partly because care packages would concentrate on practical help with a lower value being placed on the less quantifiable aspects of social work support.[76]

Increased pressure on social services departments arises from a greater number of child abuse referrals, higher levels of unemployment since 1979, higher levels of crime, policies of de-institutionalisation and demographic factors. The House of Commons Social Services Committee estimates that expenditure on the personal social services needs to increase by 2 per cent a year in real terms simply to keep pace with rising demand.

Over the period from 1980/81 to 1984/85 net expenditure (gross expenditure less money recouped from charges) on the personal social services increased by 2 per cent less than was required to meet increased demand, and gross expenditure increased by 3 per cent less than was required. Between 1980/81 and 1985/86 almost two-thirds of local authorities fell short of the target increases of 2 per cent a year, and the most recent expenditure plans indicate that between 1988/89 and 1990/91 real expenditure on the personal social services will fall by 0.7 per cent.[77] Presumably, the amount for 1991/92 will have to be increased since the new community care plans come into effect in April 1991.

In March 1990 a report from the Association of Directors of Social Services claimed that 36 per cent of local authority social services departments had had to cut services, stop new projects or impose charges as a result of pressure to keep the poll tax down. The report estimated that 75 per cent of local authorities would have insufficient resources to implement the government's community care proposals.

These figures give cause for considerable concern: they raise doubts about the genuineness of the government's stated intention of improving community care. The myth that community care is cheaper than institutional care has long since been dispensed with, but this may not necessarily deter the government from seeing the impending changes as an opportunity to cut costs.

In spite of government protestations to the contrary, privatisation lies at the heart of the proposals: commercial and voluntary sector provision will be expanded, local authority provision will contract and informal carers will be expected to carry a bigger load.

The government decided against the enforcement of competitive tendering in the domiciliary services, but this was largely because of the undeveloped state of private and voluntary agencies in this area. However, the government expects local authorities to encourage independent suppliers and make 'wider use of service specifications, agency agreements and contracts.'[78] It also intends to monitor local authorities' progress in fostering provision by private companies and voluntary agencies.

This will be achieved through the annually updated three-year community care plans which local authorities are required to produce for the Secretary of State's approval. The White Paper says:

Social services authorities will be expected to make clear in their community care plans what steps they will be taking to make increased use of non-statutory service providers or, where such providers are not currently available, how they propose to stimulate such activity. In particular, they should consider how they will encourage diversification into the non-residential care sector.[79]

The Secretary of State can insist upon changes to any plans that do not make sufficient use of independent suppliers. It seems probable that compulsory competitive tendering will be introduced, once voluntary and commercial suppliers of domiciliary services are in a stronger position.

The chairperson of the UK Homecare Association has claimed that, because the profit margins in the domiciliary services are relatively small, there is a danger of corner-cutting and slipping standards.[80] Nevertheless, companies trading in domiciliary care are now beginning to multiply – some from a base in the residential sector. Companies such as Home Care and Nursing Services, Care Concern and Care Services provide home helps, nursing auxiliaries and care attendants, meals cooked in the home and home nursing for the terminally ill. Crossroads Care, a voluntary, non-profit organisation reaches 12,000 families, and provides each year more than one million care hours in the home for physically disabled and mentally handicapped people.[81]

However, not all voluntary associations are in agreement with The White Paper's recommendation that greater reliance should be placed upon the independent sector. The Spastics Society, for example, has said of this proposal: 'We are deeply concerned about any assumptions that the public provision of care for disabled people can be in the main shifted to the private and not-for-profit sector without serious consequences for disabled people.'[82]

As far as informal carers are concerned, the evidence that families may be unable to take on extra responsibilities, and the less certain evidence that elderly people may prefer care by professionals, with help and support from the family, rather than entirely by kin, are conveniently ignored. The exploitation of informal carers – especially women – does not appear to enter into the calculations.

It would be untrue to say that there is no evidence to support the government's proposals. There have been many demonstration projects, but most of these have been on a very small scale. As the King's Fund Institute observes:

The challenge is achieving the spread of those good services. Currently they tend to be small scale, geographically isolated and add-ons to mainstream provision. Future policy at both national and local levels needs to be directed towards integrating such schemes into mainstream service provision across the country without sacrificing quality of care.[83]

It should be noted, too, that most of the experimental schemes have not included commercial enterprises.

The new community care arrangements are consistent with the Conservative government's general policy aims in that they have privatisation as one of their major objectives. However, the Thatcher government's antipathy towards local government is less clearly seen in the personal social services than it is in either education or housing. Local authorities are to be given the leading role in the organisation of community care, but the decision to give them this responsibility was taken with the greatest possible reluctance and only after every other possibility had been explored.

Furthermore, as already noted, there will be extensive central control of local authorities who will be expected to surrender some of their responsibility for direct provision of services. Although there will always be a need for residential care and some people will always prefer it, community care does have a potential for service improvement. However, a policy of community care has to be based on hard reality, not on romantic notions of the caring community nor on an ideology favouring charges and commercial provision.

The interweaving of statutory, voluntary and informal care may be a way forward, but there is no alternative to social services departments remaining the main providers. It must also be remembered that the voluntary sector has an important role as critic and that this may be impeded by interweaving.

If, however, local authorities are going to continue to be responsible for personal social services, then they need to look at alternative methods of service organisation and delivery. In particular, more research is needed to ascertain how the voice of the consumer may best be heard.

NOTES

1. Home Office, *Report of the Committee on Local Authority and Allied Personal Social Services*, Cmnd 3703 (Seebohm Report), London: HMSO, 1968.
2. See P. Parsloe, *Social Services Area Teams*, London: Allen and Unwin, 1981; O. Stevenson, *Specialisation in Social Services Teams*, London: Allen and Unwin, 1981.
3. London Borough of Brent, *Report of Public Inquiry into the Death of Jasmine Beckford*, 1985; London Borough of Lambeth, *Whose Child? Report of Public Inquiry into the Death of Tyra Henry*, 1987; London Borough of Greenwich, *A Child in Mind: Protection of Children in a Responsible Society*, Report of Public Inquiry into the Death of Kimberley Carlile, 1987.
4. Department of Health, *Caring for People*, Cm 849, London: HMSO, 1989.
5. P. Abrams, 'Community care: Some research problems and priorities', *Policy and Politics*, no. 6, 1977, pp. 125–51.
6. A. Walker (ed.), *Community Care*, Oxford: Blackwell, 1982, p. 4.
7. Social Services Committee, *Community Care with Special Reference to Adult Mentally Ill and Mentally Handicapped People*, HC 13–1, London: HMSO, 1985; Audit Commission, *Making a Reality of Community Care*, London: HMSO, 1986; King's Fund Institute, *Promoting*

Innovation in Community Care, Briefing Paper no. 3, London: King's Fund Institute, 1987; R. Griffiths, *Community Care: Agenda for Action*, London: HMSO, 1988.

8. R. Griffiths, *op. cit.*, p. iv.
9. King's Fund Institute, *op. cit.*, p. 4.
10. Audit Commission, *op. cit.*, p. 4.
11. R. Griffiths, *op. cit.*, p. iii.
12. *Ibid.*, p. 5.
13. Department of Health, *op. cit.*
14. R. Griffiths, *op. cit.*, p. vii.
15. *Ibid.*, p. 15.
16. Department of Health, *op. cit.*
17. D. R. Phillips, J. Vincent and S. Blacksell, *Home from Home*, Sheffield: Joint Unit for Social Services Research and Community Care, 1988.
18. *Ibid.*, p. 7.
19. Source: Audit Commission, *op. cit.*, p. 111.
20. H. Harman and S. Harman, *No Place Like Home*, London: NALGO, 1989.
21. Centre for Policy on Ageing, *Home Life: A Code of Practice for Residential Care*, London: CPA, 1984.
22. M. Hunt, *The Cost of Caring*, Batley: West Yorkshire Low Pay Unit, 1989.
23. *The Guardian*, 18 October 1989.
24. Department of Health, *op. cit.*, p. 22.
25. *Ibid.*, p. 25.
26. J. Wolfenden, *The Future of Voluntary Organisations*, London: Croom Helm, 1978.
27. S. Hatch and I. Mocroft, *Components of Welfare*, London: Bedford Square Press, 1983, p. 2.
28. Department of Health and Social Security, *Growing Older*, Cmnd 8173, London: HMSO, p. 3.
29. C. Phillipson, *Planning for Community Care: Facts and Fallacies in the Griffiths Report*, University of Keele: Centre for Social Gerontology, 1988, p. 4.
30. M. Bulmer, *The Social Basis of Community Care*, London: Allen and Unwin, 1987, p. 72.
31. Central Statistical office, *Social Trends*, no. 19, London: HMSO, 1989.
32. Office of Population Censuses and Surveys, *The Prevalence of Disability Among Adults*, London: HMSO, 1988.
33. Central Statistical Office, *Social Trends*, no. 19, London: HMSO, 1989.
34. J. Finch and D. Groves, 'Community care and the family; A case for equal opportunities?', *Journal of Social Policy*, vol. 9, pt. 4, 1980.

35. C. Phillipson, *op. cit.*, p. 6.
36. P. West, R. Illsley and K. Kelman, 'Public preference for the care of dependency groups', *Social Science and Medicine*, vol. 18. no. 4, 1984, pp. 287–95. Cited by C. Phillipson, *op. cit.*
37. C. Phillipson, *op. cit.*, p. 8.
38. G. Allan, *Family Life*, Oxford: Blackwell, 1985, p. 137.
39. See P. Willmott, *Social Networks, Informal Care and Public Policy*, London: Policy Studies Institute, 1986.
40. R. Griffiths, *op. cit.*, p. 26.
41. Department of Health, *op. cit.*, p. 24.
42. D. Billis and M. Harris, *An Extended Role for the Voluntary Sector*, PORTVAC Working Paper 3, London: Brunel University, 1986.
43. D. Leat, *Voluntary Organisations and Accountability: Theory and Practice*, Coventry: University of Warwick, 1987.
44. *Ibid.*, p. 43.
45. S. Hatch and I. Mocroft, 'Factors affecting the location of voluntary organisation branches', *Policy and Politics*, vol. 6, no. 2, 1977, p. 166.
46. M. Brenton, *The Voluntary Sector in British Social Services*, London: Longman, 1985, p. 79.
47. *Ibid.*, p. 197.
48. Department of Health, *op. cit.*, p. 6.
49. P. Beresford and S. Croft, 'Welfare pluralism: The new face of Fabianism', *Critical Social Policy*, no. 9, 1984, p. 25.
50. D. Leat and P. Gay, *Paying for Care*, London: Policy Studies Institute, 1987, p. 1.
51. *Ibid.*, p. 15.
52. *Ibid.*, p. 52.
53. Department of Health and Social Security, *Health Service Development: Care in the Community and Social Finance*, Circular HC (83) 6/LAC (83) 5, London: DHSS, 1983.
54. P. Cambridge and M. Knapp (eds.), *Demonstrating Successful Care in the Community*, Canterbury: Personal Social Services Research Unit, 1988.
55. See R. Hadley and M. Mcgrath, *Going Local: Neighbourhood Social Services*, London: Bedford Square Press, 1980.
56. K. Young, 'The East Sussex approach', in S. Hatch (ed.), *Decentralisation and Care in the Community*, London: Policy Studies Institute, 1985, pp. 7–19.
57. J. R. Price. 'Decentralisation in Islington', in S. Hatch (ed.), *op. cit.*, pp. 20–24.
58. P. Barclay, *Social Workers: Their Role and Tasks*, London: Bedford Square Press, 1982, p. 197.
59. All *op. cit.*

60. H. Glennerster, 'Decentralisation and inter-service planning', in S. Hatch (ed.), *op. cit*, pp. 55–7.
61. A. Jones, 'Postscript', in S. Hatch (ed.), *op. cit.*, pp. 64–8.
62. D. Challis, 'The community care scheme: An alternative approach to decentralisation', in S. Hatch (ed.), *op. cit.*, p. 40.
63. D. Challis and B. Davies, *Case Management in Community Care*, Aldershot: Gower, 1986.
64. P. Cambridge and M. Knapp, *op. cit.*, p. 5.
65. P. Beresford, 'Consumer views: Data collection or democracy?', in I. Allen (ed.), *Hearing the Voice of the Consumer*, London: Policy Studies Institute, 1988, pp. 37–51.
66. See R. Bhaduri, 'Race and culture: The "invisible" consumers', in I. Allen (ed.), *op. cit.*, pp. 21–7.
67. G. Wagner, *A Positive Choice*, London: HMSO, 1988.
68. Audit Commission, *op. cit.*, p. 11.
69. J. Finch, 'The deceit of self-help: Preschool playgroups and working class mothers', *Journal of Social Policy*, vol. 13, pt. 1, 1984.
70. R. Griffiths, *op. cit.*, p. 16.
71. B. Hardy *et al.*, *Collaboration and Cost-Effectiveness: Final Report*, Loughborough: Centre for Research in Social Policy, 1989.
72. Audit Commission, *op. cit.*, p. 70.
73. M. Bayley and A. Tennant, 'Straight across: Inter-service collaboration in Dinnington', in S. Hatch (ed.), *op. cit.*, pp. 25–39.
74. N. Deakin and M. Wicks, *Families and the State*, London: Family Policy Studies Centre, 1988, p. 30.
75. Source: Report from the Association of Directors of Social Services and the Local Authority Conditions of Service Advisory Board, 1989.
76. B. Hearn, *Community Care*, 12 October 1989.
77. Social Services Committee, *Public Expenditure on the Social Services*, Fourth Report, 1985/86, HC 387–3, and Sixth report, 1987/88, HC 687.
78. Department of Health, *op. cit.*, p. 23.
79. *Ibid.*
80. *The Guardian*, 17 November 1989.
81. *Ibid.*
82. *Ibid.*
83. King's Fund Institute, *op. cit.*, p. 6.

CHAPTER 8

CONCLUSION: THE THATCHER LEGACY

Before the election campaign of 1987 began, the Labour Party claimed that the government had run out of ideas. This may have been no more than wishful thinking, and during the campaign the Conservative Party managed to project itself as the most radical of the contenders for office.

During her third term Mrs Thatcher became the longest serving Prime Minister this century, and she has had, therefore, an unparalleled opportunity to change British society. No-one could complain that the government has not been an active one. The number of Acts, statutory instruments, White and Green Papers, consultative documents, guidelines and codes of practice gives the impression of intense activity, and each period of office has been marked by major pieces of legislation affecting health and social services, and by Acts which have brought about the denationalisation of important sectors of industry.

Frantic activity, however, does not of itself produce change. There also has to be a clear purpose and a degree of co-ordination to ensure coherence. Furthermore, legislation frequently fails to achieve its objectives and it may have unintended consequences.

The aim of this chapter is to assess the achievements of the Conservatives' years in office. In evaluating the government's achievements reference will be made to the policy objectives identified in Chapter 1: privatisation, curbing local government and promoting inequality.

PRIVATISATION

In Chapter 2 the point was made that privatisation can mean reduced government provision, reduced government finance and reduced government regulation, and that reduced government provision and finance usually means the transfer of responsibilities to non-statutory agencies. Easily the most common meaning attributed to privatisation, however, is the sale of public assets. In this the government has had a measure of success in that twenty-three separate sales have gone ahead, and most of them have been greatly over-subscribed. Even water privatisation, which every opinion poll showed to be a deeply unpopular measure, was almost six times over-subscribed.

Thus, popular capitalism has been extended: in 1980 there were just over three million shareholders but by the end of 1989 the number had risen to just under twelve million. But there is no evidence to suggest that those buying shares in privatised industries have then gone on to buy other shares, and the Conservatives' boast of a share-owning democracy does not stand up to serious examination. *The General Household Survey* for 1987 reveals that the typical investor in privatisations is male, middle-aged, professional and lives in the South-east. More than a third of all shareholders had investments solely in privatised companies. The North had the lowest percentage of share-owners and shareholding among women, manual workers and young people was low.[1]

Privatisation is always preceded by extensive television and newspaper advertising; in the most recent privatisations, about £42 million was spent on advertising the water sell off and the estimated cost of promoting the sale of the electricity industry was over £100 million. Nor are these the only costs involved, since fees also have to be paid to the city: £330 million in the case of water and £824 million in the case of electricity. Investors have frequently been offered special inducements, but the biggest inducement of all has been the under-pricing of many of the issues and the chance of an immediate profit.

The privatisation programme has also had its failures. The BP flotation in 1987 coincided with a stock market collapse, so that when the shares started trading they stood at 88p – well below the partly paid offer price of 120p – and investors stood to lose heavily. In the end the Chancellor and the Bank of England came up with a 70p a share safety net.

The electricity privatisation also ran into difficulties over nuclear power stations. For two years critics argued that nuclear power stations should not be included in the sale, but the government remained adamant. In November 1989, however, the government reversed its decision because the banks and financial institutions refused to carry the huge financial risk of de-commissioning nuclear power stations. The government's embarrassment was increased when Lord Marshall, chairman of National Power, resigned because of the climbdown.

Almost at the same time there was an investigation into the circumstances surrounding the sale of Rover to British Aerospace. The House of Commons Public Accounts Committee, the Trade and Industry Committee and the European Commission all expressed grave concern over the payment of 'sweeteners' to British Aerospace to make purchase of the Rover Company a more attractive proposition.

The other major sale of public assets has been the sale of council houses, and there can be little doubt that the sale of individual houses to tenants has, from the government's point of view, been a success. Between 1980 and the end of 1987 about 1.1 million houses were sold. However, high interest rates in 1989 and 1990 brought about a sharp reduction in sales, and some of those who had already bought their houses found themselves in financial difficulty.

The sale of the remaining rented houses to private or housing association landlords has been less successful. The 1988 Housing Act was heralded as promoting 'tenants' choice': the government assumed that there was widespread dissatisfaction with local authorities as landlords and that tenants would apply in large numbers to transfer to an alternative landlord. This simply has not happened. Nearly all transfers have taken place on the initiative either of prospective landlords or of mainly Conservative local authorities. Clearly, the sale of council houses either as rented accommodation or into owner occupation increases private provision and finance and reduces the role of the public sector.

After housing, the service in which privatisation has made the most progress is the NHS, inroads have been made on several interrelated fronts. Robin Cook, Labour's health spokesperson, charged the government with being 'concerned less with the quality of health care than with widening the role of the market in its provision – by increased competition, by more commercial medicine and by larger public subsidy of private medicine'.[2] This is obviously a partisan statement, but there is corroborating evidence.

Charges, for example, have been increased beyond the rate of inflation under the Conservatives. One of the purposes of health service charges is to transfer a proportion of the cost of treatment to the patient. The charges for prescriptions have seen the sharpest rise – an increase of no less than 1,425 per cent between 1979 and 1990. Indeed, for about half of the prescriptions the charge exceeds the drug's cost, and people are now finding it cheaper to buy the simpler remedies over the pharmacist's counter. Dental charges have also increased, the supply of spectacles has been entirely privatised, and new charges for dental checks and eyesight tests have been introduced. Charges in the NHS have the effect of making private health care relatively more attractive.

There has also been an increase in private practice within the NHS and the private sector itself has expanded considerably. The evidence for this assertion is to be found in Chapter 4 which indicates that, although the greatest growth in private provision has occurred in outpatient services and in hospital and nursing-home facilities, the private market is now moving into primary health care. These developments have been helped by a doubling in the number of people covered by private health care insurance between 1979 and 1988. It is instructive to note that 24 per cent of professional workers and 22 per cent of employers and managers were covered by private insurance in 1986, as compared with 1 per cent of unskilled workers, 2 per cent of the semi-skilled and 3 per cent of skilled manual workers.[3]

Contracting out has also become a more prominent feature of the NHS under the Conservatives. This takes two forms: the contracting out of clinical work to private hospitals and competitive tendering for the provision of non-medical services such as cleaning, catering and laundry services. Competitive tendering in the NHS actually declined between 1980 and 1983 when it became mandatory. After two years of compulsory competitive tendering in-house providers had won 57 per cent of all contracts, and by 1988 this proportion had risen to 85 per cent.[4]

The implementation of the National Health Service Act will give further encouragement to the private sector since private health care companies will be able to bid for District Health Authority contracts, and for the provision of clinical services to the patients of

GPs who are managing their own budgets. The Act will also facilitate the further development of internal markets with competition between suppliers and opted-out hospitals acting as independent contractors.

Competition among state-financed institutions has also been heightened in other services. In education, for example, schools are expected to compete with one another in a system of open enrolment and universities and polytechnics are required to engage in competitive bidding for students.

The community care proposals also involve a form of internal market with social workers devising packages of care for clients, drawing upon commercial and non-profit suppliers. It is plain that the government sees the re-organisation of community care as an opportunity to develop the role of the market in domiciliary care to complement its dominance in residential care. The personal social services provide a good example of a transfer of responsibility for provision from the state to the commercial, voluntary and informal sectors.

In a number of instances the government has 'fixed the odds' in favour of private provision. One example of this is the discounts offered to tenants purchasing local authority houses: these were altered in 1984 when sales showed signs of flagging and they were increased on flats in 1986 because few buyers could be found for flats. Increased rents has also tipped the balance in favour of purchase, although this has been more than outweighed, at least in the short term, by increased interest rates. A second example concerns private pensions. The government offered a 5-year subsidy to people moving from the state earnings-related pension scheme to take out a private pension. The state scheme was also made less attractive by reducing the benefits available.

Responsibility for provision may change without corresponding changes in the source of finance. This is what is planned in the community care services, with local authorities losing some of their responsibility for provision but retaining responsibility for the allocation of resources. The effect is similar when a District Health Authority pays a private hospital to perform operations on NHS patients. Another instance in which the government subsidises private concerns occurs in the area of industrial training. In both the Youth Training Scheme and Employment Training the government pays private training organisations to provide programmes.

On the other hand the sale of local authority housing estates to private developers or private landlords involves a change of provision *and* finance. When schools opt out of local authority control (provision) responsibility for their finance switches to central government.

The privatisation of finance occurs when the government reduces subsidies or increases charges. Local authority housing provides an example of the former and we have already looked at the role of charges in the NHS. There are two particularly interesting examples of government reliance on private finance for some of its policies. The first example is the government's emphasis on private investment in its inner city programmes in which private funds are seen as a preferred alternative to public finance. The second example concerns the financing of the City Technology Colleges, and the government's expectation that 80 per cent of this funding would come from private industry. There was, however, disappointment for the government on both counts: investment by industry in the inner cities has remained relatively small, and only 20 per cent of the funds for the first City Technology Colleges came from non-government sources.

A reduction of government regulation is another form of privatisation. The government's record in this respect is a mixed one. There has been considerable deregulation in the economic, financial and industrial spheres and deregulation of the private rented sector in housing, but in spite of its frequently articulated preference for a non-interventionist state, the Conservative government has used its years in office to increase central government power and control. Every chapter of this book contains examples of greater government intervention: in social security, health, education, housing and the personal social services. The increased regulation of the poor and unemployed in the social security system and in the sphere of training has been particularly marked.

What is sometimes not appreciated is that privatisation of provision and finance requires extra regulation. No government can simply hand over services for vulnerable groups to a completely unregulated private sector, because the political repercussions of any abuse might be too serious and the reputation of private market provision might be damaged.

Gamble explains the increased intervention in a different way. He argues that the twin objectives of the Conservative governments of the 1980s have been the creation of a free economy and a strong state. Intervention arises from attempts to restore the authority of the state and secure the compliance of other agencies and interests. Gamble writes:

The problem for the Thatcher Government is that its own diagnosis of the crisis of state authority constantly impelled it towards intervention – whether in the internal affairs of trade unions, the spending priorities of local authorities, the curricula of schools and universities, or the patterns of family behaviour.[5]

This brings us to the final point in this section: the relationship between authority, the market and rights. King, in an analysis similar to that of Gamble, argues that the New Right theories adopted by the Conservative government under Mrs Thatcher consist of two conflicting elements: a liberal element which emphasises freedom from state control, individualism and free markets and a conservative element which emphasises authority and order and the use of government to achieve these.[6]

King argues that these two elements have combined in an attack upon the citizenship rights enshrined in the welfare state. Gamble advances the same argument when he identifies the Conservative challenge to the social democratic concept of citizenship as an attempt to block the extension of equal civil, political and social rights to all citizens. He argues that a central aim of Conservatism has been 'to discredit the social democratic concept of universal citizenship rights, guaranteed and enforced through public agencies, and to replace it with a concept of citizenship rights achieved through property ownership and participation in markets'.[7]

The notion among Conservatives that citizenship is based upon participation in free markets can be connected with consumption-sector theory, which claims that the main cleavages in British society, cutting across class divisions, are based upon consumption patterns. Of particular significance is the distinction between those who obtain goods and services through the private market and those who are forced to rely upon publicly-provided services. The split between the private and public sectors extends beyond consumption into employment, so that the use of private services and employment in the private sector are perceived as status enhancing, while the consumption of public sector goods and services and public-sector employment are perceived as stigmatising.[8] Defining citizenship in terms of market participation is therefore one aspect of the Conservative government's aim of promoting inequality.

THE PROMOTION OF INEQUALITY

Income and wealth

The Conservatives have reversed the trends established in the 1970s of a narrowing of both income and wealth distribution. Between 1973 and 1979 all but one of the five most highly paid occupational groups experienced a fall in their real incomes: members of the most highly paid occupational group of all (professional, management, administration) saw their incomes fall by 5 per cent in real terms. The five lowest paid occupational groups all experienced rises of income in real terms ranging from 2 to 7 per cent. Between 1979 and 1987 the median gross weekly earnings of the lowest decile of male manual workers increased by 92 per cent in cash terms, as compared with the highest paid non-manual decile whose incomes increased by 150 per cent. Among women, the median increases for the lowest decile of manual workers was 97 per cent and for the highest non-manual decile it was 143 per cent.[9]

A Labour Research Department survey of fifty-two large UK companies in 1988 found that in only twelve of them had the percentage pay increases awarded to the lowest paid workers exceeded those awarded to the highest paid director. The Chairman of British Airways, for example, had received a pay increase of 117 per cent compared with the 6 per cent awarded to the company's lowest paid workers. In nine other companies the top director had received an increase of 30 per cent or more.[10]

Under the Conservatives, then, pay differentials have widened. Dominic Byrne comments:

it is in the period since 1979 that the growth in pay inequality has been most dramatic. Over that period the proportion of the British work-force falling below the Council of Europe's minimum 'decency threshold' for wages increased from 36 per cent to 42.3 per cent . . . Around 8.8 million workers earned less, excluding overtime, than the Council of Europe level.[11]

Byrne argues that the greater disparities in income result from a combination of a *laissez faire* approach to the wages of the more highly paid and a deliberate policy of 'driving down the wages of the lower paid'. Policies aimed at reducing the wages of the lower paid have included:

1. The curtailment of employment rights.
2. The weakening of the trade unions.
3. The use of the New Workers' Scheme (discontinued in 1989) which subsidised employers who agreed to take on young workers at low rates of pay and the similar effect of the Jobstart Scheme for the long term unemployed.
4. The prohibition of fair wages clauses in contracts awarded by public bodies to outside companies.
5. Reducing the protection offered by wages councils.[12]

Those dependent on state benefits have fared particularly badly during the 1980s, eligibility conditions having been made more stringent and the rates of many of the benefits having been cut. The House of Commons Social Services Committee has reported on the operation of the first twelve months of the new social security system. It calculated that single people had lost up to £8.84 a week and that single parents, childless couples and elderly people had lost substantially.[13] A study published by the National Association of Citizens' Advice Bureaux revealed that 80 per cent of the claimants seen by the bureaux were worse off as a consequence of the new system.[14]

The Social Services Committee said that couples with children had gained marginally. However, this conclusion was based solely on a comparison of income support levels with supplementary benefit rates. When other changes are taken into account couples with children are also seen to be considerably worse off. Particularly significant to families with children has been the loss of single payments and their replacement by loans. It is alarming that families with children who accept a social fund loan have to try to make ends meet on 85 per cent of their normal income support entitlement. Furthermore, all families on income support have to pay 20 per cent of the community charge and the whole of their water charges, and although the rates of income support include an allowance to cover the community charge payment, it is quite insufficient to compensate for the extra expenditure. Housing benefit has also been drastically cut: many claimants have lost entitlement altogether and the majority of those still in receipt of benefit are worse off.[15]

Families have also suffered as a consequence of the freezing of child benefit for three years in succession and the greater emphasis being placed upon means-tested family credit. This can be seen as one example of a greater reliance on means tests throughout the whole of the social security system.

Between 1979/80 and 1988/89 the number of people in receipt of supplementary benefit/income support increased from just under 3 million to 4.9 million. As a proportion of average earnings, the value of the benefit has declined steadily since 1979. Supplementary benefit for a couple with two children aged 6 and 8 was equivalent to 51.1 per cent of average weekly earnings in April 1979. In April 1987 supplementary benefit for the same family equalled 43 per cent of average earnings, and in April 1988 the level of income support available to this family amounted to only 37.3 per cent of earnings.[16]

Research conducted by a team at Bristol University asked a sample of the population in London what weekly income they thought was necessary to stay out of poverty. The incomes thought to be needed exceeded the amounts available under the social security system by 61 per cent. A separate survey by the same group identified a 'threshold income' below wh. multiple deprivation commonly occurred. The threshold for childless couples under pensionable age was 57 per cent above income support levels. For couples with children the threshold income was 151 per cent of income support payments, and for single parents severe deprivation occurred when levels of income fell below 168 per cent of the amounts available from income support.[17]

Over the last ten years the gap between benefits and wages has widened and the new social security system has served only to heighten the disparity. It is not surprising, therefore, to find multiple deprivation among benefit recipients – deprivation in terms of health, education, housing, diet, clothing and participation in community activities. Bradshaw and Morgan demonstrate that children whose parents are in receipt of supplementary benefit suffer from deficiencies of iron and calcium and are below a basic clothing standard.[18]

The new benefit system, then, has considerably worsened the position of the poor and widened the gulf between those on benefit and those in receipt of wages. Income inequalities among those in emploment have been widened by inequitable wages policies, but even more important than wages policies as a means of promoting inequality have been changes in the tax system.

John Hills has produced an excellent guide to the workings of the fiscal system and most of the statistics quoted here are drawn from that source.[19] Hills points out that the government has failed in its stated aim of reducing the level of taxation. In its first three years in office tax revenues from all sources increased *as a proportion of national income*. Between 1982/83 and 1984/85 the level of taxation remained relatively stable. Between 1984/85 and 1988/89 the tax ratio fell very slightly, but in April 1989 it was still higher than it had been when the Conservatives took office.

What has happened is that the tax system has become less progressive, the changes having benefited those on high incomes who now surrender a smaller proportion of their earnings in the form of tax. Four sets of changes have contributed to this:

1. Income tax: the basic rate of tax has been reduced from 33 per cent to 25 per cent, the top rate of tax has been reduced from 83 per cent to 40 per cent and investment is now treated more favourably following the removal of the investment income surcharge. Since April 1990 married women have been taxed separately from their husbands, and Hills calculates that this benefits mainly those with high earnings or investment income. Several concessions have been introduced which allow the better off to avoid their full tax liability. Notable among these are the Business Expansion Scheme, personal equity plans and the halving of stamp duty on share transactions.
2. Value Added Tax (VAT) has been greatly increased. Although VAT is slightly progressive, it is less progressive than income tax. Thus, the policy followed by the Conservative government of reducing income tax and increasing VAT necessarily favours the better off.
3. National Insurance Contributions (a form of income tax) have been increased. The contributions are levied on earnings but not on investment income.
4. In 1989 in Scotland and in 1990 in England and Wales the wholly regressive community charge replaced the less regressive rates.

Hills sums up the combined effect of the tax and benefit changes since 1979:

There has been . . . a major redistribution from those on low incomes to the better off . . . Overall, the bottom 60% of the income distribution has lost, while the top 30% – especially the top 10% – has gained . . . The losses for the bottom 50% average out at nearly £8.50 per family . . . while the top 10% have gained nearly £40 per family . . . the bottom half of the population has lost £6.6 billion, of which £5.6 billion has gone to the top 10%; indeed £4.8 billion has gone to the top 5%.[20]

So much, then, for changes in the distribution of income. Table 8.1 indicates that the Conservatives have also virtually halted the trends of the 1970s in relation to wealth. In 1971 the most wealthy 1 per cent of the population owned 31 per cent of marketable wealth, but by 1979 this proportion had fallen to 22 per cent. Between 1979 and 1985 the proportion of wealth held by the most wealthy 1 per cent fell by only 2 per cent. The proportion of marketable wealth owned by the most wealthy 10 per cent of the population fell from 65 per cent in 1971 to 54 per cent in 1979, but there was no change at all between 1979 and 1985.

Changes in income distribution in favour of the rich and the more generous treatment of investment income have an effect upon capital accumulation and investment. To some extent this is what has been happening in Britain in the 1980s. Two other changes, however, have had a more direct impact upon the accumulation and retention of wealth by a small proportion of the population.

An inheritance tax has replaced the capital transfer tax. The level at which tax becomes payable has risen from £25,000 to £110,000 and the rates have been changed from an amount varying between 10 per cent and 75 per cent, to a single rate of 40 per cent. This clearly benefits those inheriting the largest sums. No tax is payable on any gifts made seven years before death, an exemption that did

Table 8.1 Distribution of wealth

United Kingdom			
Percentage of wealth owned by	1971	1979	1985
Most wealthy 1 per cent	31	22	20
Most wealthy 10 per cent	65	54	54
Most wealthy 25 per cent	86	77	76

Source: *Social Trends*, nos. 15 and 19, Central Statistical Office, HMSO.

not apply to capital transfer tax. Several concessions have also been made in relation to capital gains tax: the amount of gain allowed tax free has risen from £1,000 a year to £5,000 a year and this allowance now applies to all gains, not just small gains as was formerly the case. These changes again work to the advantage of the better-off, but a change which has the opposite effect is the replacement of the flat rate tax of 30 per cent with the individual's top rate of tax (either 25 per cent or 40 per cent).

Nearly all of the changes made by the Conservatives during the 1980s with respect to wages, benefits, taxation and the treatment of wealth have worked in the same direction. They have benefited the rich at the expense of the poor, and Britain in 1990 is a much more unequal society than it was in 1979. It is also a more deeply divided society. We have so far looked at divisions of income and wealth. In very broad terms these may be thought of as divisions based on social class. Cutting across these are several other divisions, and below we look at four of the more important, each of which became more pronounced during the 1980s: geographical divisions, labour market divisions, racial divisions and gender divisions. Taken together, they constitute a quite dramatic increase in inequality.

Geographical inequalities
It has become a commonplace of political and economic discourse to talk about a North–South divide. Lewis and Townsend describe the North–South divide as 'one of the distinctive characteristics of Britain in the 1980s'.[21] There is general agreement among the writers on this subject and in the media that the divergence between North and South has widened during the period of Conservative government. The evidence to support this conclusion is substantial and convincing. It cannot be dealt with fully here for lack of space but an attempt will be made to summarise the main features and dimensions of the divide.

During the 1980s population growth has been very uneven; in the most general terms there has been a decline of population in the less prosperous North and gains in the prosperous South. This generalisation conceals wide variation, however, the heaviest losses having been in Merseyside, Manchester, Cleveland and parts of Scotland. Greater London itself has also lost population.

The most significant gainers have been Berkshire, Buckingham-shire, East Anglia, Hampshire, parts of South-west England and the South coast generally. All of these areas showing substantial growth lie south of a line drawn from the Wash to the Severn. There are, however, some exceptions. For example, the rural areas of North Yorkshire and parts of Cumbria have experienced popula-tion increases as did the area around Aberdeen during the North Sea oil boom.

To a large extent population changes reflect changes in prosperity and employment opportunities. Areas with the highest levels of unemployment are likely to be net exporters of population. The North has been hit by changes in the British economy; changes which were already apparent before the Conservatives took office, but which accelerated during the 1980s. In particular, there has been a rapid erosion of Britain's manufacturing base. Between March 1979 and March 1989 employment in manufacturing fell by 28.1 per cent. Employment in metal manufacturing and chemicals fell by 40.8 per cent. During the same period employment in the service sector increased by 14.5 per cent.[22] New, high-technology industries have prospered (especially during the late 1980s) and there has been an expansion of small businesses. Service and high technology industries and new small businesses are concentrated in the South, whereas the traditional industrial base of the North has been in manufacturing.[23]

In the light of these structural changes, it is not surprising to find regional variations in unemployment. This is illustrated in Table 8.2. In both of the months shown unemployment in Northern Ireland, the North, the North-west, Yorkshire and Humberside, Wales and Scotland was very much higher than it was in the South-east, East Anglia and the South-west. It is interesting to note that as unemployment fell from 14 per cent in January 1986 to 7 per cent in January 1989 the disparities between the regions actually increased. In other words, unemployment has fallen most sharply in those areas where it was least severe.

Regional statistics, however, conceal local differences. Winyard reports, for example, that at the beginning of 1987, when the UK unemployment rate was 11.9 per cent, fifty-one 'travel-to-work areas' had unemployment rates of more than 20 per cent. Winyard notes that, 'Not only is unemployment far higher in the North, but also people stay on the register for longer periods.'[24]

Table 8.2 Regional unemployment

United Kingdom

Region	January 1986 %	January 1989 %
South-east	10.9	4.4
East Anglia	11.5	3.8
South-west	12.9	5.2
West Midlands	15.8	7.3
East Midlands	13.1	6.3
Yorks and Humberside	16.0	8.3
North-west	16.7	9.6
North	19.5	10.9
Wales	17.9	9.2
Scotland	16.4	10.3
N. Ireland	21.6	15.8
UK	14.0	7.0

Source: Unemployment Unit, *Unemployment Bulletin*, February 1986 and February 1989.

Comparing 1979 with 1986 Lewis and Townsend reveal widening differences between the North and the South in terms of per capita GDP, disposable income and consumer expenditure. In 1979 per capita GDP was 7.8 per cent higher in the South than in the North. By 1986 the gap had grown to 20.5 per cent. The disparity in per capita personal disposable income in favour of the South widened from 11.8 per cent in 1979 to 15 per cent in 1986. In 1979 people in the South spent 12.5 per cent more per head than people in the North, but by 1986 the difference had widened to 23.4 per cent.[25] Share ownership is also unevenly spread with a heavy concentration in the South-east and much lower levels in the North.

Most of the evidence produced in this section deals with variations between the North and the South and most of the statistics refer to regions. However, it would be a mistake to assume that the differences *within* regions are any less significant. Poverty and deprivation are by no means confined to the North. Parts of Bristol and London, for example, are extremely deprived with high unemployment, poor housing, poor schools, poor health facilities and strained police/ community relationships. Similarly, there are pockets of prosperity, some of them quite extensive, in the North. Furthermore, from a financial point of view it may be worse to be unemployed in London than in Manchester because of the differences in the cost of living.

Labour market divisions

The major division here, of course, is between the employed and the unemployed. The first two Conservative governments presided over an economy which produced ever increasing numbers of unemployed people. In January 1983 the figure passed the 3 million mark, reaching a peak in August 1986 and then declining slowly but steadily. In October 1989, however, there were still 986,000 more people unemployed than there had been in October 1979.

A word of warning must be given about unemployment statistics: the official figures are totally unreliable as a means of gauging changes in the level of unemployment. Since 1982 the government has made twenty-nine changes to the way in which the unemployed are counted, each change resulting in a downward shift in the number said to be unemployed. Fortunately, in 1983 the Unemployment Unit began to produce statistics based on the pre-1982 system of counting, and these give a much more accurate picture of changes in the level of unemployment.

The discrepancy between the official figures and those produced by the Unemployment Unit varies, but is usually between 500,000 and 700,000. In October 1989, for example, the Unemployment Unit figure exceeded the Department of Employment count by more than 589,000. Table 8.3 shows the progress of unemployment giving both the official figures (DE Count) and the Unemployment Unit figures (UU Index).

Table 8.3 Unemployment totals, 1979–89: seasonally adjusted (excludes school leavers)

United Kingdom		
Date	DE Count	UU Index
October 1979	1,277,300	–
October 1980	1,895,700	–
October 1981	2,725,500	–
October 1982	3,059,500	–
October 1983	2,941,200	3,278,700
October 1984	3,099,700	3,451,800
October 1985	3,173,300	3,532,800
October 1986	3,166,200	3,571,900
October 1987	2,713,600	3,298,800
October 1988	2,118,800	2,956,100
October 1989	1,674,100	2,263,200

Source: Unemployment Unit.

As unemployment grew the number of long-term unemployed also expanded. The official definition of long-term unemployment is more than twelve months without work, although employment training, which is designed for the long term unemployed, requires entrants to have been on the register for more than six months. Although a short period of unemployment may be unwelcome and will certainly cause hardship, it is not necessarily disastrous. However, how long does a period of unemployment have to be before people become disheartened and experience a loss of self worth? As the period of unemployment lengthens, financial reserves (if any) are exhausted and increasing debt may follow. Eventually entitlement to unemployment benefit ceases and means-tested income support is then the only alternative. Between 1979 and 1987 the proportion of unemployed men who received supplementary benefit alone increased from 43 per cent to 61.4 per cent.

In January 1986 long-term unemployment stood at 1,371,632. Since 1986 the number has fallen steadily, declining to 821,419 by January 1989. Although this is still far too many it represents a substantial improvement. However, the picture is less optimistic when the figures are looked at a little more closely. Some of those classified as short-term unemployed may be intermittently unemployed and this may be just as demoralising as a long spell off work. Another point to bear in mind is that in 1988 only 35 per cent of the 400,000 new jobs created were full time: 34 per cent were part time and 31 per cent were in self employment. Furthermore, the Government Actuary's financial estimates predict a rise in unemployment during 1990/91 of 80,000. This could very well be an underestimate since the government's spending plans are based on an estimated growth in the economy of only 1.25 per cent in 1990/91. This includes the proceeds from North Sea oil, and if oil is excluded then the rate of growth is reduced to only 0.75 per cent. Christopher Huhne says that this 'would represent the lowest growth rate since 1981 and is almost certain to lead to a rise in unemployment'.[26] The Unemployment Unit shares this view.

The Conservatives have created greater cleavages between the employed and the unemployed. Apart from the reductions in benefits noted earlier, the treatment of the unemployed has become increasingly demeaning. Several factors have contributed to this, but the government's attitude to the unemployed has been the most crucial factor. Norman Tebbitt's advice to the unemployed to 'get on their bikes' to look for work implied that many people were voluntarily unemployed and this statement was probably symptomatic of the government's whole approach to unemployment. Blaming the victim has always been popular with governments anxious to shrug off the blame attaching to themselves but the Conservative governments of the last decade have been particularly prone to this.

Another aspect of the disregard for the feelings of the unemployed was the reduction in the number of mainstream staff in DSS offices at a time when the number of claimants was rising. Putting greater pressure on DSS staff increases the possibility of mistakes and makes incivility and friction more likely. Staff cuts have also occurred in Jobcentres and there have been repeated threats of privatisation.[27]

The cuts in mainstream staff in DSS offices and Jobcentres have been accompanied by an expansion of those staff concerned with regulating the poor. The DSS established Specialist Claims Control Teams in 1980 and it has appointed over 1,000 additional social security investigators. In 1983 the Department of Employment set up Regional Benefit Investigation Teams.

The government has imposed increasingly stringent tests on those in receipt of unemployment benefit. Restart interviews are now automatic and compulsory after each six months of unemployment. To the availability-for-work test has been added the actively-seeking-work test in which the unemployed person has to demonstrate and provide evidence that he or she has taken all necessary steps to obtain employment. After a certain period a job cannot be refused on the grounds of low pay or travelling distance from home.

A Claimant Advisor may offer a Restart interviewee a place on the Employment Training Scheme. In a purely formal sense such an offer does not have to be accepted, but a refusal will contribute to the impression a Claimant Advisor forms of the claimant's seriousness in seeking work.

The Employment Training Scheme is a classic example of blaming the victim. The Unemployment Unit says of it:

The Government are changing the terms of the debate about long term unemployment. By concentrating public attention on the training, employability and motivation of the unemployed, the Government hope to divert attention both from poverty and personal hardship experienced by claimants and away from the failure of their economic policies to create enough jobs.[28]

The Unit is highly critical of the White Paper, 'Training for Employment' which claims that the long-term unemployed share a combination of negative characteristics such as: lack of skills and motivation; inappropriate skills; problems of numeracy and literacy; lack of qualifications; ignorance of 'in-work' benefits; unrealistic expectations of pay levels; lack of flexibility and adaptability and dependence on state benefits.[29]

It appears that the unemployed are segmented into two groups each of which is accorded different treatment: those who have been unemployed for more than six months and those who have not. The second group may be further divided into two segments: those for whom the present unemployment is a single episode and those who are intermittently unemployed. The notion of segmentation is useful in identifying different categories among the unemployed, but it also has a wider usefulness in analysing cleavages in the labour market generally.

This is not the place to explore the subtleties of dual or segmented labour market theories.[30] However, the idea that there are two or more sectors or segments in the labour market has some relevance for the present discussion.

The simplest variant of the theory is to split the labour market into two sectors. One sector is composed of trained, skilled workers with stable employment, good working conditions, opportunities for advancement and for further training and with good pay. The secondary sector consists of low-paid, largely unskilled or semi-skilled workers with poor working conditions, little or no job security and no chances of promotion. A high proportion of these workers may be part time. It is this sector that has suffered most from the low pay strategies of the Conservatives and from unemployment. It is the same workers in the public sector who have had their employment privatised and further marginalised.

Segmented labour market theories help to explain the disadvantaged position of women and ethnic minorities in employment, and it is to these groups that we now turn. It should be noted that the purpose is not to discuss the various dimensions of inequality affecting women and minority groups. What needs to be considered is whether these groups are better or worse off as a result of ten years of Conservative rule. Have inequalities of gender and race been widened or narrowed?

Gender inequalities

Writing in 1987, Glendinning says that 'women, of all ages have borne much of the brunt of the increasing poverty and social inequality of the last eight years'.[31] I would agree with this view. Although there have been a few gains, these have been outweighed by the losses.

The gains can be divided into four categories:

1. There is now a greater degree of *formal* equality within the social security system. For example, when a couple claim income support they can choose whether the man or the woman is to make the claim.

2. The law against sex discrimination was strengthened by the Sex Discrimination Act of 1986 which removed the restrictions on the hours women could work, allowing both night work and shift work, and gave women the right to work until the same age as their male colleagues. The Employment Act of 1989 further extended equal employment opportunities for women and removed restrictions on the types of employment available to them.

3. The Job Training Scheme has been replaced by Employment Training which has better provision for married women. There are 15,000 places for married women who do not qualify for benefit in their own right. This is something of a doubtful privilege since such women receive only £10 a week. One good feature of the scheme is that single parents are entitled to child care payments, although the benefit of this development is reduced by the exclusion of lone mothers with children below school age.

4. As from April 1990 husbands and wives will be taxed separately. This is certainly less sexist, but the married couple's allowance goes to the man unless he has insufficient income to benefit from it.

It is difficult to be certain of the impact of unemployment upon women. Figures relating to female unemployment are unreliable and there is substantial under-recording. It is *probably* the case that women have not been so seriously affected by long-term unemployment as have men in comparable occupations.

However, many women are forced into part time, low-grade jobs – more often than not in the public sector. As Table 8.4 demonstrates, between 1985 and 1987 some 60 per cent of all women of

Table 8.4 Employment status of population of working age by sex, 1985–7

Great Britain

Type of employment	Men %	Women %
Full time	63	31
Part time	2	24
Self employed	11	4
On government scheme	2	1
Total	78	60

Source: *Social Trends*, Central Statistical Office.

working age were in employment with 31 per cent working full time and 24 per cent part time. Among men of working age, 78 per cent were in employment with 63 per cent working full time and 2 per cent part time.

Part-time employees have fewer rights than those in full time work and their work is less secure. Full time work is also very often the passport to various forms of occupational welfare such as pension rights, private health insurance, subsidised meals and paid holidays.

In 1987 31 per cent of the female workforce worked in the public sector as compared with 21 per cent of males. In 1988 slightly more than 82 per cent of employed women worked in service industries as compared with 57.5 per cent of employed men. Most of the public sector and service industry jobs taken by women are in cleaning, catering and laundry work.

In spite of equal pay legislation women have continued to be paid less than men. In 1988 women's average gross hourly earnings represented 74.9 per cent of men's earnings, which is slightly down on the peak of 75.5 per cent in 1977 but is an improvement on the 1985 figure of 73.9 per cent. These are not dramatic changes, but one might have hoped that Britain's first woman Prime Minister would have taken a tougher line on women's pay. The reduction of wages council protection will affect women's earnings since 75 per cent of the labour force in the industries concerned are women.

Changes to the social security system have reduced the living standards of the majority of recipients; but, since women are the main users of the system, they are the main losers. Women are disproportionately represented among income support recipients for two main reasons: first, there is a high proportion of elderly and disabled women in the population; and second, lone parenthood is increasing and the proportion of lone parents dependent upon state benefits has also increased (by 1986 about 40 per cent of the income of lone parents came from state benefits[32]). Lone parents, 91 per cent of whom are women, are among the poorest members of the population. The replacement of single payments by social fund loans will also have a disproportionate effect on women in general and on lone parents in particular.

Women are also being hit by the changes in child benefit and family credit. As mentioned elsewhere, child benefit has been frozen for three consecutive years. All families with children are disadvantaged by this, but, since child benefit is nearly always paid to women, it is they who are most disadvantaged. Increasingly, poor families are forced to rely upon family credit, which is of course means-tested and to make matters worse, free school meals have been withdrawn from over 500,000 children whose parents are on family credit. An allowance is made for this, but it is insufficient to pay for a school meal.

Two other benefit changes directly affecting women are the reduction in widows' benefits and the replacement of the universal maternity grant by statutory maternity pay, administered by employers, which is subject to contribution conditions and liable for tax.

The harsher conditions attaching to the receipt of unemployment benefit affect all claimants, but the consequences for women are particularly unfortunate. The available for work condition is interpreted to mean *immediately* available, and women have to demonstrate that they have made adequate arrangements for the care of dependants. Furthermore, they may have to accept work further away from home than they are accustomed to travelling, which may in itself present child care problems. The actively seeking work condition also discriminates against women who, because they are usually responsible for child care and domestic work, have less time to devote to formal jobsearch.

This raises the whole question of responsibility for care. The bulk of domiciliary care is already provided by families, but Mrs Thatcher has made it plain that she expects families to take on *extra* responsibilities, and this is also apparent in the White Paper on *Caring for People*. Janet Finch writes:

In the 1980s, the Conservative government has become increasingly explicit about its desire to encourage families to take care of their members. This is seen as part of its policy to make citizens more self-reliant, and less prone to look to the state for financial and practical support when they are out of work, chronically sick, elderly and infirm and so on.[33]

This issue is discussed more fully in Chapter 7 where it is argued, with no claim to originality, that community care usually means family care and family care means care by women. It also argues that the Conservative emphasis on family care ignores much recent research indicating that social changes are restricting the family's capacity to care. Not the least among these changes is the greater participation of women in the labour market and their increased career expectations. Stereotyped gender roles are changing only slowly and women still take on most of the caring and domiciliary tasks, which has fairly obvious implications for equal opportunities policies. The government has failed to provide adequate day-care facilities for children to enable women to go out to work. Increasingly, firms are making their own provision, but where this is not available, women have to rely on friends, relatives and informal self help arrangements, or else pay for private care.

Racial inequalities

It must be stressed again that this section of the chapter does not attempt to look at the level and nature of racial discrimination in Britain. It is concerned with the effects of Conservative policies since 1979. In this section I shall use the term black or ethnic minority to refer to all non-white groups. I recognise the dangers of lumping together people with quite different cultures but the problems I am concerned with are experienced by members of all minorities in Britain.

It also has to be remembered that all too often it is the black population that is seen as the problem, when the real problem is society's treatment of black people: it is not black people who need to change, but the discriminatory attitudes and practices used against them. The final point by way of preface is that it is a mistake to assume that all black people are deprived. In one sense only is this true: all black people are discriminated against no matter what positions they occupy. I shall concentrate upon deprivation among black people because this is where the government's policies have been most damaging.

The section on gender began with a summary of some of the gains made by women. I would have been pleased to start this section in similar fashion, but could find very little evidence of improvements. As Hilary Arnott says:

> To look at the black experience in Britain since 1979 is to expose the effects of Conservative policies at their harshest, with few if any palliative gestures to hide the stark reality of life for deprived minorities in the 1980s.[34]

It is not so much that the Conservatives have deliberately introduced racist policies as that they have ignored the harmful impact of their policies on ethnic minorities. When problems have arisen such as in the urban riots they have explained them away as resulting from a lack of proper parental and school discipline (blaming the victim again) or as the work of political agitators.

Ethnic minorities, over represented as they are in the secondary labour market referred to earlier, are forced to take jobs (frequently in the service sector) with low pay, poor working conditions, no training and little security. According to de Sousa, similar discrimination occurs in the Youth Training Scheme (YTS):

> The Youth Training Scheme has, from its inception, been riddled with racist practices. The abuses and discrimination which Black (Afro-Caribbean and Asian) workers face in the labour market are replicated in every aspect of the scheme. From the moment they seek training – whether voluntarily or because of benefit withdrawal – to the day they leave, Black trainees are subject to considerably worse conditions than their white colleagues.[35]

The Training Agency frequently claims that it insists on non-discriminatory practices, but 'all the evidence points to widespread exclusion of Black trainees from prestigious employer based schemes . . . most likely to lead to full-time jobs, top-ups to the allowance and higher quality training'.[36] Just under 30 per cent of black trainees obtain work as opposed to just over 45 per cent of their white counterparts. De Sousa blames the Training Agency, the Careers Service and the YTS schemes for this situation.

As is demonstrated in Table 8.5, black people suffer disproportionately from unemployment. It will be observed that the disparities occur at different levels of overall unemployment, and that all ethnic minorities experienced higher rates of unemployment than the white population in the 1980s. The plight of the Pakistani/Bangladeshi

Table 8.5 Unemployment rates by ethnic origin, 1985 and 1988

Great Britain		
Ethnic Origin	1985 %	1988 %
All people of working age	10.7	8.7
White	10.3	8.5
West Indian/Guyanese	21.0	14.9
Indian	17.0	11.9
Pakistani/Bangladeshi	31.0	24.0
All other ethnic origins	17.0	9.7

Source: Unemployment Unit.

minority is particularly serious with unemployment rates almost three times the level of those among the white population.

Cuts in social security benefits have important implications for ethnic minorities because of their higher rates of unemployment. There have also been successive attempts throughout the 1980s to restrict the benefits available to immigrants. The latest of these was contained in the Immigration Act of 1988, which requires anyone wishing to bring their family to this country to demonstrate that there is support and accommodation available and that the marriage was not entered into primarily for immigration reasons.[37] The purpose of the new rules is to ensure that there is no recourse to social security benefits or access to housing.

Because of low incomes, high unemployment and plain discrimination black people are forced into the worst housing. They have therefore suffered more than most from cuts in the housing programme. They have also been among the major victims of the failure of the government's inner city policies. The inner cities have been hit by reductions in rate support grant and by rate capping. The position will worsen once the full effects of the poll tax and the revenue support grant are felt after the expiry of the four-year transitional period.

CENTRALISATION AND DEMOCRACY

Mrs Thatcher has talked at length and often about popular capitalism and consumer choice, and she has also said much about freedom and democracy. Independence, self help and active citizenship have all been praised. Yet throughout her period of office there has been a strong aut ɔritarian tendency. Mrs Thatcher prides herself on her strong and determined leadership, but this frequently means overruling colleagues and ignoring advice. However, Mrs Thatcher's personal style is less important than the policies she has supported, some of which are distinctly anti-democratic.

The government's disregard for democratic processes is seen in the voting procedures originally proposed and eventually adopted for opting out in housing and education. The 1988 Housing Act, as we have seen, offered tenants the opportunity to opt out of local authority control. An election would be held to decide the final outcome, but quite astonishingly the government decreed that abstentions would count as 'yes' votes. In education, schools were given a similar opportunity to opt out of local government control. Again, an election would decide the outcome, but a simple majority of those *voting* (as opposed to those *on the register*) was all that was required. There was intense opposition to these proposals but the only concession made in both instances was to require a second ballot if less than 50 per cent of those entitled to vote did so. The government clearly wished to tilt the balance in favour of opting out.

In the 1980s the powers of the central state were considerably enhanced as the practice of discussion with affected parties and major interests was abandoned. The government confronted opposition and frequently overcame it, and the extra powers given to ministers – especially in education and housing and potentially in the personal social services – were extensive.

Centralisation gained considerable impetus from the government's attack on local authorities which, as we saw in Chapter 2, has been one of the major features of Conservative policy. The means used to emasculate local government have been varied. Local authorities have been forced to sell the best of their housing stock into owner occupation, and to agree to the transfer of houses remaining in the rented sector to alternative landlords. They have also lost houses to Housing Action Trusts and been forced to raise the rents of the houses still within their control. Local authorities' ability to plan and develop a co-ordinated housing policy has been curtailed. Council housing is rapidly becoming a residual service for specific categories of clients: the poor, the unemployed, the elderly and the disabled.

Inner city initiatives have demonstrated the extent of the government's contempt for local government. There has been a heavy reliance on private market initiatives forcing local government out, and the Urban Development Corporations, where they exist, have virtually supplanted local authorities as planning authorities.

The Metropolitan County Councils, the Greater London Council and the Inner London Education Authority have all been abolished. The main reason for this abolition was their control by Labour councils and their opposition to government policies.

Local education authorities have lost their polytechnics. In the school system we have the possibility of schools opting out, although by 1990 there had been no rush to do so. The city technology colleges, outside local authority control, have also failed to develop at the speed the government hoped for. Nevertheless, the policies are in place and resources are being made available.

Local authorities are to retain overall control of community care services, but they are to be responsible for planning, finance and regulation rather than direct provision. Local government was allocated these responsibilities with great reluctance only after the government had explored every other possibility.

The government has met with less success than it had anticipated in its policy of compelling local authorities to put services out to competitive tender. The 1988 Local Goverment Act required competitive tendering, as from 1 April, 1989, in seven areas of service: school meals, other catering, refuse collection, street cleaning, building cleaning, grounds maintenance and vehicle maintenance. A report on the first three months of the system claimed that 77 per cent of contracts had been won by in-house tenders.[38]

Throughout the 1980s the government made attempt after attempt to control and curb local government expenditure through cash limits, rate-capping and grant withdrawal. How successful have they been?

As Table 8.6 indicates, between 1980/81 and 1987/88 there were two years in which reductions in expenditure in real terms were achieved. The overall trend, however, has been upward – an increase in real terms of 11.6 per cent. At first glance it appears that the government has not been particularly successful in bringing about reductions in local government expenditure. However, since

Table 8.6 Local government expenditure in real terms*

United Kingdom		
Year	£ billion	Percentage change
1980–1	35.2	–
1981–2	34.0	−3.4
1982–3	34.8	+2.3
1983–4	37.9	+8.9
1984–5	38.2	+0.8
1985–6	36.4	−4.7
1986–7	37.9	+4.1
1987–8	39.3	+3.8

* Cash outturns adjusted to 1986/87 price levels.

Source: Social Trends, nos. 17, 18 and 19, Central Statistical Office, HMSO.

1983/84 local government expenditure has fallen slightly as a proportion of GNP and one would question the usefulness of the Retail Price Index as a measure of inflation within local government. Furthermore, many authorities, had they been given the option, would have chosen to spend more on services. Authorities that have been rate-capped and lost grant have had to cut services or put off planned improvements.

Nevertheless, the government takes the view that local authority expenditure has not been effectively controlled, and one of the main purposes of the community charge is to try to remedy this. In his Autumn Statement in November 1989 the Chancellor of the Exchequer accused local authorities of 'massive overspending', and held them responsible for the fact that public expenditure for 1989/90 was expected to be £1 billion higher than originally planned. The Chancellor said: 'As the House knows, new arrangements for the finance and control of local authority expenditure in England and Wales are being introduced on 1 April 1990. This year's outturn shows how necessary these new measures are.'[39]

A strong and independent system of local government is a necessary feature of a democratic system of government. It constitutes a restraint on excessive centralisation. Since the Conservatives came to power they have considerably weakened local government and greater centralisation has been the consequence.

The 1980s have also seen infringements, actual or potential, of civil liberties. The measures include the withdrawal of the right to belong to a trade union at GCHQ; the drawing up of a poll tax register; and, under the Local Government Act of 1989, the restrictions placed on the political activities of all local government officers earning over £13,500 a year.

The government has been obsessed with secrecy as is indicated by the prosecution of Clive Ponting and Sarah Tisdall over the disclosure of material covered by the Official Secrets Act and by their efforts to prevent the publication of *Spycatcher* by Peter Wright.

The government has spent more heavily than its predecessors on promoting its policies. The bill for the privatisation of public sector companies amounted to £2.4 billion, White Papers have become glossy booklets, and the expenditure of the Central Office of Information increased from £67 million in 1985/6 to £195 million in 1988/9. At the same time the government has made great efforts to centralise the control of information.

They have also tried on more than one occasion to influence the editorial policy of the BBC and have complained of biased reporting. In 1989 government information and press officers claimed that they were under considerable pressure from ministers to give a much more party political slant to press releases and general information for public consumption.

OVERALL ASSESSMENT

Rhetoric or action?
It is sometimes asserted that the rhetoric of the Conservative administration has exceeded its achievements. This is probably true of any government: all politicians have a tendency to confuse intent with accomplishment and to exaggerate their own influence upon events.

The Conservative government may not have achieved all that it intended, but it has nevertheless brought about substantial change. Simply restricting the analysis to the period between the third election success and 1990, we have had a Housing Act, an Education Act, Acts dealing with local government and with industrial relations, an Immigration Act, a Public Order Act and a National Health Service and Community Care Bill. In addition, the Social Security Act of 1986 has been implemented.

Every area of social policy has been affected in some way during the 1980s, and the purpose of this book has been to indicate the scale and nature of the changes. The main pillars of the welfare state – social security, the National Health Service, education, housing and the personal social services – have been, or are in the process of being, transformed. Implementation may, of course, moderate the impact of the changes, and it is also possible to argue that it is the structure and organisation of services that have been altered and that the underlying principles remain intact. Nevertheless, there is a common thread running through all the social policy changes: a belief in markets and competition. The implication is that the social services are a wasteful burden, and that increasing social expenditure was a major factor contributing to Britain's economic problems in the late 1970s. The impression given by the government is that public services are outdated and inferior to services available from private market suppliers.

The economy

The control of inflation has been the government's top priority and a tight money policy has been the chosen means by which this was to be achieved. This has meant high interest rates and the control of public expenditure.

Although in its economic forecasts the government has been constantly over-optimistic about the future course of inflation, it has managed to bring the rate down. But Britain still has a higher rate than many of its European competitors and a higher rate than both the United States and Japan. Inflation began to rise again in 1988/89 and the higher interest rates took longer than expected to make their effect felt. At the beginning of 1990 inflation stood at 7.7 per cent, but a forecast for April suggested a rate of inflation in excess of 10 per cent. High interest rates obviously hit those paying off a mortgage, retail outlets suffer as consumer expenditure falls and industry is faced with higher costs of borrowing to finance investment. Nor is it easy to predict with any degree of accuracy the precise effects of anti-inflationary policies and there is always the danger of sliding into a recession with a consequent rise in unemployment.

Just such a recession occurred in the early 1980s and between 1979 and 1982 the GDP declined. The cost in terms of unemployment has already been commented upon. The economy began to pick up in 1983, although it took three years for this to begin to be reflected in lower unemployment figures. Between 1983 and 1989 there was a period of sustained growth (reaching 5 per cent at one point). The estimated rate of growth for 1990/91 is only 1.25 per cent (including oil) and if this proves to be correct it will bring down the average rate of growth for the four years ending in 1990/91 to 3 per cent. One of the problems associated with the recovery is that most of the growth has been in the service sector; Britain's manufacturing capacity was greatly reduced during the early 1980s and the position has not since been retrieved.

It had always been the government's aim to reduce income taxation in the hope of increasing incentives. However, the main reductions had to wait until inflation was under control. The budgets of 1986, 1987 and 1988 all contained reductions in the rates of income tax, with the rich, as we have seen, benefiting most. It was largely the revenue from North Sea oil and the denationalisation programme that financed income tax cuts.

Another aspect of the government's economic strategy was the deregulation of both labour and financial markets. The deregulation of labour markets has already been referred to. In the financial sphere, currency exchange restrictions were abolished.

The movement towards a free economy also demanded, according to the government, action to curb the power of the trade unions. The public sector unions had been particularly troublesome and this partly explains the government's commitment to compulsory competitive tendering.

Reconstructing welfare

We have seen how the government has reconstructed individual services and how it has promoted both privatisation and greater inequality. The task now is to take a more general look at this process, especially in terms of public expenditure.

The government's aim has been to control, and if possible reduce, public expenditure. One of the ways in which savings may be made is by reducing the size of the civil service, and Mrs Thatcher appointed Sir Derek Rayner, Managing Director of Marks and Spencer, to look at management efficiency in the public services. Sir Derek, who reported directly to Mrs Thatcher, interpreted his role as looking for staff reductions. In 1979 there were 732,000 civil servants. By January 1983 the number had been reduced to 606,000. In 1989 civil servants numbered 576,000. In 1990, however, the trend was reversed and the number rose to 587,000.

The government has also begun to implement a policy of hiving off civil servants who do executive work into new agencies. By the end of 1990 over 66,000 civil servants will have been hived off. There are, however, firm plans for a further 104,000, and eventually as many as 450,000 may be involved. David Hencke comments:

Besides splitting the executive and policy-making functions of civil servants, the agencies open the way to ending uniform pay and conditions and replacing the concept of public service with a growing emphasis on business management and the commercialisation of services.[40]

There is a parallel programme of relocating civil servants out of London and the South-east in an attempt to cut costs.

In 1978/79 the ratio of public expenditure to GDP was 43.25 per cent, rising to 46.75 per cent in 1982/83. It fell slightly in 1983/84, but rose again in 1984/85 (the year of the miners' strike) to 46.25 per cent. The proportion then fell each year until it reached 38.75 per cent in 1989/90. A slight rise to 39 per cent is expected in 1990/91, but the proportion will revert to 38.75 per cent in 1991/92. The Chancellor expects a further fall in 1992/93 to the lowest level since the mid-1960s.

In real terms (allowing for increases in the Retail Price Index) total public expenditure increased by 11 per cent between 1978/79 and 1989/90. Table 8.7 shows how individual departments fared during the same period.

The most striking of these figures is the 233 per cent increase in the expenditure of the legal departments. Another big increase is 63 per cent for the Home Office, representing increased expenditure on law and order. Defence, which received massive increases in the first half of the 1980s, has more recently fallen away somewhat, but still records an overall increase of 17 per cent.

Of the services covered in this book, the most obvious loser has been housing with a 79 per cent cut in expenditure. Education has received a modest 10 per cent increase (less than 1 per cent per year) and as a proportion of GDP education expenditure declined from 5.5 per cent in 1980/81 to 4.9 per cent in 1986/87. The increase in health and personal social services expenditure appears substantial at 37 per cent. In fact, this amounts to no more than level funding. The reader is referred to Chapter 4 for the reasoning lying behind this statement.

Social security is an interesting case. Writing about the period

Table 8.7 Increases in public expenditure 1978/9–89/90

United Kingdom Department	Real rise 1978/79 to 1989/90 %
Ministry of Defence	17
Foreign Office – other	17
Foreign Office – Overseas Development	– 13
EEC	20
Ministry of Agriculture, Fisheries and Food	6
Department of Trade and Industry	–68
Export Credits	–71
Department of Energy	–
Department of Employment	64
Department of Transport	–11
Department of Environment – Housing	–79
Department of Environment – other	–13
Home Office	63
Legal Departments	233
Department of Education	10
Office of Arts and Libraries	29
DHSS – Health	37
DHSS – Social Security	36
Scotland	–
Wales	6
N. Ireland	11
Chancellor's Departments	23
Other departments	–63
Reserve	–
Special sales of assets	–
Total	11

Source: C. Huhne, *The Guardian*, 31 January 1989.

from 1978/79 to 1986/87, Hills disputed the DHSS's view that two-thirds of the increase in expenditure could be attributed to an increase in the number of claimants – especially an increase in the number of unemployed people, but also an increase in the number of elderly people – and one-third could be attributed to real increases in the average amounts of benefit paid. Hills points out that this is not the same thing as real increases in benefit levels. Part of the increase in the average amounts paid reflects higher rents leading to higher housing benefit payments, and part stems from the lower incomes of those coming on to supplementary benefit as compared with earlier years. Hills says that where benefits have been increased they have failed, in a number of instances, to keep pace with rising prices, and they have certainly fallen 'well behind the growth rates of earnings or national income as a whole'. Hills concludes that: 'The increase in real spending can mainly be ascribed to increased numbers of claimants, which are, in turn, mainly attributable to increased unemployment and demographic changes'.[41]

It is instructive to look at the public expenditure figures for the three-year period from 1987/88–1989/90. In 1987/88 real expenditure fell by 0.7 per cent and this was followed by a further fall of 0.8 per cent in 1988/89. In November 1989 it was estimated that in 1989/90 there would be a rise of 0.9 per cent.

The problem is that spending plans always under-estimate the level of inflation. Thus, in 1989/90 the real increase fell below what had been originally planned. The projections published in November 1989 were £11.8 billion lower than indicated in the 1987 plans and £3.5 billion lower than in the 1988 plans.[42]

The plans for 1990/91 indicate a real increase in expenditure of 2.3 per cent, or 3.9 per cent if debt interest is excluded. This involves a £5.5 billion addition to the government's previous plans, including an extra £2.4 billion for the NHS, £500 million extra for higher education and £250 million over two years for policies relating to homelessness. These increases depend crucially upon inflation not exceeding the government's estimates and past experience does not engender optimism. Indeed, the first four months of 1990 indicated that the government had again underestimated the rate of inflation.

In general terms, then, government expenditure has not been reduced since 1979. Even allowing for inflation, there has been an increase since 1978/79 of 11 per cent. Most of this increase, however, occurred in the first half of the 1980s. Between 1987/88 and 1989/90 public expenditure was subjected to severe restraint. As a proportion of GDP, public expenditure has fallen. It has been cushioned by the proceeds from North Sea oil and denationalisation, but, when the oil dries up and there is nothing left to sell, public expenditure is bound to suffer.

The government has shown itself, to no-one's surprise, to be hostile to public expenditure and the standards of public services have declined. The Retail Price Index is a totally inappropriate measure of inflation in most of the social services and consequently statements of 'real terms expenditure' are misleading.

In more than a decade one might have hoped for improvements in the quality of service. Instead, the reverse has happened. In housing, for example, the number of homeless families has more than doubled since 1979. Rents are higher and rising and there is greater polarisation in social housing and between the public and the private sectors. The changes made under the Housing Act are, at best, an irrelevance.

In the National Health Service there are staff shortages, wards are being closed and patients turned away to join lengthening queues. The encouragement of private markets, the development of internal markets and greater reliance on charges hardly seem appropriate responses to the problems facing the service – problems stemming largely from underfunding.

The personal social services are hampered by staff shortages and funding has not kept pace with growing need. Greater demands are being made on families and no extra help is made available to help them meet these demands. Contracting out and greater dependence on the commercial and voluntary sectors will not solve these problems.

The changes made to the education system seem designed to create greater divisions. Competition rather than co-operation is to be the distinguishing feature of the system. Schools, colleges, polytechnics and universities are meant to be run like businesses and pupils and students are to be helped towards a better appreciation of the enterprise culture.

The new social security system is even less generous than the one it replaced. It is more heavily dependent upon means tests and the emphasis on the detection of fraud is based on the largely unsupported assumption that there is widespread abuse. Much less attention is paid to under-claiming, and unemployed claimants have to prove not only that they are available for work but also that they are actively seeking it.

Nevertheless, the welfare state has not yet been dismantled. The major services, much changed and with inadequate resources, are still in place. Furthermore, support for the welfare state in the population at large seems undiminished and there is less satisfaction with Mrs Thatcher's handling of it.

The annual survey, *British Social Attitudes*, is a rich source of data on people's views of the welfare state. The 1985 survey found that only 5 per cent of respondents would welcome reductions in health, education and social benefits even when coupled with tax cuts.[43] Significantly this compares with 9 per cent who favoured this option in 1983.[44] In 1987 one half of respondents supported rises in taxes to pay for increased social provision. This represents a substantial change from 1983 when only one-third favoured this course of action.

Support for the National Health Service is particularly strong. The researchers responsible for the report, published in 1988, say:

In sum, our various pieces of evidence suggest strongly that the NHS continues to matter a great deal to the British public. Among all the possible targets for increased public expenditure (including other 'popular' ones such as education and housing), it commands by far the greatest and most consistent support . . . most people express continuing contentment with standards of medical and nursing care in hospitals, as with primary health-care services such as GPs and dentists.[45]

A *British Social Attitudes* report published in 1989 found that 88 per cent of respondents wanted more state spending on health; 75 per cent wanted more state spending on education; the same percentage wanted more spending on pensions; and 41 per cent wanted more state spending on jobless benefits.[46]

A poll conducted by International Communications and Marketing Research, in conjunction with *The Guardian*, in September 1989, found that 58 per cent of respondents thought that it was preferable to pay higher taxes and have better services than to pay lower taxes and have worse services; only 21 per cent took the opposite view. The same survey reported that 62 per cent of respondents were against selling off profitable state industries and running them as private companies. The percentage assenting to the proposition 'There is one law for the rich and one for the poor' increased from 66 per cent in 1988 to 71 per cent in 1989. The report concludes that 'The sense of living in an unfair society has strengthened over the past year'. Finally, 70 per cent disagreed with the view that the National Health Service is safe in Mrs Thatcher's hands.[47]

Support for the welfare state, then, seems assured, but the Conservatives have won three elections and it is they who have set the political agenda. In the introduction to this book a brief reference was made to Gamble's interpretation of Thatcherism as a hegemonic project. Gamble sees Thatcherism as preparing the ground for the new hegemony rather than itself constituting that hegemony.

The conclusion must be that Thatcherism as a hegemonic project has been only partially successful. It has failed to diminish public supprt for the welfare state, but it has succeeded in restoring the authority of the state – although the vehement protests against the poll tax in March 1990 may pose a threat to this. In addition, the Conservatives have gone part of the way towards the establishment of a free economy, and it is the Conservative agenda that has dominated British politics since Mrs Thatcher took over leadership of the party. Gamble writes:

The ascendancy of the Conservatives was marked not simply by their success in winning elections, but by their apparent domination of the political argument and the policy agenda. They appeared to have succeeded in reconstructing the political terrain in Britain in such a way that any party seeking to become or remain the main opposition to the Conservatives would be forced to move a long way towards the new policy positions being staked out by the Thatcher Government in order to compete effectively.[48]

This point is borne out by Labour's Policy Review which accepted more unreservedly than ever before the role of the private sector.[49]

Much of the Conservatives' electoral success has resulted from the sustained growth in the economy since 1983. There are now some signs of this faltering and Conservative electoral impregnability seems less assured: opinion polls at the beginning of March 1990 put the Labour Party 18 per cent ahead of the Conservatives.

However, the next general election is unlikely to be held before 1992, and if the economy can be put back on course the Conservatives could very well secure a fourth term in office. A further six years would bring the realisation of the hegemonic project a stage nearer. It will be interesting to see if Mrs Thatcher and her supporters can successfully dictate the terms on which the next election is fought.

THE LEGACY

What is the legacy of the Conservatives' term of office since 1979? Above all else, Britain is a much more unequal society with more people living in poverty. There is no doubt about this and some of the evidence is reviewed in this book. Many of the poor are among the millions who have experienced unemployment during the 1980s, but anyone drawing social security benefit is inevitably poorer as a result of the changes made to the social security system. Lone parents and disabled and elderly people, for example, are among the poor in receipt of state benefits, but couples with children are also worse off. Many of the poor are concentrated in the inner cities where conditions have actually deteriorated under the Conservatives. In a society which has become more materialistic, a society which has encouraged conspicuous consumption, poverty may more readily lead to resentment and unrest. The inner city 'riots' were an example of this.

Britain is also a more divided society. As Loney said before the election of 1987: 'the Thatcher government has not achieved the abolition of the welfare state or the civilised values on which it was founded, but it has had the chance to show us how far, given the opportunity, it can divide Britain.'[50] Since 1987 the divisions have become wider than ever: divisions in the labour market, divisions of race and gender and divisions between the rich and the poor. There are wider cleavages, too, between council tenants, private sector tenants and owner occupiers.

The distinction between public squalor and private affluence has heightened during the 1980s. Public services have deteriorated and private provision has prospered. It is not just in terms of resources, however, that the public sector has suffered but also in terms of status, and one result is that those working in the public sector are becoming increasingly demoralised.

Finally, Britain has become less democratic. It is ironic that the party which talks so much about freedom in the market place should have restricted civil liberties. It is equally ironic that the Prime Minister who applauds the movement towards democracy in Eastern Europe should have presided over the virtual dismantling of local democracy in Britain and the concentration of greater power in the hands of the central state.

This then is the legacy of Thatcherism. The question arises as to whether Thatcherism will survive when Mrs Thatcher is no longer leader of the Conservative Party. The moderate wing of the Party has been much weakened under Mrs Thatcher and it is doubtful whether any new leader could take the Conservatives all the way back to the kind of party presided over by Mr Macmillan and Mr

Heath. Some accommodation with the Thatcherites in the Party will have to be reached. As Mr John Biffen, one of the moderates in the Conservative Party, has said:

Tomorrow's Toryism will keep faith with the past decade, but in its approach to spending and taxation there will have to be changes in reality and rhetoric. Many believe that the Conservative Party is for turning and can make the adjustments easily enough. They are right.[51]

Even if Mr Biffen's assessment is correct, many of the changes made in the last decade may be irreversible or may take at least another decade to remedy. Even if Thatcherism were to disappear with Mrs Thatcher, its effects would continue to be felt for many years. The main task of any new Prime Minister, Conservative, Labour or Liberal Democrat, would be to try to heal the rift which now divides Britain.

NOTES

1. Office of Population Censuses and Surveys, *The General Household Survey for 1987*, London: HMSO, 1989.
2. R. Cook, *Life Begins at 40: In Defence of the NHS*, London: Fabian Society, 1988, p. 4.
3. Central Statistical Office, *Social Trends No. 19*, London: HMSO, 1989, p. 132.
4. K. Ascher, *The Politics of Privatisation*, London: Macmillan 1987, pp. 167–208; and Department of Health, *Working for Patients*, Cm 555, London: HMSO, 1989, p. 69.
5. A. Gamble, *The Free Economy and the Strong State*, London: Macmillan, 1988, p. 233.
6. D. S. King, *The New Right: Politics, Markets and Citizenship*, London: Macmillan, 1987.
7. A. Gamble, *op. cit.*, p. 16.
8. P. Dunleavy is the most persuasive of consumption-sector theorists. See P. Dunleavy, 'The political implications of sectoral cleavages and the growth of state employment – parts I and II', *Political Studies*, vol. 28, nos. 2 and 3, 1979; P. Dunleavy and C. Husbands, *British Democracy at the Crossroads*, London: Allen and Unwin, 1985.
9. Source: Central Statistical Office, *Social Trends*, no. 19, London: HMSO, 1989.
10. Reported in *The Guardian*, 6 September 1989.
11. D. Byrne, 'Rich and poor: The growing divide', in A. Walker and

C. Walker (eds.), *The Growing Divide*, London: Child Poverty Action Group, 1987, p. 29.

12. *Ibid.*, pp. 27–8.
13. Social Services Committee, *The April 1988 Social Security Changes*, HC 437–1, London: HMSO, 1989.
14. National Association of Citizens' Advice Bureaux, *The Social Security Act: First Impressions*, London: NACB, 1988.
15. For evidence see Sixth Report of the Social Security Advisory Committee, London: HMSO, 1988; P. Waterhouse, 'Housing Benefit', *Community Care*, 28 January 1988.
16. Child Poverty Action Group, *The Real Value of Social Security Benefits*, London: CPAG, 1988.
17. P. Townsend, *The Guardian*, 29 November 1989.
18. J. Bradshaw and J. Morgan, 'Budgeting on benefit', *New Society*, 6 March 1987.
19. J. Hills, *Changing Tax? How the Tax System Works and How to Change It*, London: Child Poverty Action Group, 1988.
20. *Ibid.*, p. 13.
21. J. Lewis and A. Townsend (eds.), *The North–South Divide: Regional Changes in Britain in the 1980s*, London: Chapman, 1989, p. xi.
22. Unemployment Unit and Youthaid, *Working Brief*, December 1989, p. 6. Most of the statistics contained in this section and in the following section on Labour Market Divisions come from Unemployment Unit and Youthaid publications.
23. See R. Martin, 'The political economy of Britain's North–South divide', in J. Lewis and A. Townsend (eds.), *op. cit.*, pp. 20–60.
24. S. Winyard, 'Divided Britain', in A. Walker and C. Walker (eds.), *op. cit.*, pp. 39–49.
25. J. Lewis and A. Townsend (eds.), *op. cit.*, pp. 15–7.
26. *The Guardian*, 16 November 1989.
27. See D. Finn and G. Lewtas, *Towards a Better Employment Service*, London: Employment Service Section and the Unemployment Unit, 1989.
28. Unemployment Unit, *Square Pegs in Round Holes*, London, Unemployment Unit, 1988, p. 1.
29. Department of Employment, *Training for Employment*, Cm 316, London: HMSO, 1988.
30. For a good introduction to the theories, and for guidance on further reading see C. Cousins, *Controlling State Welfare*, Brighton: Wheatsheaf, 1987.
31. C. Glendinning, 'Impoverishing women', in A. Walker and C. Walker (eds.), *op. cit.*, p. 50.
32. Source: Central Statistical Office, *Family Expenditure Survey 1986*, HMSO: London, 1987.

33. J. Finch, *Family Obligations and Social Change*, Cambridge: Polity Press, 1989, p. 3.
34. H. Arnott, 'Second class citizens', in A. Walker and C. Walker (eds.), *op. cit.*, p. 61.
35. E. de Sousa, 'YTS – the Racism Riddle', *Unemployment Bulletin*, no. 29, Spring 1989, p. 23.
36. *Ibid.*
37. Source: J. Campling, 'Social policy digest', *Journal of Social Policy*, vol. 18, pt. 1, 1989, p. 131.
38. *The Guardian*, 30 August 1988.
39. Reported in *The Independent*, 16 November 1989.
40. *The Guardian*, 30 August 1988.
41. J. Hills, 'What happened to spending on the welfare state?', in A. Walker and C. Walker (eds.), *op. cit.*, pp. 88–100.
42. *The Guardian*, 2 November 1988 and 22 November 1989.
43. R. Jowell and S. Witherspoon (eds.), *British Social Attitudes*, Second Report, Aldershot: Gower, 1985.
44. R. Jowell and C. Airey (eds.), *British Social Attitudes*, First Report, Aldershot: Gower, 1985.
45. R. Jowell, S. Witherspoon and L. Brook (eds.), *British Social Attitudes*, Fifth Report, Aldershot: Gower, 1988.
46. R. Jowell, S. Witherspoon and L. Brook (eds.), *British Social Attitudes: An International Report*, Aldershot: Gower, 1989.
47. *The Guardian*, 18 September 1989.
48. A. Gamble, *op. cit.*, p. 209.
49. The Labour Party, *Meet the Challenge Make the Change*, London: Labour Party, 1989.
50. M. Loney, 'A war on poverty or on the poor?', in A. Walker and C. Walker (eds.), *op. cit.*, p. 19.
51. *The Observer*, 30 April 1989.

AFTERWORD

In November 1990, just over a month after this book was first published, Mrs Thatcher was replaced as Prime Minister and Leader of the Conservative Party by Mr Major.

The initial challenge to Mrs Thatcher came from Mr Heseltine. In the ensuing election Mrs Thatcher failed by just two votes to secure an outright victory, and immediately announced her intention of entering the second ballot.

However, opposition to the Prime Minister in her own party had been growing for some time, and the view that she had become a liability in electoral terms was being openly expressed. This was probably not a majority view, but the fact that it was being expressed at all was significant.

Leading members of the Conservative Party now put enormous pressure on Mrs Thatcher to withdraw from the contest. Mr Hurd and Mr Major resolutely maintained that they would not seek to replace Mrs Thatcher, and that as long as she remained in contention they would not put themselves forward as candidates for the leadership.

After much deliberation Mrs Thatcher withdrew from the second ballot and the way was open for Mr Major and Mr Hurd to contest the leadership with Mr Heseltine. Mr Major, who received Mrs Thatcher's public endorsement, gained 49.7 per cent of the vote – two short of the number of votes required for an outright victory. However, Mr Hurd and Mr Heseltine conceded defeat and pledged their support for Mr Major and a third ballot was therefore avoided.

Mr Major now had to consolidate his victory by attempting to stamp his own brand of Conservatism on a party which had been through a period of division and uncertainty.

One of his problems in attempting to establish his authority was that he had been a protégé of Mrs Thatcher and a strong supporter of many of the policies with which her administration had been associated. He had to convince people that he had a distinctive contribution to make which, while not rejecting outright the policies of the Thatcher governments, would be sufficiently different in content, tone and emphasis as to constitute a new approach.

He has had to contend with the *Conservative Way Forward* group of MPs who are dedicated to a continuation of Thatcherite policies – especially the privatisation of welfare – and the *Bruges Group* whose members are opposed to any softening of attitudes towards the European Community.

THE FIRST NINE MONTHS

Europe
Among the factors contributing to Mrs Thatcher's loss of support was her hard, uncompromising stance on Europe. There has been little change in *policy* with regard to the European Community but a considerable change in attitude and style. The Major government remains equivocal about a single European currency and it is resistant to the notion of political union. On the other hand, the new government does not summarily reject European initiatives and it does not adopt a hectoring tone in its dealings with other heads of state and foreign secretaries. It has shown itself ready to discuss issues and consider compromises.

The poll tax and local government
Mrs Thatcher was wholly committed to the deeply unpopular poll tax, and it was chiefly on this issue that Mr Heseltine chose to challenge her. It was not unexpected, therefore, when the new Prime Minister gave Mr Heseltine the task of finding an alternative.

In April 1991, as Secretary of State for the Environment, Mr Heseltine announced details of the new council tax which is to come into effect in April 1993. It constitutes a return to a tax based on property values. Every house in the country will be given a value by the Inland Revenue. Households will be placed in one of eight bands according to the value of the house they occupy. The greater the house value, the higher the band and the higher the council tax. There will be a flat-rate 25 per cent discount for people living alone, and for students, youth trainees and student nurses. Those on income support will be exempt.

The Department of the Environment has published two consultative documents on local government in England. The first deals with the structure of local government and proposes the establishment of a local government commission which would make suggestions for reform area by area. A single uniform structure for the whole country is rejected, but a greater number of unitary authorities is anticipated.[1]

The second paper deals with the internal management of local authorities. Among its more important proposals is a greater streamlining of the committee system allowing chairpersons to make decisions, removing the requirement for minority party representation and the further development of cabinet-style government. Other suggestions include the appointment of council managers, the election of executives and directly elected mayors.[2]

The Citizen's Charter

Mr Major has made the Citizen's Charter the centre-piece of Conservative Party policy in the expectation that it will have great electoral appeal.

The paper, published in July 1991, contains seventy proposals covering the National Health Service, transport, the Post Office and other utilities, law and order, benefits, tax, council house and housing association tenancies, the personal social services, local government, services for unemployed people and complaints procedures. Service standards will be published and rights of redress and compensation will be spelled out.[3]

Many of the details are still to be worked out and a full analysis of the proposals is not possible in the space available. Nevertheless, several key features need to be identified.

1. The discussion surrounding the Charter has emphasised the negative aspects of public services, although the systematic denigration of public provision, which characterised the 1980s, has been moderated.

2. The Charter considerably extends the privatisation of public services and promises that the opting out of hospitals and schools will be speeded up. British Rail is to be de-nationalised, the Post Office monopoly of the delivery of mail is to be broken and London buses are to be de-regulated. Compulsory competitive tendering in the National Health Service and local government is to be widened.

3. Internal markets, promoting competition within public services, are to be strengthened. Opting out is seen as essential to this process, but there will also be national league tables on hospital efficiency and on the performances of schools and local authorities.

4. The government has said little about the cost of implementing these proposals. The need for greater investment in public services is ignored.

Social security

One very significant improvement has been made to the system of social security since Mr Major came to power: child benefit, which seemed to be in grave danger of withering away during the 1980s, was increased in 1991 and the government has said that in future the level of benefit will be tied to the retail price index. This is a very welcome change, especially since child benefit is not means-tested. Elsewhere in the social security system, however, there is just as great a reliance on means testing and the social fund remains. Melanie Phillips argues that if John Major wishes to prove that he is more compassionate than his predecessor he must abolish the social fund – the worst 'of all Mrs Thatcher's acts of sanctimonious indifference against the poor . . . the totem of the social injustice of the Thatcher years'.[4]

Benefit levels remain pitifully low. The basic unemployment benefit now represents about 12 per cent of average male earnings and Michael Meacher claims that this puts Britain at the bottom of the European league.[5]

The National Health Service

In spite of intense pressure from the medical profession urging the government not to press ahead too quickly with its reforms of the NHS, the provisions of the National Health Service and Community Act (insofar as they affected the NHS) were implemented in April

1991 without the government having made any concessions either in content or timing.

The government forced the pace in the creation of NHS Hospital Trusts. In April 1991 fifty-seven trusts were formed. There were 118 applications for the second wave and this will be followed by two more waves in 1993 and 1994.

The creation of the trusts has not been without its problems. To the embarrassment of the government, the trust which it had regarded as its flagship, Guy's and Lewisham, was one of those that experienced serious financial difficulties. Within weeks of its creation the trust announced cuts amounting to £12.8 million and the loss of 600 jobs (later to be reduced to 400). There were disagreements within the management team about policy and in July the finance director resigned. Another trust, in Bradford, was forced to make cuts of £7 million involving the loss of 300 jobs and there have been some job losses at the Manchester Central Trust.

The picture is not, however, one of unrelieved gloom. Some trusts have shown modest gains and in others there has been little change.

There have also been problems in operating the system in which GPs manage their own budgets. Two particular problems have arisen. One is the effect which a large number of budget holders might have on the ability of district health authorities to fulfil their role of setting and meeting local health strategies. The Health Secretary, William Waldegrave, has accepted that some regulation of GP budget holders might be necessary.

A second problem has been alleged queue-jumping by patients of GPs who manage their own budgets and the danger of a two-tier NHS system developing. Mr Waldegrave has now produced new guidelines to try to prevent queue-jumping, but these will not take effect until April 1992.

On the whole Mr Waldegrave has shown greater flexibility in the handling of the health reforms than did his predecessor Kenneth Clarke, who is now Secretary of State for Education.

Unemployment and anti-inflation policy

The new government has continued the economic policies followed by Mr Major himself when he was Chancellor of the Exchequer. This has meant the use of a single instrument, high interest rates, to combat inflation. Since Mr Major came to power Britain has slid deeper into recession. The Chancellor of the Exchequer, Mr Lamont, insists that the economy will begin to pick up in the second half of 1991. At the time of writing (August 1991) Mr Lamont claims that the signs of recovery are now showing, but financial and industrial institutions are much less convinced of this. Certainly, in the first six months of 1991, the number of bankruptcies almost doubled compared with the same period in 1990. Many small businesses have been forced to close: accountants Touche Ross report an increase of almost 50 per cent in the number of manufacturing companies put into receivership in the first six months of 1991 as compared with the same period in the preceding year. Industrial production in April was down 6.6 per cent on April 1990, and it is anticipated that Gross Domestic Product will fall by 2 per cent in 1991.[6]

One consequence of these policies has been a continuing rise in the number of people unemployed. This is not an unforeseen result of high interest rates. It was fully understood that unemployment would increase. When questioned about the unemployment figures, Mr Lamont, the Chancellor of the Exchequer, said that higher unemployment was a price worth paying if it enabled us to beat inflation. Those actually paying the price may, of course, take a quite different view.

When Mr Major took up office in November 1990 unemployment stood at 2,724,200 in the United Kingdom; by June 1991 the figure had risen to 3,365,700; an increase of more than 23 per cent.[7]

High interest rates have other undesirable consequences. They prevent people from buying their own homes and they cause some of those who have already bought to fall into arrears with mortgage repayments. A report issued by Shelter in June 1991 claimed that arrears reached a record of 790,000 in March, almost a 50 per cent increase from a year earlier.[8] Figures from the Lord Chancellor's Department, released in August, showed that the courts had ordered 33,778 mortgage repossessions during the first six months of 1991. This represents a 50 per cent increase over the number of repossession orders made in the same period of 1990. Repossession orders made by the courts, however, tell only part of the story, since there is a substantial number of voluntary repossessions every year.

The 1991 Budget
From the point of view of social policy the budget was largely neutral. The most significant changes were the raising of child

benefit and the increase in VAT to 17.5 per cent to pay for poll tax relief.

Rates of income tax remained unchanged, although in the longer term the government is still committed to reducing the basic rate to 20 per cent. At least the budget was not biased in favour of the better-off as were so many of the budgets during the 1980s.

Those with company cars were treated less favourably, with an increase in the rate of tax and liability for national insurance contributions, and the higher rate of mortgage tax relief was abolished. These changes are minor when compared with a reduction in the top rate of tax from 83 per cent to 40 per cent during the 1980s, and the government appears to have no intention of substantially redistributing the tax burden.

An £8 billion deficit is anticipated in 1991/92, and this is likely to rise to at least £12 billion in the following year. In July the spending departments submitted bids for an extra £15 billion for 1992/93. However, the Treasury is preparing to apply a tight squeeze on public spending in the Autumn, and the Chief Secretary to the Treasury, Mr David Mellor, is already looking for savings. Social security expenditure remains something of a problem, since it rises as unemployment rises.

In his budget speech Mr Lamont made it plain that the firm control of public spending remained a fundamental strategy and that he would be aiming for budget balance in the medium term.

Conclusions

It is only nine months since John Major became Prime Minister, and perhaps it is too soon to allow firm conclusions to be drawn. The pace of change has certainly slowed down, but given the legislative programme of the late 1980s and the Gulf war, this is not surprising.

With one or two exceptions, the changes made since Mr Major took over have been relatively minor. However, it has to be borne in mind that Mr Major had been a member of the Thatcher cabinet since 1987 and that he had occupied three important offices: Chief Secretary to the Treasury, Foreign Secretary (for a brief period) and Chancellor of the Exchequer. He was therefore centrally concerned with public spending decisions and with economic policy generally. As a member of the cabinet he accepted collective responsibility for the Housing Act, the Education Act, the National Health Service and Community Care Act and for several Acts dealing with local government and industrial relations. Furthermore, Mr Major's support in the leadership contest came mainly from the right of the party and included Mrs Thatcher herself.

Mr Major has brought about two reversals of policy in relation to the poll tax and child benefit and launched a new policy initiative in the form of the Citizen's Charter. He has also brought the word 'poverty' back into the language. Mrs Thatcher simply refused to acknowledge the existence of poverty, and other words such as 'vulnerable' had to be found.

Perhaps Mr Major's most significant contribution has been in terms of style of leadership and style of government. Mrs Thatcher's style was combative and confrontational. She was not inclined to discuss proposals at length and ministers were frequently pushed to one side or forced to take more precipitate action than they might have wished.

By contrast, Mr Major is a better listener and he is much more ready to enter into discussions and negotiation and to accept compromise. He is much less authoritarian in his approach, treating his ministers as members of a team. Relationships with the civil service have also improved as Mr Major has been less inclined to use outside policy advisers. As Travis and Hencke observe:

Under Mrs Thatcher, policy making tended to be a centralised affair dominated by Number 10. Mrs Thatcher relied heavily on a group of outside policy advisers to the detriment of Whitehall departments. . . . Under John Major, these departments have experienced a sense of liberation from a system which meant that Number 10 not only had the last word but often the first word as well on policy development.[9]

The change in style is undoubted, but there are few signs as yet of a fundamental change in direction. For example, the Major government has pressed ahead with the National Health Service reforms, and indeed has accelerated the opting-out programme. The internal market is still the preferred method of delivering health care and nothing has been done to curb the development of private markets in health.

In education, privatised school inspection and auditing schemes are proposed; these are new ideas emanating from the present Secretary of State. The opting out scheme is proceeding and it is anticipated that the election manifesto will contain a commitment to encourage most schools to opt out of local authority control. The city technology colleges have run into difficulties through lack of industrial sponsors, and in order to save the programme the Major government has been diverting substantial sums of public money into the colleges. Competition among schools is being heightened with the publication of league tables, and competition within the system of higher education has been endorsed as has the student loans scheme.

Nothing has been done to halt the residualisation of public sector housing. No extra resources are being made available for housing investment but the government has devised a novel way of sharing out the resources. The idea is based on the City Challenge scheme, the results of which were announced by Mr Heseltine at the end of July. Under this scheme cities were invited to compete for urban regeneration funds. The criteria for judging the projects included the degree of community and private sector involvement. There are now plans to extend this form of allocation to the resources for council house repairs.

Income support, family credit, housing benefit and the social fund are still in place and there has been no improvement in the position of those dependent upon state benefits; high unemployment has greatly increased the numbers drawing benefit.

So it would seem that Thatcherism and the policies it gave rise to are far from dead. Indeed, in some cases, there has been an extension and an intensification of such policies. Many of the people who held ministerial office under Mrs Thatcher are still in government, although occupying different posts. The government is still wedded to privatisation, and the Citizen's Charter involves an extension of opting out, compulsory competitive tendering and market provision. There is little sign that the trend towards greater inequalities which characterised the 1980s is likely to be reversed, although some slowing down of the trend may occur.

There is to be a general election in the very near future and it will become increasingly difficult in the months ahead to separate substance and rhetoric. Nevertheless, the manifestos, when they appear, will give some indication of the future direction of social policy. The Conservative manifesto will repay careful analysis to see how far it constitutes a rejection or a confirmation of Thatcherism.

NOTES

1. Department of the Environment, *The Structure of Local Government in England*, London: HMSO, 1991.
2. Department of the Environment, *The Internal Management of Local Authorities in England*, London: HMSO, 1991.
3. Cabinet Office, *The Citizen's Charter*, Cm 1599, London: HMSO, 1991.
4. *The Guardian*, 15 February 1991.
5. *The Guardian*, 11 July 1991.
6. Reported in Unemployment Unit and Youthaid, *Working Brief*, August/September 1991.
7. Both figures adjusted. Unemployment Unit figures used.
8. *The Guardian*, 26 June 1991. Shelter includes all those two months or more in arrears; the Council of Mortgage Lenders issues figures based on arrears of six months or more.
9. *The Guardian*, 11 July 1991.

BIBLIOGRAPHY

Abrams, P., 'Community care: Some research problems and priorities', *Policy and Politics*, no. 6, 1977.

Abrams, P., 'Social change, social networks and neighbourhood care', *Social Work Service*, no. 22, 1980.

Abrams, P., Abrams, S. and Davison, J., *Patterns of Neighbourhood Care*, Association of Researchers in Voluntary Action and Community Involvement, Occasional Paper no. 1, 1979.

Alcock, P., *Poverty and State Support*, London: Longman, 1987.

Allan, G., *Family Life*, Oxford: Blackwell, 1985.

Allen, I. (ed.), *Hearing the Voice of the Consumer*, London: Policy Studies Institute, 1988.

Archbishop of Canterbury's Commission on Urban Priority Areas, *Faith in the City*, London: Church House Publishing, 1985.

Arnott, H., 'Second class citizens', in A. Walker and C. Walker (eds.), *The Growing Divide*, London: Child Poverty Action Group, 1987.

Ascher, K., *The Politics of Privatisation: Contracting Out Public Services*, London: Macmillan, 1987.

Audit Commission, *Making a Reality of Community Care*, London: HMSO, 1986.

Audit Commission, *Managing the Crisis in Council Housing*, London: HMSO, 1986.

Audit Commission, *Managing Social Services for the Elderly More Effectively*, London: HMSO, 1985.

Audit Commission, *Urban Regeneration and Economic Deviupment: The Local Government Dimension*, London: HMSO, 1989.

Barclay, P., *Social Workers: Their Role and Tasks*, London: Bedford Square Press, 1982.

Barnes, A. J. L. and Barr, N. A., *Strategies for Higher Education: The Alternative White Paper*, Aberdeen: Aberdeen University Press, 1989.

Barr, N. A., 'Review article: The White Paper on Student Loans', *Journal of Social Policy*, vol. 18, pt. 3, 1989.

Barr, N. A., *Student Loans: The Next Steps*, Aberdeen: Aberdeen University Press, 1989.

Bayley, M. and Tennant, A., 'Straight across: Inter-service collaboration in Dinnington', in S. Hatch (ed.), *Decentralisation and Care in the Community*, London: Policy Studies Institute, 1985.

Bean, P., Ferris, J. and Whynes, D. (eds.), *In Defence of Welfare*, London: Tavistock, 1985.

Becker, S. and MacPherson, S. (eds.), *Public Issues Private Pain, Poverty, Social Work and Social Policy*, London: Social Services Insight Books, 1988.

Bennett, F., 'What future for social security?', in A. Walker and C. Walker (eds.), *The Growing Divide*, London: Child Poverty Action Group, 1987.

Beresford, P., 'Consumer views: Data collection or democracy?', in I. Allen (ed.), *Hearing the Voice of the Consumer*, London: Policy Studies Institute, 1988.

Beresford, P. and Croft, S., 'Welfare pluralism: The new face of Fabianism', *Critical Social Policy*, no. 9, 1984.

Berger, P. L. and Neuhaus, R. J., *To Empower People: The Role of Mediating Structures in Public Policy*, Washington, DC: American Enterprise Institute for Public Policy Research, 1977.

Berthoud, R., *Challenges to Welfare*, Aldershot: Gower, 1985.

Berthoud, R., 'The social fund – will it work?', *Policy Studies*, vol. 8, pt. 1, 1987.

Berthoud, R. and Hinton, T., *Credit Unions in the United Kingdom*, London: Policy Studies Institute, 1989.

Berthoud, R. and Kempson, E., *Credit and Debt in Britain*, London: Policy Studies Institute, 1990.

Beveridge, Sir W., *Social Insurance and Allied Services*, Cmd 6404, London: HMSO, 1942.

Bhaduri, R., 'Race and culture: The "invisible" consumers', in I. Allen (ed.), *Hearing the Voice of the Consumer*, London: Policy Studies Institute, 1988.

Billis, D. and Harris, M., *An Extended Role for the Voluntary Sector*, PORTVAC Working Paper 3, London: Brunel University, 1986.

Birch, S., 'Increased patient charges in the National Health Service: A method of privatising primary care', *Journal of Social Policy*, vol. 15, pt. 2, 1986.

Birmingham Consultants for the Rescue of the NHS, *Counting the Cost of Cost-Cutting*, Birmingham: BCRNHS, 1989.

244   Bibliography

Blackman, T., Evason, E., Melaugh, M. and Woods, R., 'Housing and health: A case study of two areas in west Belfast', *Journal of Social Policy*, vol. 18, pt. 1, 1989.

Blaug, M., 'Education vouchers – it all depends on what you mean', in J. Le Grand and R. Robinson (eds.), *Privatisation and the Welfare State*, London: Allen and Unwin, 1984.

Bosanquet, N., *After the New Right*, London: Heinemann, 1983.

Bradshaw, J. and Morgan, J., 'Budgeting on benefit', *New Society*, vol. 79, no. 1262, 6 March 1987, pp. 17–19.

Brenton, M., *The Voluntary Sector in British Social Services*, London: Longman, 1985.

Bulmer, M., *Neighbours: The Work of Philip Abrams*, Cambridge: Cambridge University Press, 1986.

Bulmer, M., *The Social Basis of Community Care*, London: Allen and Unwin, 1987.

Bulmer, M., Lewis, J. and Piachaud. D. (eds.), *The Goals of Social Policy*, London: Unwin Hyman, 1989.

Burrows, L., *The Housing Act 1988*, London: Shelter, 1989.

Butler, D. and Kavanagh, D., *The British General Election of 1987*, London: Macmillan, 1988.

Byrne, D., 'Rich and poor: The growing divide', in A. Walker and C. Walker (eds.), *The Growing Divide*, London: Child Poverty Action Group, 1987.

Byrne, D., Harrison, S., Keithley, J. and McCarthy, P. M., *Housing and Health: The Relationship Between Housing Conditions and the Health of Council Tenants*, Aldershot: Gower, 1986.

Byrne, D., MacNeill, K., Pond, C. and Smail, R., 'The 1988 budget and the poor', *Low Pay Review*, no. 33, 1988, pp. 3–12.

Cambridge, P. and Knapp, M. (eds.), *Demonstrating Successful Care in the Community*, Canterbury: Personal Social Services Research Unit, 1988.

Campling, J., 'Social policy digest', *Journal of Social Policy*, vol. 18, pt. 1, 1989.

Carr, J., 'New roads to equality', *Fabian Society Tract*, no. 517, London: Fabian Society, 1987.

Cawson, A., *Corporatism and Welfare: Social Policy and State Intervention in Britain*, London: Heinemann, 1982.

Central London Social Security Advisers' Forum, *Beyond the Limit*, London: CLSSAF, 1989.

Centre for Policy on Ageing, *Home Life: A Code of Practice for Residential Care*, London: CPA, 1984.

Challis, D., 'The Community Care Scheme: An alternative approach to decentralisation', in S. Hatch (ed.), *Decentralisation and Care in the Community*, London: Policy Studies Unit, 1985.

Challis, D. and Davies, B., *Case Management in Community Care*, Aldershot: Gower, 1986.

Charlesworth, A., Wilkin, D. and Durie, A., *Carers and Services: A Comparison of Men and Women Caring for Dependent Elderly People*, Manchester: Equal Opportunities Commission, 1984.

Child Poverty Action Group, *The Real Value of Social Security Benefits*, London: CPAG, 1988.

Child Poverty Action Group, *School Meals – Not Suitable in All Respects*, London: CPAG, 1987.

Cook, R., *Life Begins at 40: In Defence of the NHS*, London: Fabian Society, 1988.

Corrigan, P., Jones, T., Lloyd, J. and Young, J., 'Socialism, merit and efficiency', *Fabian Society Tract*, no. 530, London: Fabian Society, 1988.

Cousins, C., *Controlling Social Welfare*, Brighton: Wheatsheaf, 1987.

Deakin, N., *The Politics of Welfare*, London: Methuen, 1987.

Deakin, N. and Wicks, M., *Families and the State*, London: Family Policy Studies Centre, 1988.

Department of Education and Science, *Better Schools*, Cmnd 9409, London: HMSO, 1985.

Department of Education and Science, *The National Curriculum 5–16*, London: HMSO, 1987.

Department of Employment, *Removing Barriers to Work*, Cm 655, London: HMSO, 1989.

Department of Employment, *Training for Employment*, Cm 316, London: HMSO, 1988.

Department of the Environment, *Alternatives to Domestic Rates*, Cmnd 8449, London: HMSO, 1981.

Department of the Environment, *An Inquiry Into the Condition of Local Housing Stock in England*, London: HMSO, 1986.

Department of the Environment, *Competition in the Provision of Local Authority Services*, London: HMSO, 1985.

Department of the Environment, *Housing: The Government's Proposals*, Cm 214, London: HMSO, 1987.

Department of the Environment, *Paying for Local Government*, Cmnd 7414, London: HMSO, 1986.

Department of the Environment, *Policy for the Inner Cities*, Cmnd 6845, London: HMSO, 1977.

Department of Health, *Caring for People*, Cm 849, London: HMSO, 1989.

Department of Health, *Working for Patients*, Cm 555, London: HMSO, 1989.

Department of Health and Social Security, *Growing Older*, Cmnd 8173, London: HMSO, 1981.

Department of Health and Social Security, *Promoting Better Health*, Cm 249, London: HMSO, 1987.

Department of Health and Social Security, *Reform of Social Security*, Cmnd 9517, London: HMSO, 1985.

Department of Health and Social Security, *The Reform of Social Security: Programme for Action*, Cmnd 9691, London: HMSO, 1985.

de Sousa, E., 'YTS – the racism riddle', *Unemployment Bulletin*, no. 29, 198(

Dilnot, A. W., Kay, J. A. and Morris, C. N., *The Reform of Social Security*, Oxford: Clarendon Institute for Fiscal Studies, 1984.

Dobson, F., *School Meals Price Survey, Autumn 1987*, London, Labour Party, 1987.

Doling, J., Ford, J. and Stafford, B., *The Property Owing Democracy*, Aldershot: Avebury, 1988.

Drabble, Margaret, 'Case for equality', *Fabian Tract*, no. 527, London: Fabian Society, 1988.

Duke, V. and Edgell, S., 'Gender and social policy: Impact of the cuts', *Journal of Social Policy*, vol. 12, pt. 3, 1983.

Duncan, S., *Public Problems, Private Solutions*, London: HMSO, 1988.

Dunleavy, P., 'The political implications of sectoral cleavages and the growth of state employment – Parts I and II', *Political Studies*, vol. 28, nos. 2 and 3, 1979.

Dunleavy, P. and Husbands, C., *British Democracy at the Crossroads*, London: Allen and Unwin, 1985.

Esam, P., Fimister, G. and Oppenheim, C., *Ability to Pay?*, London: CPAG, 1989.

Esam, P., Good, R. and Middleton, C., *Who's to Benefit? A Radical Review of the Social Security System*, London: Verso, 1985.

Esam, P. and Oppenheim, C., *A Charge on the Community*, London: Child Poverty Action Group and the Local Government Information Unit, 1989.

Evans, A. and Duncan, S., *Responding to Homelessness: Local Authority Policy and Practice*, London: HMSO, 1988.

Evers, A., Nowotny, H. and Wintersberger, H. (eds.), *The Changing Face of Welfare*, Aldershot: Gower, 1987.

Finch, J., 'The deceit of self-help: Preschool playgroups and working class mothers', *Journal of Social Policy*, vol. 13, pt. 1, 1984.

Finch, J., *Education as Social Policy*, London: Longman, 1984.

Finch, J., *Family Obligations and Social Change*, Cambridge: Polity Press, 1989.

Finch, J. and Groves, D., 'Community care and the family: A case for equal opportunities?', *Journal of Social Policy*, vol. 9, pt. 4, 1980.

Finn, D. and Lewtas, G., *Towards a Better Employment Service*, London: Civil and Public Services Association, Employment Service Section and the Unemployment Unit, 1989.

Flynn, R., 'Political acquiescence, privatisation and residualisation in British housing policy', *Journal of Social Policy*, vol. 17, pt. 3, 1988.

Forbes, I. (ed.), 'Market socialism', *Fabian Tract*, no. 516, London: Fabian Society, 1986.

Ford, J., *The Indebted Society: Credit and Default in the 1980s*, London: Routledge, 1988.

Ford, J., 'Problematic statistics? The case of mortgage default', *Journal of the Chartered Building Societies Institute*, March 1989, pp. 16–18.

Ford, J., 'Pity the poor home owners – again', *Roof*, November 1989.

Forrest, R. and Murie, A., *The Right to Buy? Need, Equity and Polarisation in the Sale of Council Houses*, Bristol: School for Advanced Urban Studies, 1984.

Forrest, R. and Murie, A., 'The social division of housing subsidies', *Critical Social Policy*, vol. 8, no. 2, 1988.

Forrest, R. and Murie, A., *Selling the Welfare State*, London: Routledge, 1988.

Friedman, M., *Capitalism and Freedom*, Chicago, University of Chicago Press, 1962.

Friedman, M. and Friedman, R., *Free to Choose*, Harmondsworth: Penguin Books, 1985.

Gamble, A., *The Free Economy and the Strong State: The Politics of Thatcherism*, London: Macmillan, 1988.

George, V. and Wilding, P., *The Impact of Social Policy*, London: Routledge and Kegan Paul, 1984.

Gibb, K. and Kearns, A., 'The assured tenancy business expansion scheme: A framework for research', reported in *Inside Housing*, vol. 6, no. 32, 1989.

Gilbert, N., *Capitalism and the Welfare Stae*, New Haven: Yale University Press, 1983.

Gittins, D., *The Family in Question*, London: Macmillan, 1985.

Glendinning, C., 'Impoverishing women', in A. Walker and C. Walker (eds.), *The Growing Divide*, London: Child Poverty Action Group, 1987.

Glennerster, H., 'Decentralisation and inter-service planning', in S. Hatch (ed.), *Decentralisation and Care in the Community*, London: Policy Studies Institute, 1985.

Glennerster, H. (ed.) *The Future of the Welfare State*, London: Heinemann, 1983.

Goodin, R. E., *Reasons for Welfare*, New Jersey: Princeton University Press, 1988.

Goodin, R. E., 'Self reliance versus the welfare state', *Journal of Social Policy*, vol. 14, pt. 1, 1985.

Golding, P. and Middleton, S., *Images of Welfare*, Oxford: Blackwell, 1982.

Gough, I., *The Political Economy of the Welfare State*, London: Macmillan, 1979.

Green, D. G., *Challenge to the NHS*, London: Institute of Economic Affairs, 1986.

Green, D. G., *Everyone a Private Patient*, London: Institute of Economic Affairs, 1988.

Green, D. G., *Medicines in the Marketplace*, IEA Health Unit Paper, no. 1, London: The Institute of Economic Affairs, 1987.

Green, D. G., *The New Right*, Brighton: Wheatsheaf, 1987.

Greenwood, J. and Wilson, D., *Public Administration in Britain*, London: Allen and Unwin, 1984.

Griffith, B., Iliffe, S. and Rayner, G., *Banking on Sickness: Commercial Medicine in Britain and the USA*, London: Lawrence and Wishart, 1987.

Griffiths, R., *Community Care: Agenda for Action*, London: HMSO, 1988.

Hadjipateras, A., *Reform of Social Security: A Checklist of the Responses of 60 Key Organisations to the Government's Green Paper*, London: Child Poverty Action Group, 1985.

Hadley, R. and Hatch, S., *Social Welfare and the Failure of the State*, London: Allen and Unwin, 1981.

Hadley, R. and McGrath, M., *Going Local: Neighbourhood Social Services*, London: Bedford Square Press, 1980.

Hall, P. (ed.), *The Inner City in Context*, London: Heinemann, 1981.

Hall, S. and Jaques, M. (eds.), *The Politics of Thatcherism*, London: Lawrence and Wishart, 1983.

Hallett, C., *The Personal Social Services in Local Government*, London: Allen and Unwin, 1982.

Hardy, B., Turrell, A., Webb, A. L. and Wistow, G., *Collaboration and Cost Effectiveness: Final Report*, Loughborough: Centre for Research in Social Policy, 1989.

Harman, H. and Harman, S., *No Place Like Home*, London: NALGO, 1989.

Harrison, S., Hunter, D. J., Johnston, I. and Wistow, G., *Competing for Health: A Commentary on the NHS Review*, Leeds: Nuffield Institute for Health Service Studies, 1989.

Hatch, S. (ed.), *Decentralisation and Care in the Community*, London: Policy Studies Institute, 1985.

Hatch, S., *Outside the State*, London: Croom Helm, 1980.

Hatch, S. and Mocroft, I., *Components of Welfare*, London: Bedford Square Press, 1983.

Hatch, S. and Mocroft, I., 'Factors affecting the location of voluntary organisation branches', *Policy and Politics*, vol. 6, no. 2, 1977.

Health Visitors' Association and General Medical Services Committee, *Homeless Families and their Health*, London: HVA and GMSC, 1989.

Henwood, M. and Wicks, M., *The Forgotten Army: Family Care and Elderly People*, London: Family Policy Studies Centre, 1984.

Higgins, J., *The Business of Medicine: Private Health Care in Britain*, London: Macmillan, 1988.

Higgins, J., 'Defining community care', *Social Policy and Administration*, vol. 23, no. 1, 1989.

Hills, J., *Changing Tax: How the Tax System Works and How to Change it*, London: Child Poverty Action Group, 1988.

Hills, J., 'What happened to spending on the welfare state?', in Walker, A. and Walker, C. (eds.), *The Growing Divide*, London: Child Poverty Action Group, 1987.

Hindess, B., *Freedom, Equality and the Market*, London: Tavistock, 1987.

Holroyd, D. J., *Social Services – What Next?*, Hadleigh: Holhouse, 1987.

Home Office, *Report of the Committee on Local Authority and Allied Personal Social Services*, Cmnd 3703, London: HMSO, 1968.

Housing Corporation, *Tenants' Choice: Criteria for Landlord Approval and Guidance. Notes for Applicants*, London: 1989.

Hunt, M., *The Cost of Caring*, Batley: West Yorkshire Low Pay Unit, 1989.

Johnson, N., *Voluntary Social Services*, Oxford: Blackwell, 1981.

Johnson, N., *The Welfare State in Transition*, Brighton: Wheatsheaf, 1987.

Johnson, N., 'The privatisation of welfare', *Social Policy and Administration*, vol. 23, no. 1, 1989.

Jones, A., 'Postscript', in S. Hatch (ed.), *Decentralisation and Care in the Community*, London: Policy Studies Institute, 1985.

Jones, P., *The Thatcher Experiment*, London: Routledge and Kegan Paul, 1980.

Jordan, B., *Rethinking Welfare*, Oxford: Blackwell, 1987.

Jowell, R. and Airey, C. (eds.), *British Social Attitudes*, First Report, Aldershot: Gower, 1984.

Jowell, R. and Witherspoon, S. (eds.), *British Social Attitudes*, Second Report, Aldershot: Gower, 1985.

Jowell, R., Witherspoon, S. and Brook, L. (eds.), *British Social Attitudes*, Fifth Report, Aldershot: Gower, 1988.

Jowell, R., Witherspoon, S. and Brook, L (eds.), *British Social Attitudes: An International Report*, Aldershot: Gower, 1989.

Kaldor, N., *The Economic Consequences of Mrs Thatcher*, London: Fabian Society, 1983.

Kerr, M., *The Right to Buy: A National Survey of Tenants and Buyers of Council Houses*, London: HMSO, 1988.

King, D. S., *The New Right: Politics, Markets and Citizenship*, London: Macmillan, 1987.

King's Fund Institute, *Promoting Innovation in Community Care*, Briefing Paper no. 3, London: King's Fund Institute, 1987.

Klein, R. and O'Higgins M. (eds.), *The Future of Welfare*, Oxford: Blackwell, 1985.

Kramer, R. M. *Voluntary Agencies in the Welfare State*, Berkeley: University of California Press, 1981.

Labour Party, *A Year of Mortgage Misery*, London: Labour Party, 1989.

Labour Party Policy Review Group, *Meet the Challenge: Make the Change*, London: Labour Party, 1989.

Laming, H., *Lessons from America: The Balance of Services in Social Care*, London: Policy Studies Institute, 1985.

Lane, J.-E., *State and Market: The Politics of the Public and the Private*, Beverly Hills: Sage, 1985.

Laurence, S. and Hall, P., 'British policy responses' in P. Hall (ed.), *The Inner City in Context*, London: Heinemann, 1981.

Leadbeater, C., 'The politics of prosperity', *Fabian Society Tract*, no. 523, London: Fabian Society, 1987.

Leat, D., *Voluntary Organisations and Accountability: Theory and Practice*, Coventry: University of Warwick, 1987.

Leat, D. and Gay, P., *Paying for Care*, London: Policy Studies Institute, 1987.

Le Grand, J., *The Strategy of Equality*, London: Allen and Unwin, 1982.

Le Grand, J. and Estrin, S. (eds.), *Market Socialism*, Oxford: University Press, 1989.

Le Grand, J. and Robinson, R. (eds.), *Privatisation and the Welfare State*, London: Allen and Unwin, 1984.

Leonard, P., 'Restructuring the welfare state', *Marxism Today*, vol. 23, no. 12, 1979, p. 7.

Levitas, R. (ed.), *The Ideology of the New Right*, Cambridge: Polity Press, 1986.

Lewis, J. and Townsend, A. (eds.), *The North–South Divide*, London: Chapman, 1989.

Lister, R., 'Conclusion II – there is an alternative', in A. Walker and C. Walker (eds.), *The Growing Divide*, London: Child Poverty Action Group, 1987.

Loney, M., 'A war on poverty or on the poor?', in A. Walker and C. Walker (eds.), *The Growing Divide*, London: Child Poverty Action Group, 1987.

Lunn, T., 'The Social fund', *Community Care*, 28 January 1988.

McCarthy, M. (ed.), *The New Politics of Welfare: An Agenda for the 1990s?*, London: Macmillan, 1989.

McEvaddy, S., *One Good School Meal*, London: CPAG, 1988.

McIntosh, M., 'Feminism and social policy', *Critical Social Policy*, vol. 1, no. 1, 1981.

McKechnie, S. and Wilson, D., *Homes Above All*, London: Shelter, 1986.

McLachlan, G. and Maynard, A. (eds.), *The Public/Private Mix for Health: The Relevance and Effects of Change*, London: Nuffield Provincial Hospitals Trust, 1982.

Malpass, P. and Murie, A., *Housing Policy and Practice*, London: Macmillan, 1982.

Manning, N. (ed.), *Social Problems and Welfare Ideology*, Aldershot: Gower, 1985.

Manwaring, T. and Sigler, N. (eds.), *Breaking the Nation*, London: Pluto, 1985.

Martin, R., 'The political economy of Britain's North–South divide', in J. Lewis and A. Townsend (eds.), *The North–South Divide: Regional Changes in Britain in the 1980s*, London: Paul Chapman Publishing, 1989.

Meacher, M., 'The good society', *New Socialist*, June 1985.

Miller, D., *Market, State and Community: Theoretical Foundations of Market Socialism*, Oxford: Oxford University Press, 1989.

Milne, R. G., 'Competitive tendering in the NHS: An economic analysis of the early implementation of HC(83)H8', *Public Administration*, vol. 15, no. 2, 1987.

Ministry of Education, *Higher Education*, Cmnd 2154 (The Robbins Report), London: HMSO, 1963.

Mishra, R., *Society and Social Policy*, London: Macmillan, 1977.

Mishra, R., *The Welfare State in Crisis*, Brighton: Wheatsheaf, 1984.

Mount, F., *The Subversive Family: An Alternative History of Love and Marriage*, London: Jonathan Cape, 1982.

Murie, A., *Housing Inequality and Deprivation*, London: Heinemann, 1983.

Murie, A., 'Housing', in P. Wilding (ed.), *In Defence of the Welfare State*, Manchester: Manchester University Press, 1986.

National Association of Citizens' Advice Bureaux, *The Social Security Act: First Impressions*, London: NACB, 1988.

National Association of Health Authorities, *Income Generation in the NHS*, Birmingham: NAHA, 1988.

No Turning Back Group of Conservative MPs, *The NHS: A Suitable Case for Treatment*, London: Conservative Political Centre, 1988.

Office of Population Censuses and Surveys, *The Prevalence of Disability Among Adults*, London: HMSO, 1988.

Office of Population Censuses and Surveys, *The General Household Survey for 1987*, London: HMSO, 1989.

Oppenheim, C., *A Tax on All the People*, London: Child Poverty Action Group, 1987.

Organisation for Economic Co-operation and Development, *Financing and Delivering Health Care*, Paris: OECD, 1987.

Pancoast, D. L., Parker, P. and Froland, C. (eds.), *Rediscovering Self-Help: Its role in Social Care*, Beverly Hills: Sage, 1983.

Papadakis, E. and Taylor-Gooby, P., *The Private Provision of Public Welfare: State Market and Community*, Brighton: Wheatsheaf, 1987.

Parsloe, P., *Social Services Area Teams*, London: Allen and Unwin, 1981.

Phillips, D. R., Vincent, J. and Blacksell, S., *Home from Home*, Sheffield: Joint Unit for Social Services Research and Community Care, 1988.

Phillips, D. R., Vincent, J. A., assisted by Blacksell, S., 'Petit bourgeois care: Private residential care for the elderly', *Policy and Politics*, vol. 14, no. 2, 1986.

Phillipson, C., *Planning for Community Care: Facts and Fallacies in the Griffiths Report*, University of Keele: Centre for Social Gerontology, 1988.

Piachaud, D., 'The growth of poverty', in A. Walker and C. Walker (eds.), *The Growing Divide*, London: Child Poverty Action Group, 1987.

Pinker, R., 'Populism and social services', *Social Policy and Administration*, vol. 18, no. 1, 1984.

Plant, R., 'Equality, markets and the State', *Fabian Tract* 494, London: Fabian Society, 1984.

Pond, C. and Winyard, S., *The Case for a National Minimum Wage*, London: Low Pay Unit, 1983.

Price, J. R., 'Decentralisation in Islington', in S. Hatch (ed.), *Decentralisation and Care in the Community*, London: Policy Studies Institute, 1985.

Riddell, T., *The Thatcher Decade. How Britain has Changed During the 1980s*, Oxford: Blackwell, 1989.

Robinson, R., 'Restructuring the welfare state: An analysis of public expenditure', *Journal of Social Policy*, vol 15, pt. 1, 1986.

Rose, H. and Rose, S., 'Moving right out of welfare and the way back', *Critical Social Policy*, vol. 2, no. 1, 1982.

Scarman, Lord., *The Brixton Disorders 10–12 April 1981*, London: HMSO, 1981.

Scruton, R., *The Meaning of Conservatism*, Harmondsworth: Penguin Books, 1880.

Skidelsky, R. (ed.), *Thatcherism*, Oxford: Blackwell, 1988.

Smith, M., 'The consumer case for socialism', *Fabian Society Tract*, no. 513, London: Fabian Society, 1986.

Social Security Advisory Committee, *The Draft Social Fund Manual*, London: HMSO, 1987.

Social Services Committee, *April 1988 Social Security Changes*, HC 437–1, London: HMSO, 1989.

Social Services Committee, *Community Care with Special Reference to Adult Mentally Ill and Mentally Handicapped People*, HC 13–1, London: HMSO, 1985.

Social Services Committee, *Public Expenditure on the Social Services*, HC 548, London: HMSO, 1988.

Social Services Committee, *Resourcing the NHS: The Government's Plans for the Future of the NHS*, HC 214–III, London: HMSO, 1989.

Stevenson, O., *Specialisation in Social Service Teams*, London: Allen and Unwin, 1981.

Svenson, M. and MacPherson, S. 'Real losses and unreal figures: The impact of the 1986 Social Security Act', in S. Becker and S. Macpherson (eds.), *Public Issues Private Pain: Poverty, Social Work and Social Policy*, London: Social Services Insight Books, 1988.

Taylor-Gooby, P., *Public Opinion, Ideology and State Welfare*, London: Routledge and Kegan Paul, 1985.

Titmuss, R. M., *Commitment to Welfare*, London: Allen and Unwin, 1968.

Titmuss, R. M., *Essays on the Welfare State*, London: Allen and Unwin, 1963.

Titmuss, R. M., *The Gift Relationship: From Human Blood to Social Policy*, London: Allen and Unwin, 1970.

Townsend, P., Davidson, N. and Whitehead, M., *Inequalities in Health* and *The Health Divide*, Harmondsworth: Penguin, 1988.

Treasury, *The Government's Expenditure Plans: 1985/6 to 1987/8*, Cmnd. 9428, London: HMSO, 1985.

Treasury, *The Government's Expenditure Plans, 1990/91–1992/93*, Cm 879, London: HMSO, 1989.

Treasury, *The Next Ten Years: Public Expenditure and Taxation into the 1990s*, Cmnd. 9189, London: HMSO, 1984.

Treasury, *Proposals for a Tax Credit System*, Cmnd 5116, London: HMSO, 1972.

Unemployment Unit, *Square Pegs in Round Holes*, London: The Unemployment Unit, 1988.

Wagner, G., *A Positive Choice*, London: HMSO, 1988.

Walker, A. (ed.), *Community Care: The Family, The State and Social Policy*, Oxford: Blackwell, 1982.

Walker. A., 'Conclusions I: A divided Britain', in A. Walker and C. Walker (eds.), *The Growing Divide*, London: Child Poverty Action Group, 1987.

Walker, A. and Walker C. (eds.), *The Growing Divide*, London: Child Poverty Action Group, 1987.

Warnock, M., *Universities: Knowing Our Minds*, London: Chatto and Windus, 1989.

Waterhouse, P., 'Housing benefit', *Community Care*, no. 696, 28 January 1988, p. viii.

Weale, A., *Political Theory and Social Policy*, London: Macmillan, 1983.

Webb, A. and Wistow G., *Planning Need and Scarcity*, London: Allen and Unwin, 1986.

Webb, A. and Wistow, G., *Social Work, Social Care and Social Planning: The Personal Social Services Since Seebohm*, London: Longman, 1987.

West, P., Illsley, R. and Kelman, K., 'Public preference for the care of dependency groups', *Social Science and Medicine*, vol. 18, no. 4, 1984.

Wilding, P. (ed.), *In Defence of the Welfare State*, Manchester: Manchester University Press, 1986.

Wilkinson, M., 'Tax expenditures and public policy in the UK', *Journal of Social Policy*, vol. 15, pt. 1, 1986.

Williams, F., *Social Policy: A Critical Introduction*, Cambridge: Polity Press, 1989.

Willmott, P., *Social Networks, Informal Care and Public Policy*, London: Policy Studies Institute, 1986.

Willmott, P. and Murie, A., *Polarisation and Social Housing*, London: Policy Studies Institute, 1988.

Winyard, S., 'Divided Britain', in A. Walker and C. Walker (eds.), *The Growing Divide*, London: Child Poverty Action Group, 1987.

Wolfenden, J., *The Future of Voluntary Organisations*, London: Croom Helm, 1987.

Wright, G., *ABC of Thatcherism*, London: Fabian Society, 1989.

Young, K., 'The East Sussex approach', in S. Hatch (ed.), *Decentralisation and Care in the Community*, London: Policy Studies Institute, 1985.

Young, S., 'The Nature of Privatisation in Britain, 1979–85', *West European Politics*, vol. 9, no. 2, 1986.

INDEX

260 Index

Taylor-Gooby, P., 70
Tebbitt, N., 109, 207–8
Tennant, A., 183
Thatcher, M., 1, 2, 3, 4, 11, 70, 72, 102,
    103, 107, 144, 149, 150–1, 154–5,
    165, 191, 197, 212, 215, 216, 221,
    225, 226, 227, 228, 229
Tindall, S., 219
Titmuss, R. M., 69
Townsend, A., 203, 205
Townsend, P., 57
Trade Union Act, 1984, 30–1
trade unions, 30–1, 219

UK Home Care Association, 185
unemployment, 5, 29–30, 45, 133, 147,
    154, 155, 204, 206–9, 210,
    214–15, 228
Unemployment Unit, 29, 206, 207,
    208–9
Universities Information Unit, 118

voluntary sector, 4, 14, 137–9, 164, 165,
    169, 173–6, 185–7, 195, 225

wages see incomes
Wages Act, 1986, 28
wages councils, 12, 28
Wagner Report, 180
Walker, A., 26, 163
Warnock, M., 125
Waterhouse, P., 48
Weale, A., 64
wealth, 32, 192, 202–3

welfare pluralism, 168–77
    Griffiths Report and, 163–5
    interweaving and, 177, 187
    see also commercial sector; informal
        sector; voluntary sector
welfare state
    and crisis, 3
    support for, 225–7
West, P., 171–2
Western Provident Association, 72
West Yorkshire Low Pay Unit, 167
Wicks, M., 183–4
Wilkinson, M., 11
Williams, Lady Rhys, 63
Willmott, P., 129, 179
Wilson, D., 15
Winyard, S., 58, 59
Wolfenden Report, 168
women
    and caring, 32, 55, 70–3, 181–2,
        185–6, 210–11
    and employment/unemployment, 56,
        171, 210–11
    and inequaltiy, 54–7, 59, 171, 186,
        210–13, 228
    and poverty, 56, 59
    and social security, 38, 54–7, 65,
        211–12
workers' rights, 28, 29, 31
Wright, P., 219

Young, H., 152
Youth Training Scheme, 28, 45, 195,
    214